Normative Foundations of the Welfare State

I0882100

This scholarly work offers analyses, perspectives and interpretations of the normative foundation of the 'Nordic welfare state model'. Welfare programmes and institutions tend to be analysed as instrumental arrangements, overlooking the fact that welfare programmes essentially are expressions of moral conceptions and values.

The authors examine the main principles in this model, exploring their origins and the relationship between them. Paying particular attention to the principles of 'universalism', 'public responsibility for welfare', and 'work for all', they consider their significance for current welfare policy and question whether external economic and ideological pressures threaten these principles. The book is divided into three parts:

- Part I considers the historical trajectories behind the Nordic welfare model.
- Part II looks more specifically at normative tensions and dilemmas in current welfare policies with a focus on women-friendly welfare, attitudes to basic income, and alcohol and drug misuse.
- Part III focuses on the possible change in the normative foundation of the Nordic welfare states.

This book is essential reading for researchers and students of the welfare state, and also to those in the fields of social policy, comparative politics and political economy.

Nanna Kildal is a Researcher at Stein Rokkan Centre for Social Studies, University of Bergen. She has written a number of articles on the 1990s welfare reforms in Europe and USA. **Stein Kuhnle** is Professor of Comparative Politics at the University of Bergen. His recent publications in English include *Survival of the European Welfare State* and *Modernizing the Korean Welfare State.*

Routledge/EUI studies in the political economy of welfare

Series editors: Martin Rhodes and Maurizio Ferrera

The European University Institute, Florence, Italy

This series presents leading edge research on the recasting of European welfare states. The series is interdisciplinary, featuring contributions from experts in economics, political science and social policy. The books provide a comparative analysis of topical issues, including:

- reforms of the major social programmes – pensions, health, social security
- the changing political cleavages in welfare politics
- policy convergence and social policy innovation
- the impact of globalization.

1 **Immigration and Welfare**
Challenging the borders of the welfare state
Edited by Michael Bommes and Andrew Geddes

2 **Renegotiating the Welfare State**
Flexible adjustment through corporatist concertation
Edited by Frans van Waarden and Gerhard Lehmbruch

3 **Comparing Welfare Capitalism**
Social policy and political economy in Europe, Japan and the USA
Edited by Bernhard Ebbinghaus and Philip Manow

4 **Controlling a New Migration World**
Edited by Virginie Giraudon and Christian Joppke

5 **The Moral Economy of Welfare States**
Britain and Germany compared
Steffen Mau

6 **Welfare State Reform in Southern Europe**
Fighting poverty and social exclusion in Italy, Spain, Portugal and Greece
Edited by Maurizio Ferrera

7 **Normative Foundations of the Welfare State**
The Nordic experience
Edited by Nanna Kildal and Stein Kuhnle

Normative Foundations of the Welfare State

The Nordic experience

Edited by Nanna Kildal and Stein Kuhnle

Routledge
Taylor & Francis Group
LONDON AND NEW YORK

First published 2005
by Routledge
2 Park Square, Milton Park, Abingdon, Oxon, OX14 4RN

Simultaneously published in the USA and Canada
by Routledge
270 Madison Ave, New York, NY 10016

Routledge is an imprint of the Taylor & Francis Group

Transferred to Digital Printing 2006

Typeset in Baskerville by Wearset Ltd, Boldon, Tyne and Wear

British Library Cataloguing in Publication Data
A catalogue record for this book is available from the British Library

Library of Congress Cataloging in Publication Data
A catalog record for this book has been requested

ISBN10: 0-415-34943-5 (hbk)
ISBN10: 0-415-42976-5 (pbk)

ISBN13: 978-0-415-34943-7 (hbk)
ISBN13: 978-0-415-42976-4 (pbk)

Printed and bound by CPI Antony Rowe, Eastbourne

Contents

Figures

Tables

Contributors

Jan Otto Andersson, Reader in Economics, Åbo Akademi University, Finland. E-mail: jananderss@abo.fi

Anette Borchorst, Associate Professor in Gender Studies and Comparative Studies, University of Aalborg, Denmark. E-mail: ab@ihis.aau.dk

Marcus Carson, Researcher, Stockholm University and Researcher/ Lecturer, South Stockholm University College, Stockholm, Sweden. E-mail: Marcus.Carson@sociology.su.se

Rune Ervik, Researcher, Stein Rokkan Centre for Social Studies, University of Bergen, Norway. E-mail: rune.ervik@rokkan.uib.no

Sven E. O. Hort, Professor in Sociology, Södertörn University College, Stockholm, Sweden. E-mail: sven.hort@sh.se

Olli E. Kangas, Research Professor, The Danish National Institute of Social Research, Copenhagen, Denmark. E-mail: olk@sfi.dk

Lars Bo Kaspersen, Associate Professor, Department of Sociology, University of Copenhagen, Denmark. E-mail: lbk@sociology.ku.dk

Olavi Kaukonen, Ministerial Adviser, Ministry of Justice in Finland; Docent in the University of Helsinki, Finland. E-mail: olavi. kaukonen@om.fi

Nanna Kildal, Researcher, Stein Rokkan Centre for Social Studies, University of Bergen, Norway. E-mail: nanna.kildal@rokkan.uib.no

Stein Kuhnle, Professor, Department of Comparative Politics, University of Bergen, Norway. E-mail: stein.kuhnle@isp.uib.no

Jørn Loftager, Associate Professor, Department of Political Science, University of Aarhus, Denmark. E-mail: loftager@ps.au.dk

Anders Nordlund, Associate Professor in Sociology, Luleå University of Technology, Sweden. E-mail: anders.nordlund@ltu.se

Stefán Ólafsson, Professor of Sociology and Director of the Urban Studies Institute, University of Iceland, Reykjavík, Iceland. E-mail: olafsson@hi.is

Birte Siim, Professor in Gender Research in Social Sciences, Aalborg University. E-mail: siim@ihis.aau.dk

Kerstin Stenius, Researcher, SoRAD (Social Research on Alcohol and Drugs), Stockholm University, Sweden. E-mail: kerstin.stenius@stakes.fi

Bo Stråth, Professor of Contemporary History, European University Institute, Florence, Italy. E-mail: bo.strath@iue.it

Preface

This book is the result of a research project directed by the editors, and financed by the Programme on Welfare Research of the Norwegian Research Council, on 'The normative foundation of the Scandinavian welfare state'. As part of the project we invited a group of scholars from all five Nordic countries to participate in a workshop on this topic, held in Bergen in May 2002. The contributors belong to the quite extensive network of scholars across social science disciplines in 'welfare (state) research' in the Nordic countries. They represent one or several of the fields of political science, sociology, history and economics. The aim of the project, and the book, is to draw attention to one dimension of welfare state development – 'normative foundation' – which appears under-researched. We are of the opinion that this aspect of modern welfare states deserves more reflection, quite particularly in an era when European governments and parliaments persistently discuss various ways to reform welfare state arrangements. The politics of welfare state 'reconstruction' or, often more bluntly, 'retrenchment', may demand more contemplation about the normative basis of public welfare policies than what was (or theoretically can be) the case in 'good economic times' of welfare state expansion in which the expectation of steady and persistent economic growth was (is) widespread. This state of affairs presumably existed in many European countries in the early 1960s, sometimes perceived as 'the golden era' of welfare state development. Today, doubt and uncertainty about prospects for economic and social development are prevalent in European politics of welfare. The book provides a range of perspectives on the Nordic experience, and may hopefully inspire future research on this topic both in and far beyond the Nordic countries.

We thank the authors for their original contributions to this book, partly based on their own on-going research. We extend special thanks to the Stein Rokkan Centre for Social Studies at the University of Bergen, which has inspired, hosted and administered our project, and a most particular thanks to Maila Solheim at the Centre, who has skilfully and diligently supervised the final editing and preparation of the manuscript for publication.

Nanna Kildal and Stein Kuhnle
Bergen

1 Introduction

Nanna Kildal and Stein Kuhnle

The concept of a Scandinavian or Nordic welfare (state) model is firmly established worldwide. But neither the model nor the empirical reality it pertains to describe or idealize is static. It may be said that when the Holy Roman Empire of the German Nation was headed for dissolution it was neither particularly holy, specifically Roman, nor much of an empire. We are far from claiming that the Scandinavian or Nordic welfare model is on the brink of dissolution, but feel tempted to ask: how well does the concept of a Nordic welfare model describe the reality of the Nordic countries? Nordic? Welfare? Model? What makes whatever it is Nordic?

There are many ways of categorizing welfare states. Yet, compared to other European welfare states the Nordic ones are always to be found in the same group – they share some basic characteristics representing similar internal welfare state logics. However, this picture of kinship and commonalities between the Nordic welfare states does not imply that ideas, values and motives underlying welfare institutions, are unambiguous and easy to define. Rather, the conceptions of welfare models conceal as much as they illuminate normative principles regulating welfare policies; the institutional patterns are mixtures of different reasons for welfare. The aim of this book is to identify, clarify and discuss the guiding principles in Nordic welfare policy development.

Nordic welfare policies have undergone many changes during the 1990s, mainly small, although a few have held greater significance (e.g. pension reform in Sweden). Some reforms imply stricter, others more generous welfare policies. The interpretations of the reforms, which mainly consist of bit-by-bit changes, are varied and even conflicting. Abrahamson (1999: 55) argues that a process of convergence is pushing diverse European welfare states towards 'a corporate welfare model'. In the field of *social welfare policies* proper, referring to Titmuss' (1958) conceptual map, a possible dualization or segmentation is a topic that has gained more attention in political debates (Ervik and Kuhnle 1996: 90–8). In Norway, 'targeting' has become a key issue as poverty was set on the agenda of the centre-right 'cooperation government' formed in October 2001 (Hatland 2001). 'The flight from universalism' and 'a shift of paradigm' are characteristics that sum up this position (Sunesson *et al.* 1998; Cox 1998; Kildal 2001; Carson, Chapter 11, this volume). On the other hand, it has been claimed that in spite of changes and reforms during the last decade the institutional characteristics of the Scandinavian universal type of welfare state are likely to remain basically intact for the foreseeable future (Kuhnle 2000).

Norms, values, motives

An important question, though, is whether seemingly insignificant piecemeal changes may be understood as merely pragmatic adjustments or rather as indications of more fundamental normative trends in the development of social policies. Actually, this character of piecemeal changes may mirror politicians' lack of reflection regarding the normative significance of welfare institutions. To the extent that norms and values are brought into current political debates they generally concern the effects that welfare programmes may have on peoples' utility calculations. Subsequently, welfare programmes may eventually lead to a change in peoples' norms and values, for instance their work ethics and sense of personal responsibility. It is often ignored, both in policy debates and in welfare research that welfare institutions are not simply arrangements of rewards and punishments, but also expressions of norms, values and social goals, such as ideas of justice and freedom and norms of solidarity and responsibility. Perceivably, these ideas influence societal norms, values and basic ways of thinking in a more complex sense than the current debates on incentives in welfare programmes allow for. The institutional design of welfare states contributes to the essential moral structure of society (cf. Pierre and Rothstein 2003).

The lack of reflection and research on normative issues may (plausibly) be understandable in times of economic growth and welfare state expansion. However, in times of economic uncertainty and ideological pressures for change, and possible deconstruction of advanced welfare states, this lack may be highly problematic as arrangements without a clearly defined rationale may easily be reduced or terminated. Western welfare states are today confronted with challenges, which not only put pressure on the efficiency of the welfare institutions, but also on their legitimacy. Thus, in the assessment of several minor and larger, more or less incremental or casual, welfare reforms during recent decades, studies of the more or less hidden governing values and principles in welfare policies are crucial for any interpretations, justifications or rejections of them.

The current external and internal challenges to the moral structures of welfare states have given normative analyses and normative theory in welfare research a more important role than has so far been the case. Normative analyses did not swell the ranks of welfare research publications during the Nordic 'golden age' of public welfare expansion. In the course of the last 20 years, however, publications on welfare issues have increasingly raised questions about the norms and values that are embedded in welfare policies, how they may be justified and which consequences they may have. According to Rawls (1971: 3), justice is the first virtue of social institutions. This implies the fair distribution of goods and burdens, rights and duties, and the treatment of everyone with equal respect. No matter how efficient and well-arranged laws and institutions are, they must be reformed or abolished if they are unjust.

Ideally speaking, society should be a transparent social order where the governing principles are known and available for public consideration and examination, defence or rejection (Bertram 1997). 'People should know and understand the reasons for the basic distribution of wealth, power, authority and freedom' (Waldron 1993: 61); a legitimate social order is one that is 'capable of explaining itself at the tribunal of each person's understanding'. Even Max Weber, who is famous for his thesis on 'ethical neutrality', argued that the analyses of the ideas, principles, norms and values that form the basis of political decisions and arrangements constitute a necessary dimension of welfare research: 'It is self-evident that one of the most important tasks of every science of cultural life is to arrive at a rational understanding of these "ideas" for which men either really or allegedly struggle' (Weber 1969 [1904]: 54).

Normative and positive research

A distinction is often made between the empirical or positive, and normative research, describing the two approaches as inconsistent: while a positive statement is a statement about *what is*, that may be right or wrong without any indication of approval or disapproval, a normative statement expresses a judgment about *what ought to be*. For instance, should the state accept responsibility for the welfare of all citizens, and if so, what kind of responsibility should it agree to? What kind of duties may a society impose on its citizens? How may social rights be justified? Where should the borders be drawn for the state's legitimate exercise of power?

Generally speaking, empirical and normative studies have diverged greatly in welfare research. Nevertheless, a combination of the two may seem an optimal research strategy. This approach makes it possible to raise the following three critical questions: what *should* the state do? What in fact *can* it do? (Rothstein 1998) and, if it cannot do what we agree upon that it ought to do, is it possible *to build state capacity*? In other words, the 'proper functioning' of social institutions cannot be achieved by means of pragmatic and normative arguments alone – the state's ability is also fundamental. Prescriptions must be feasible; 'ought implies can'. Thus normative theory should be 'a reflection on practice' (Weale 1983: 9). The empirical question of what options we have to relieve the life conditions of the worst-off, raises for instance immediate normative questions about the conceptions of 'worst-off' and 'relief'. In fact, most of the concepts that are used in welfare and other social science research are normatively impregnated and should be thoroughly reflected on.

Normative theory, as a part of moral philosophy, is concerned with the justification of principles for the design of the basic institutions of society, cf. John Rawls' *Theory of Justice* (1971). Such prescriptions and constructions of reasons take place in the border area between science and philosophy. As normative theory constructs reasons and judges the legitimacy of principles and ideas, social scientists may be better able to empirically unveil, analyse and throw light on more or less hidden values and normative dilemmas attached to the governing principles of the policies. In this way normative theory may contribute to productive thinking concerning the moral dimensions of politics (Hausman and McPehrson 1996; Rothstein 1998).

The aim of this book is to analyse welfare policy development by going beyond their pragmatic and instrumental dimensions and to call attention to central ideas and motives that have been important for the designing of the Nordic welfare state model, and to ideas and values that are currently emerging. Are important changes of ideas and principles taking place, or are the ideational motives that once inspired the development of the Nordic welfare state institutions still active? The aim is to offer analyses, perspectives and interpretations of (parts of) the normative foundation of what is described as the 'Nordic welfare (state) model'. We discuss questions such as: what are the main normative principles in this model; what is the relationship between them; what are their origin; what is their significance for current welfare policy; to what extent do external economic and/or ideological pressure threaten these principles?

The conception of a Nordic (welfare) model

A small note on terminology is required here. 'Scandinavia' and 'the Nordic countries' refer in principle to different geographical and political entities, but have come to be used interchangeably by scholars and media in- and outside of the Nordic area. Geographically the concept of Scandinavia covers the mountainous peninsula surrounded by the Arctic Ocean in the north, the Atlantic in the west and the 'northern Mediterraneans', the North Sea and the Baltic, in the southwest and the southeast, thus what is today the nation states of Norway and Sweden. Due to the intertwined history of the Nordic area, the concept is very often used to include the archipelago of Denmark, Finland – 'the land of lakes and forests', and the islands of Iceland and the Faeroes. The 'Nordic countries' is a more precise concept than 'Scandinavia' when we refer to the area which covers the present nation states of Denmark, Finland, Iceland, Norway and Sweden, but the lack of a generally accepted noun for the term 'the Nordic countries' tempts most writers to opt for 'Scandinavia' as a synonymous or equivalent concept. The noun 'Norden' is a most familiar word in Scandinavia (*sic!*) and in the Nordic countries, but is not in general use outside of the area, although it has been introduced in a book, and even in the title of the book, in English (Øystein Sørensen and Bo Stråth (eds) *The Cultural Construction of Norden*, Oslo: Scandinavian University Press, 1997). Our book is about the normative foundations of the *Nordic* welfare states, but when the concepts 'Scandinavian welfare states' or 'Scandinavian countries' occur, 'Scandinavian' is almost without exception tantamount to 'Nordic'.

The conception of a Nordic model has gained wide acceptance in the social science literature as well as in journalistic essays. It can probably be traced to observations outlined in the book *Sweden: The Middle Way* which Marquis Childs, an American reporter, published in 1936. It was argued that Sweden had found an admirable middle way between Bolshevism and un-regulated, laissez-faire capitalism. Although the Swedish case was then, and during most of the period after the Second World War has been, identified as *the* empirical embodiment of the Scandinavian model, in fact all five Nordic countries took off in the same developmental direction during the 1930s. All of the Nordic countries got their crisis compromises in that decade, leading to new tension-reducing institutional solutions for mediation between agricultural and industrial interests as well as between the interests of organized labour and employers. This is the Nordic *Sonderweg*: crucial steps, unique in Europe, towards building a broad political consensus on a platform of a state-regulated socially modified capitalism were taken before the Second World War. Since then, with the exception of the wartime period, economic growth, democratization and social policy development have largely gone hand in hand in the Nordic countries.

According to Erikson *et al.* (1987), the core of the Scandinavian Model:

> lies in *broad public participation* in various areas of economic and social life, the purpose of which is to promote economic efficiency, to improve the ability of society to master its problems, and to enrich and equalize the living conditions of individuals and families. In social policy, the cornerstone of the model is *universalism*.
>
> (Erikson *et al.* 1987: vii)

By this is meant that the Scandinavian countries – 'at least on paper' – have set out to develop a welfare state that includes the entire population. Global programmes are preferred to selective ones (Erikson *et al.* 1987: vii–viii). The universalist Nordic welfare model is often depicted as the 'social democratic model' or 'social democratic regime' (Esping-Andersen 1990), but at important crossroads Nordic social democrats have only hesitantly endorsed the principle and practice of universalism, especially in income transfer programmes (Hatland 1992; Kildal and Kuhnle, Chapter

2 in this volume). One may claim that universalism has come about more through pragmatic, reformist consensus-building policy-making than through a historically embedded, clear visionary programme. But once achieved, several political parties, the social democratic ones in particular, have been all too happy with being associated with this principle.

Kuhnle (1990) lists 11 components of welfare systems which taken together, with partial exceptions, set Nordic countries apart from other welfare states. Among these are the relative size of governmental welfare provision; size of welfare employment (broadly speaking); public employment as a proportion of total employment; redistribution; high legitimacy for state/public welfare provision; and universal, citizenship-based social rights. 'Their universal embrace has anchored the Scandinavian welfare states' claim to a special status' (Baldwin 1990: 51–2). The principle of universalism is also part of the Beveridgean post Second World War development in Britain, and indeed, Nordic postwar developments are inspired by Beveridge (1942) and Labour's introduction of the National Health Insurance in UK in 1948.

Esping-Andersen and Korpi (1987) label the Scandinavian welfare states *institutional* welfare states as a contrast to 'marginal' or 'residual' welfare states and the 'corporatist' or so-called 'reciprocal' ones, based on earlier attempts at classification of welfare state models (see e.g. Wilensky and Lebeaux 1958; Titmuss 1974). A few years later Esping-Andersen (1990) renamed the various categories of welfare state models, and replaced 'institutional' with *social democratic* (welfare regime). The underlying view is that the institutional alias social democratic model prescribes the welfare of the individual to be the responsibility of the social collective; that all citizens should be equally entitled to a decent standard of living; and that full social citizenship rights and status should be guaranteed unconditionally (Esping-Andersen and Korpi 1987: 40). The social democratic model/regime label may be perceived as unnecessary politicized and imprecise since many political forces have contributed to and are responsible for the present characteristics of the Nordic welfare states, but we all agree that the hallmark of the contemporary Nordic 'institutional' welfare state is aptly expressed in terms of three essential features: social policy is *comprehensive;* the social entitlement principle has been *institutionalized* (social rights); and social legislation has a solidaristic and *universalist* nature.

Themes and structure of the book

Studies of norms and ideas are of various kinds. Normative research may be said to cover a continuum, from empirical studies of peoples' attitudes to philosophical justifications of principles and institutions. In this book the chapters are mainly based on empirical studies and conceptual analyses, of ideational displacements and resistance to changes and attitudes, although the book also includes discussions of arguments that have been put forward in favour of particular principles of welfare. The book is divided into three parts.

Part I, *Normative foundations: historical perspectives*, considers the historical trajectories behind the Scandinavian or Nordic welfare model. As the principle of 'universalism' may be said to be of prime significance in the moral logic of the Scandinavian welfare states, Nanna Kildal and Stein Kuhnle begin (Chapter 2) with a comprehensive analysis of the principle of universalism. Six questions are discussed: what is universalism? When was it introduced? What were the arguments? Who put them forward? What happened in the 1990s, and what is the prospective fate of universalism ? The following Chapter 3, by Bo Stråth, discusses the organization of the Nordic countries in view of some influential historical discourses on the concept of '*Volk/folk*' and '*folkhem*', a home for the people. His argument is that the social democratic occupation of the '*folk*' concept and the semantic field surrounding it, was crucial for the way in which society was organized in the North of Europe.

Chapter 4, authored by Lars Bo Kaspersen, offers a creative analysis of the development of the Danish welfare state. It is argued that the normative foundation of any state is, *inter alia*, to be searched for in the rationality of the state itself, in (its) decisions about survival and recognition. This argument rests on examples from Danish history. The political reform agenda in Nordic social politics in the late twentieth century is perceptively analysed by Anders Nordlund in Chapter 5, where he raises the question of how it is that economic and political pressure for radical changes have not resulted in a profound change in the Nordic welfare states. The reform agenda of the political parties are seen as a key to understand the obvious discrepancy between pressures for policy changes and actual policy outcomes.

Part II, *Normative tensions*, directs the attention more specifically to normative tensions and dilemmas in current welfare policies. In Chapter 6 Birte Siim and Anette Borchorst analyse the concept of 'the women-friendly welfare state', which has had a considerable influence on welfare theory and research during the 1990s. The authors argue that the concept is biased towards social democratic welfare states, which assume a particular notion of women's needs. In the following chapter (Chapter 7), Jan Otto Andersson and Olli Kangas present results from a recent study that explores the conspicuous difference in Swedish and Finnish attitudes to 'basic income', the most universalistic solution to income protection in a situation where ordinary jobs have become a scarce resource.

Olavi Kaukonen and Kerstin Stenius focus in Chapter 8 on the normative differences between Swedish and Finnish solutions to specific social problems of marginalized groups. The authors discuss postwar changes in the treatment of alcohol and drug misusers in the two countries in order to get a better understanding of why and how the universalistic ambitions of the policies may be threatened today – and what possibly protects the persistence of a comprehensive norm. In Chapter 9, Sven E. O. Hort discusses the conceptual relationship between the normative basis of the welfare state and theorizing and modelling based on empirical welfare state research. He compares the changing approaches or underlying models to social policy and the political attempts at evaluating and reorganizing social welfare in Sweden from the early 1990s to the second half of the first decade of the new millennium.

In the last part of the book, Part III *Towards a paradigm shift?*, the focus is on a possible change in the normative foundation of the Nordic welfare states. The first chapter in this section, Chapter 10 by Rune Ervik, addresses changes in the pension discourses in Norway and analyses those in terms of an altered balance between different normative principles. The case made in the subsequent chapter, Chapter 11 by Marcus Carson, is that important developments taking place in Sweden's welfare state can be identified and analysed in terms of cognitive–normative changes that constitute a paradigmatic drift. The relationship between equality and efficiency as guiding principles is central to the author's analysis of policy discourses and reforms in housing and health. The aim of the following chapter, Chapter 12 by Stéfan Ólafsson, is to give an account of the principles on which the Icelandic welfare system is based, of how it deviates from the general conception of the Scandinavian (Nordic) model and of the turn towards more liberalist principles during the 1990s. The consequences of this turn are examined in the light of normative foundation of different types of welfare regimes. The centre of attention in the last chapter, Chapter 13 by Jørn Loftager, is the relationships between the welfare state, capitalism and democracy. The overall concern is to discuss the kind of welfare system that can nurture democracy as deliberative democracy.

References

Abrahamson, P. (1999) 'Activation and social policies: comparing France and Scandinavia. Introduction', in MIRE *Comparing Social Welfare Systems in Nordic Europe and France*, Paris: Drees.

Baldwin, P. (1990) *The Politics of Social Solidarity; Class Bases of the European Welfare States 1875–1975*, Cambridge: Cambridge University Press.

Bertram, C. (1997) 'Political justification, theoretical complexity, and democratic community', *Ethics*, 107: 563–83.

Beveridge, Sir W. H. (1942) *Social Insurance and Allied Services*, London: Cmd 6404, HMSO.

Childs, M. (1936) *Sweden: The Middle Way*, New Haven: Yale University Press.

Cox, R. H. (1998) 'The consequences of welfare reform: how conceptions of social rights are changing', *Journal of Social Policy*, 27 (1): 1–16.

Erikson, R., Hansen, E. J., Ringen, S. and Uusitalo, H. (eds) (1987) *The Scandinavian Model: Welfare States and Welfare Research*, New York: M. E. Sharpe.

Ervik, R. and Kuhnle, S. (1996) 'The Nordic welfare model and the European Union', in B. Greve (ed.) *Comparative Welfare Systems: The Scandinavian Model in a Period of Change*, Houndmills/London: Macmillan.

Esping-Andersen, G. (1990) *The Three Worlds of Welfare Capitalism*, Cambridge: The Polity Press.

Esping-Andersen, G. and Korpi, W. (1987) 'From poor relief to institutional welfare states: the development of Scandinavian social policy', in R. Eriksson, E. J. Hansen, S. Ringen and H. Uusitalo (eds) *The Scandinavian Model: Welfare States and Welfare Research*, New York: M. E. Sharpe.

Hatland, A. (1992) *Til dem som trenger det mest? Økonomisk behovsprøving I norsk sosialpolitikk*, Oslo: Universitetsforlaget.

Hatland, A. (2001) 'Mer målrettet velferdspolitikk?', NHO, *Horisont*, (4).

Hausman, D. M. and McPehrson, M. S. (1996) *Economic Analysis and Moral Philosophy*, Cambridge: Cambridge University Press.

Kildal, N. (2001) *Workfare Tendencies in Scandinavian Welfare Policies*, Genéve: ILO InFocus Programme on Socio-Economic Security paper series.

Kuhnle, S. (1990) 'Den skandinaviske velferdsmodellen-skandinavist? Velferd? modell?', in A. R. Hovdum, S. Kuhnle and L. Stokke (eds) *Visjoner om velferdssamfunnet*, Bergen: Alma Mater.

Kuhnle, S. (2000) 'The Nordic welfare state in a European context: dealing with new economic and ideological challenges in the 1990s', *European Review*, 8 (3) July: 379–98.

Pierre, J. and Rothstein, B. (eds) (2003) *Välfärdsstat i otakt*, Malmö: Liber.

Rawls, J. (1971) *A Theory of Justice*, Cambridge: Harvard University Press.

Rothstein, B. (1998) *Just Institutions Matter. The Moral and Political Logic of the Universal Welfare State*, Cambridge: Cambridge University Press.

Sunesson, S., Blomberg, S., Edebalk, P. G., Harrysson, L., Magunsson, J., Meeuwisse, A., Petersson, J. and Salonen, T. (1998) 'The flight from universalism', *European Journal of Social Work*, 1 (1): 19–29.

Titmuss, R. M. (1958) 'The social division of welfare', in R. M. Titmuss *Essays on the Welfare State*, London: Allen & Unwin.

Titmuss, R. M. (1974) *Social Policy*, London: Allen & Unwin.

Waldron, J. (1993) *Liberal Right*, Cambridge: Cambridge University Press.

Weale, A. (1983) *Political Theory and Social Policy*, London: Macmillan.

Weber, M. (1969 [1904]) '"Objectivity" in social sciences', in M. Weber *The Methodology of the Social Sciences*, New York: The Free Press.

Wilensky, H. and Lebeaux, C. N. (1958) *Industrial Society and Social Welfare*, New York: Russel Sage Foundation.

Part I

Normative foundations

Historical perspectives

2 The Nordic welfare model and the idea of universalism[1]

Nanna Kildal and Stein Kuhnle

Introduction

Basically we subscribe to the view that there is such a thing as a Scandinavian or Nordic (welfare) model or type (or welfare regime), characterized among other things by the general adoption of the principle of universalism. The questions we shall discuss are: what is meant by universalism? When did the (defined) principle of universalism become embedded in the Nordic welfare states? Why did it, with some exception for Iceland (see Chapter 12), become so important in Scandinavia and 'Norden'? Who promoted the principle, with which arguments? Is universalism still a major component of recent social and welfare policy reforms in the Nordic countries?

What is universalism?

The concept of universalism signifies the general, what concerns everything of a special kind, or the totality. The concept is central in different European traditions of thought; in theology it connotes a religious view that asserts the ultimate salvation of *all* souls (*inter alia* in opposition to Calvinist predestination). In moral philosophy the concept denotes different moral theories arguing for principles of universal validity, independent of particular traditions, cultures or relations. In sociology, universalism is primarily attached to Talcott Parsons and the universalizing of citizens' relationships during the nineteenth century, replacing particular group-memberships. In the area of politics, the principle of universalism was initially expressed in the eighteenth century idea of human rights. In welfare policy, universalism as a distributive principle has been discussed since the nineteenth century. It is associated with equity and redistribution; yet the content of universal ideas in welfare policies remains somewhat unclear. Universal welfare policies are often contrasted with selective policies of a residual, means-testing kind, targeted at the poor. However, it is important to bear in mind that selective policies also comprise insurance-based, reciprocal ones; they comprise programmes targeted at individuals who cannot provide for themselves, as well as programmes restricted to the working population. Generally speaking, the conceptual confusions in the fields of both welfare policy and welfare theory are striking. Regarding universalism, its conceptual polysemy may partly be due to a conflation of (at least) two dimensions of the principle: *membership* and *allocation.*

Membership

Democratic governance has, so far at least, been closely interconnected with the nation state. As the democratic constitutional state guarantees equality before the law and the equal political status for all citizens, the main characteristic of a universal welfare state is the high degree of population coverage – people are attributed social rights by virtue of membership in a particular community; all members of society are, as a matter of right, beneficiaries of welfare schemes. This has to be qualified, however: everyone is covered as a member of a specific population category (i.e. people under or beyond a certain age, sick people, families with children, etc.) that represent certain politically-defined need situations with more or less strict entry criteria. Thus, taken literally, there are very few universal benefits in the Nordic countries: family allowances or child benefits, which are given to all families with children until they reach a certain age (18 in Norway), and old-age benefits being the most universal ones.

The terms 'all members' and 'everyone' are also ambiguous in another sense: sometimes the terms refer to 'all citizens' (Kuhnle 1990: 15; Hatland 1992: 23; 2001: 35), at other times, to 'all residents'. 'The Nordic countries have established a universal model of social protection, where benefits and services based on residence are combined with earnings-related social insurance programme' (Palme 1999: 9). Residence is obviously the most comprehensive principle and the most generous to immigrants, guest-workers etc.[2] In addition to the normative confusion produced by mixed definitions of membership *within* a universal welfare state, *between* welfare states this mix may produce serious gaps in the social protection systems.[3] In a world of increasing migration, these gaps represent a great normative challenge to principles of justice for all democratic governments – especially for welfare states that claim to be universal.

Allocation

A distinction is often made between 'universal' and 'discretionary' allocations of benefits, the latter being associated with 'selective' policies and gatekeepers that determine the applicants' eligibility on the basis of humiliating and integrity-violating investigations (Rothstein 1998: 21). However, no comprehensive universal welfare state manages without discretionary allocations, naturally more so for service provisions than for income transfers or support. Certainly, in terms of income security, the ideal-typical universal allocation is an unconditional, flat-rate 'basic income' unconditionally paid to all – a benefit which no country has yet introduced. Not only are all social benefits category-based, most of them are also subjected to various degrees of professional discretion. For instance, in order to enter the categories of sick or disabled, with entitlements to sickness benefits or disability pensions, more or less 'strong' or 'weak' discretionary assessment (Dworkin 1977) has to be carried out. Such assessments apply more extensively to the provision of health and social care services. The fact that the gatekeepers make a lot of priorities between clients/patients, using access criteria that may or may not be standardized, obviously weakens the social rights of the welfare state, and thus the universality of the allocation of benefits. Nevertheless, a welfare state that not only aims at securing a basic security for all, but also at compensating for social and natural inequalities due to brute bad luck, is compelled to allocate benefits on the basis of discretionary assessments of non-economic needs. As Titmuss noticed some 30 years ago:

> Universalism is not, by itself alone, enough: in medical care, in wage-related social security and in education. This much we have learnt in the past two decades from the facts about inequalities in the distribution of incomes and wealth.
>
> (1968: 134–5)

He therefore advocated a particular infrastructure of universal policies that incorporated 'positive selective discrimination' in income maintenance, housing, health care, education etc., i.e. complex professional discretionary assessments of needs.[4]

Furthermore, even standardized services may be allocated on a less than an ideal 'instant' universal basis than the legal or formal right to them may indicate. The fulfilment or implementation of legal obligations may take time because of scarce resources, bad organization or more or less intentionally biased allocation. Most services are de facto rationed and the claimants are, for example, put in waiting queues varying from days to years (for expensive or specialized medical treatment). Partly as a response to the problem of health queues, there has been a trend towards developing private health centres, which charge market prices for treatment. Moreover, the introduction of user fees, which have become widespread in Scandinavia and range from being insignificant to approaching market fees, contributes to a weakening of the principle of universalism as a principle of allocation in the Nordic welfare system.

It follows from the discussion above that the distinction between 'objective' and 'discretionary' assessments of needs is not essential for the demarcation between universal and selective policies. A distinction between kinds of needs is, however, important. A primary function of the welfare state is to protect its members against social risks. Characteristic for the development of the Nordic welfare states is that an increasing number of risks, such as unemployment, illness and the like, have been recognized as matters of public responsibility and matters of individual social rights. Thus, the categories of citizens with 'undisputable' legitimate needs for protection have gradually expanded. Risks that have not been granted this recognition are subsumed under residual social support mechanisms like the Social Assistance Act. As a consequence, a demarcation line is drawn between the testing of legitimate needs based on professional norms, without concern for the person's immediate economic or social circumstances, and the testing of economic needs, i.e. testing of 'means' at disposal and 'means' necessary to cover discretionary defined needs or, simply, testing of the *ability to pay*. Only the latter needs test should be classified as selective, 'since they select in relation to individuals' economic standing' (Rothstein 1998: 20). Even if professionals and local administrators are granted considerable discretionary power as to who should receive, for example, health services – what, when, how and how much – from the universal welfare state, *financial capacity* is the vital criterion for receiving support within selective welfare. Financial capacity of the individual can be defined *pre* or *post hoc*, thus selective policies take two qualitatively different forms: selective policies either take the form of insurance-based (and 'rights-based') policies for the economically active or policies are targeted at the economically weakest part of the population and paid from general (often local) governmental revenues. Only the second kind of selective policies implies *post hoc means-testing* by professional and/or administrative personnel, in the former case no actual means-testing is carried out since allocation of benefits is based on rather precise rights-based rules which relate benefits to income levels, previous income and/or period of employment. Most benefits fall within one of these two types. An important distinction thus exists between *post hoc* discretionary means-testing and a kind of *pre hoc* rights-based income-testing.

We have established that the concept and principle of universalism can refer to at least two dimensions: membership and allocation. Schemes that are universal in terms of population coverage normally have certain filters for coverage, such as eligibility (age, years of employment, income earned etc.) and in terms of benefit formulas (e.g. equal benefits or benefit in-cash or in-kind based on certain criteria). One example can illustrate that filters of both kinds may have become more important over time. During the period 1959–1967 the Norwegian old age pension system was at its most universal, taking various dimensions of the concept of universalism into account: the criterion of economic means-testing was done away with and the criterion of 'work-merit' was not introduced. Thus, all people beyond a certain age received a pension, and, significantly, the size of the pension was equal for all beneficiaries. After 1967, total pension benefits were made unequal as the filter of work merits was introduced. From the early 1990s a history of documented unpaid care work was added as a new criterion for earning a supplementary pension beyond the minimum pension. Nordic welfare states are not necessarily universal if by universal is meant equal benefits. Flat rate or uniform benefits were in one period considered especially egalitarian as they were regarded as an indication of the state's refusal to perpetuate market inequalities (Baldwin 1990: 52). To complicate matters, we should add that the concepts of universalism and selectivity are often used as entries to different ideological perspectives of welfare policies rather than as useful analytical tools (Hatland 1992: 22).

Universal welfare – when?

If we consider education as part of the welfare state, the Nordic countries stand out as relatively early proponents of a universal education. An early step towards democratization and universalization of education was the demand for general literacy for all; women as well as men. This 'need' or 'demand' was in principle created in the sixteenth century, as – with the coming of the Reformation – the then two Nordic kingdoms of Denmark-Norway-Iceland and Sweden-Finland became Evangelical Lutheran. The Church took responsibility for making the population literate.[5] Introduction of a general and compulsory system of elementary education came in the nineteenth century: elementary schools were a duty of local authorities and every child had the right to an elementary education of a certain length and of a broader secular content than the former church schools had offered (Sysiharju 1981: 420–1). Denmark was first, with a Public Education Act of 1814 which introduced seven years of compulsory education, and obliged all municipalities to set up primary schools (Flora 1983: 567); compulsory elementary education (length not specified) was introduced by law in Sweden in 1842 (ibid.: 613); compulsory education for all children from the age of seven to confirmation (*c.* age 14) was legislated in 1848 in Norway (ibid.: 608); and a system of general elementary schools was in principle established by legislation in 1866 in Finland. Elementary education for all citizens was also introduced partly under the influence of ideas behind the American and French revolutions.

Before the idea and institution of social insurance came firmly on the agenda in European countries after the introduction of relatively comprehensive social insurance legislation in Germany in the 1880s, the welfare responsibility and role of states and governments were, since the sixteenth century, to develop and maintain state-supported welfare or poor relief programmes. By the seventeenth century, virtually every European state had some sort of centrally established public welfare programme (Leichter 1979: 22), among which the Elizabethan Poor Law of 1601 is probably the best-known case. The motivation was not always simply paternalistic or moral/religious, but also to maintain law and order. Early welfare measures, particularly health, were also related to the doctrine of mercantilism as a healthy population was considered good for the creation of national wealth and strength. Public health was one of the first areas in which the state began playing an active role, motivated not least by the fact that epidemic diseases such as cholera, typhus and smallpox tended to be socially indiscriminate, affecting rich and poor alike. Some of the first positive exertions of state authority came in the area of public health; the first public health laws were introduced in 1832 in France and 1848 in England (Leichter 1979: 31). The provision of free, state-supported, and state-administered medical assistance to the *needy* was introduced as a reaction to industrialization and urban-related health problems in the nineteenth century. In England, such assistance was supplied under the poor laws, but at a social and political price: until 1885, to request free medical assistance resulted in pauperization (i.e. losing one's political rights and being subject to placement in a workhouse). France was one of the first nations to provide free medical treatment and hospitalization for the needy. It did so in 1893 with the National Law for Free Medical Assistance (Leichter 1979: 32). Sweden and Norway were among the countries which by the latter part of the nineteenth century employed doctors to provide free or inexpensive medical services to the *needy*, i.e. those *without means*, and to supervise public health programmes (Leichter 1979: 32). These early *selective* legislation for the needy can – at least *post factum* – be looked upon as a step towards universalizing public health care.[6] The Nordic countries have a long tradition of health and medical services. Denmark passed a health law in 1858, followed by Norway in 1860, Sweden in 1874, and Finland in 1879 – all laws introducing control over and regulation of health and hygiene by local authorities (Kuhnle 1981b).

After 1850, *die Arbeiterfrage* or 'social question' frequently appeared in parliamentary discussions and deliberations in Denmark, Norway and Sweden. Though modest attempts at worker insurance following the emergence and growth of industrialization have been attempted in several countries, it was Bismarck's regime in Germany that introduced a new concept of state-legislated social insurance in 1883, with all industrial workers being insured against sickness in a compulsory programme.[7] This law was only one in a series of social insurance schemes to be implemented in Germany in the 1880s. The shift in the concept of poor law relief to the idea of social insurance was a dramatic and significant change in terms of attitudes to public responsibility for certain types of risks or individual misfortunes. Scandinavian debates, and to some extent social policy developments, were influenced by the German legislation (Kuhnle 1981a, 1996), but decisions varied as to priority of insurance needs, form of organization, extent of population or worker coverage, whether insurance should be voluntary or compulsory. What is of particular interest here is coverage or membership of schemes, and it can be established that all first laws were limited in terms of coverage, except the Swedish old age and disability pension law of 1913 which, with minor exceptions, was universal in scope, although with varying rules of eligibility for variegated benefits (e.g. means-tested supplement for those who had not paid contributions). The intention was to provide both the urban and rural populations with economic security in old age (Palme 1999). All early pension laws in the Nordic countries prescribed some elements of income and/or means-tested pensions,[8] and not until the post Second World War period was the right to receive a national pension independent of a means test instituted, thus making the schemes truly universal (1946 in Sweden, 1957 in Norway and Finland, 1964 in Denmark and 1965 in Iceland) (Kuhnle 1981b). The Danish pension scheme of 1891 has been described as universal (Knudsen 2000: 9, 21), but that stretches the concept of universality too far: only deserving poor people at the age of 60 or more – who had not received poor relief during the previous ten years – were entitled to a pension (Kuhnle 1981a).[9] Industrial accident insurance, first introduced in one form or other between 1894 and 1903, covered only industrial workers (and in Iceland fishermen), but was gradually extended to cover all employees (Denmark 1916, Sweden 1927, Finland 1948, Norway 1958, Iceland 1965) (Kuhnle 1981b). Sickness insurance was made voluntary in the first legislation in Denmark and Sweden in 1892 and 1891, respectively, while Norway started out with a compulsory insurance which in principle covered all wage earners below a fixed, relatively high income limit, thus proving much more supportive of the principle of universality than legislation in the other Nordic countries. The principle of universality was even more emphatic: as the first country in the world Norway introduced in 1909 the family-friendly principle in sickness insurance that the spouse (i.e. in practice wife) and children of the employee/worker were automatically insured without having to pay an extra premium (Kuhnle 1983). Thus, a much larger part of the population was covered than statistics on the insured would indicate. Other European countries introduced corresponding family-friendly schemes only from the 1930s onwards. It was only after the Second World War, however, that all Nordic schemes were made truly universal, encompassing all citizens (residents) (Sweden 1955, Norway 1956, Iceland 1956, Denmark 1960, Finland 1963). With the exception of Norway, unemployment insurance has been voluntary in the Nordic countries, thus less universal than other schemes. Unemployment insurance in Norway has been compulsory since 1938, adopted for nearly all wage earners, and organized by the state. However, any person becoming unemployed in the other Nordic countries can claim economic assistance based on some kind of means test.

> It was during the postwar period that the cornerstones of the modern welfare state were laid. Where previously Scandinavia had hardly

> differed from international trends, the new period gave rise to a uniquely Scandinavian model. This model is characterized by considerable inter-Nordic convergence.
>
> (Esping-Andersen and Korpi 1987: 47)

The postwar construction of the welfare state went through two phases: the first was characterized by the general acceptance and establishment of universal population (or relevant category of population) coverage with a flat-rate benefit system; the second phase from the 1960s is marked by the introduction of earnings-related and adequate benefits, and thus also maintenance of status (and to a larger extent income) achieved in gainful employment.

Why universal welfare?

Originating in Europe at the end of the nineteenth century, the development of public health and social security has spread worldwide. The evolution of welfare states, in one form or other, is a near global phenomenon. But *universal* social programmes are less common; they were long the hallmark of the welfare states of UK and the Nordic countries. New Zealand was, in 1898, the third country in the world (after Iceland and Denmark) to introduce non-contributory old age pensions, providing means-tested pensions, and more importantly, introduced unemployment benefits based on a system of compulsory earnings-related contributions in 1930 (Kaim-Caudle 1973).[10] One should be aware, however, that universal social security programmes from the early post-1945 period in Britain have offered very low benefit levels, thus in practice, and as intended by the 'architect' Beveridge (1942), giving the market much greater space relatively than in the Nordic countries. Though we have stressed that by universalism we refer among other things to population coverage of programmes, and that the Nordic countries and Britain show similarities in this respect, a careful comparison would remind us that other aspects of social security and welfare programmes can be conducive to the development of institutionally very different types of welfare states, with Britain often placed in the category of 'residual', 'marginal' or 'liberal' welfare states. The Nordic–British contrast is not a topic to be pursued here. Rather, we shall focus on: why was it that the idea of universal welfare and social security programmes, relatively generous although not always 'adequate' (variously defined) in terms of benefit levels, developed earlier and stronger in the Nordic countries than most places elsewhere? Why did residency (and citizenship) status become principally as important as employment status in northern Europe, but not – or only much later emerging as a possibility – elsewhere? What arguments and possible structural factors were conducive to the emphasis on one or the other principle of membership of state welfare programmes?

Arguments supporting universalism

Goul Andersen (1999) has listed arguments that have been used in debates on universal (general, adequate) welfare schemes. Arguments against are that universal schemes are too expensive; taxes are too high; high taxes have negative effects on the market; less social equality is achieved; lead to inefficient priorities; create dependency cultures; increase transaction costs; and create too high expectations among citizens. Arguments in favour of universal programmes have been (or are): such programmes are market conform (meaning that they make for fewer negative incentives for saving, employment, etc.); administratively simpler; do not give incentive to abuse; create greater social equality; are non-stigmatizing; create and support community feeling and social cohesion; and support and increase citizens' resources and thus their autonomy.

Many of these arguments, *pros* and *cons,* can be found in political debates and government documents at various times in the Nordic countries. At this stage we shall try to order pro-arguments in distinct, broader categories and only briefly discuss some arguments that have been used in favour of universal programmes. Then we list some possible structural and contextual factors, which may have been conducive to universalism.

The basis for universalistic Nordic welfare states, empirically a post Second World War phenomenon, can be traced both to idealistic and pragmatic ideas promoted and partly implemented in many early examples of social insurance legislation immediately before and after the turn of the twentieth century. Arguments in favour may tentatively be grouped in four main categories.

Community-building

Early social security programmes were initiated concomitant to political and economic 'modernization', in an era where state- and nation-building were on top of the agenda of state leaders in European countries and national identity- and community-building was important. New social groups pressed for political inclusion, and whether this fight was successful or not, social inclusion was considered important both by authoritarian state leaders (e.g. Germany, Austria) and more democratically oriented leaders (e.g. Nordic countries). Early programmes did not include all groups (although the Swedish pension law of 1913 came close), groups were excluded on different grounds (non-employed; economically well-off; morally 'unworthy' people), but an idea of universalism can perhaps be said to have been at least a *latent* element of the 'nation-building' project. In Norway, the concept of a 'people's insurance' appeared around 1900 and the first parliamentary worker's commission formulated among its proposals in 1894 that 'because of the greatness of the cause and the interest it has aroused, the pension scheme should cover the entire population' (Hatland 1992: 55, *our translation*). In the far-off days before the First World War, important voices considered welfare and national efficiency complementary; welfare was supposed to prevent waste of human resources in a highly different, unequal and 'class-saturated' society.[11]

Risk exposure

The protection against social risks caused by a century of turmoil, war and change, and last, but not least, the novel idea of prevention, contributed to the recognition of the ideas of social rights and universalism (Titmuss 1968). 'We are all in the same boat' is a normatively impregnated description of this risk-situation: every citizen is potentially exposed to certain risks and all capable citizens should share responsibility for meeting welfare needs arising from such risk exposure. For instance, in 1918, the non-socialist government's proposal for an old age and disability pension covering all workers, rich and poor, was justified by the society's risk-pattern; only very few citizens could afford a long-lasting loss of income, and thus nearly the whole population had a self-interest in the equalizing of risks. In this respect the Norwegian non-socialist parties went against the international trend – the implementation of 'class insurance' for the less well-off (except for Sweden) (Hatland 1992: 56). Moreover, the high degree of universalism in 'population coverage' also went against the Norwegian social democratic party, which, as late as in 1946, proposed an old age pension restricted to workers below a certain income limit. Soon afterwards, however, in the same year, the idea of a 'people's insurance' was transformed into a universal idea and implemented as a universal child allowance (ibid.: 70).

It can be claimed that socialist or social democratic parties in the 1880s had a solidaristic vision of universal social programmes, e.g. in 1885 it was claimed that 'the state should guarantee a general old-age pension with state subsidy for all classes of society' (*Det Norske Arbeiderparti* 1918: 11, *our translation*). However, at that time it implied improving (selectively) the life chances of workers and the poor and not an idea of all classes and citizens being part of public programmes offering benefits to everybody, which have become part of post Second World War social democratic programmes.

The famous Beveridge report *Social Insurance and Allied Services* (1942) sought to establish 'a comprehensive programme of social reform directed to deal not only with Want but with the four other giant evils of Disease, Ignorance, Squalor and Idleness' (quote from Beveridge 1943: 10). The universalistic ambition of the report – the aim to expand the risk-pool from particular classes to embracing all citizens – immediately made it a success. It inspired for instance the design of the Norwegian White Paper on a National Insurance Scheme that was presented in 1948 (Seip 1994: 152–3).[12]

Human dignity

Early social programmes were selective. They either provided tax-financed means-tested minimum benefits targeted at the poor (cf. the Danish old age pension from 1891), or contribution-based income-maintenance schemes, both types of programmes in fact excluding 'unworthy' people from coverage (beggars, drunkards, 'lazy good-for-nothing people') (cf. also the Norwegian old age pension system 1923 and 1936); the very poor and weak were excluded in the Swedish pre-Second World War sickness and unemployment insurance programmes (Olsson 1990: 149). Only after the Second World War did the concept of 'unworthy' people lose ground concomitant to the rise of the concept of human rights (civil, political, social rights, cf. UN Declaration in 1948): all citizens are 'equal' or of equal worth.

According to Titmuss, an essential historical reason for adopting the twin concepts of *social* rights and universalism in welfare politics was to remove *the humiliating* loss of status, dignity and self-respect that goes with exclusion from programmes and entitlements. 'There should be no sense of inferiority, pauperism, dignity or stigma in the use of a publicly provided service; no attribution that one was being or becoming a "public burden"'(Titmuss 1968: 129).

According to Jose Harris (1994), the biographer of Beveridge, the Beveridge proposals were also mainly results of his long-term *aversion* against the Poor Law, selectivity and all forms of means-tested benefits. He fought the ethic of 'clientage, concealment, and calculated improvidence' that assumedly ultimately would corrupt the whole society (Harris 1994: 26).

Also in the Norwegian socio-political debates the dignity-argument was salient, expressing first and foremost a deep dissatisfaction with the existing poor relief system that offered only limited help to a heterogeneous group with quite different problems in a highly paternalizing and stigmatizing way. Although the Conservatives and other non-socialist parties, on grounds of economic and administrative efficiency arguments, were driving forces for ending the means-tested old age pension and making it universal, the Norwegian social democratic Prime Minister Einar Gerhardsen justified his proposal for moving from a means-tested to a universal old age pension with dignity arguments; old people's self-respect and social standing were even more important than economic equalization (Hatland 1992: 74). This way of arguing was also salient in the justification of a universal child allowance in 1946; the positive effects of not distinguishing between children of poor and rich families.

Economic and bureaucratic efficiency

The principle of universal social programmes, i.e. no selectivity on moral or economic grounds, has also been argued for on a pragmatic basis. This was, for example, the case in Norway in the 1950s when the Conservatives and other non-socialist parties pressed for the reform of the means-tested old age pension in favour of a universal (flat rate) pension because as many as 75–80 per cent of all old people received means-tested pensions. To make pensions universal – a matter of citizen's right – it was argued, would save huge amounts of administrative cost. The Conservative Party (*Høire*) in Norway was the first party to include in its programme, in 1949, the aim of a universal pension scheme (Sejersted 1984: 528). Other arguments (often heard in these debates), included the claim that means-testing penalizes the will to work and save, and the problem linked to the demarcation line; different municipal practices undermined the legitimacy of the means-testing arrangements.

A social democratic myth

Political actors are seldom consistent over time, and parties of similar ideological predisposition have not always advocated the same arguments across countries. It has been claimed by several authors (e.g. Seip 1981; Bull 1982; Esping-Andersen 1985; Bergh 1987; Marklund 1988), that universalism is an idea that is particularly strong within the social democratic movement. This was not always so (Hatland 1992). Social democratic parties were long in favour of means-testing of the wealthy both before and after reaching governmental power, partly for class solidaristic reasons, partly for economic (too expensive) and partly as a matter of principle (affluent people do not need public benefits) (ibid.: 62). According to Hatland, the main social democratic contribution to a system of universal social security in Norway, was their struggle for means-testing insurance schemes which seem to have stronger inherent attributes to develop into systems of universal social insurance schemes than insurance schemes originally established for certain occupational groups. However, from the 1960s until this day, social democratic parties, having substantial experience as government parties, have tended to make the universal welfare state part of their image and trade mark, the great defenders of the universal, solidaristic welfare state where the rich and the middle classes are consciously included as members and beneficiaries of uniform public programmes to promote egalitarianism and fight social differentiation, and as a means to corroborate broad social and political support for the welfare state (Sosialdemokrati 2000). The argument has been that universal programmes make for a 'better', more generous welfare state than selective, means-testing, partly stigmatizing programmes for which the middle classes and well-off assumedly take no or little interest in paying taxes to maintain (see e.g. Rothstein 1998). 'Forced solidarity' makes, it may be argued, paradoxically, for a better welfare state for economically, socially and politically weak groups than 'selective solidarity', even when that in principle should yield more economic resources available for weak groups.

Universalism: a vision, a compromise or an overlapping consensus?

As we have shown in this preliminary analysis, different kind of arguments has been used in favour, directly, and not least indirectly, in favour of universalism. Even if this analysis is tentative and has to be substantiated through a closer analysis of historical documents, we have not found a clear political vision behind the political initiatives towards universalism. On the other hand, universalism can hardly be conceived of as a pure interest-based compromise, a result of a bargaining process. The interpretation that we will suggest is that universalism was a result of a long, dynamic argumentative process developing towards an 'overlapping consensus' (Rawls 1993: lecture IV). Political actors were critical to different parts of the traditional social security system, and universalism was the alternative they gradually come to agree on. The driving force seems, in other words, to have been the same as was inspiring Beveridge's proposals for universalism; a deep discontent with the existing selective system.

Structural and contextual factors conducive to Nordic universalism

Can it be that certain social–structural conditions have been conducive to fostering arguments in favour of universalism? Let us indicate four possible 'causal' factors, which independently or in combinations may have favoured a social and political climate for universalism in the Nordic countries:

- *Historical-institutional pre-requisites.* The early fusion of the church and state bureaucracies since the Reformation in the 1500s made for a more unified and stronger public interest in and responsibility for welfare matters in general, and citizens would direct their welfare demands towards government (central and/or local). Local communities had a long, pre-Reformation history of responsibility for poor relief or support. There was no 'competition' between state and church for provision of education and health services in the modern state- and nation-building period as was the case in many other countries of Catholic Europe. And there was limited space for market and other non-governmental solutions (Kuhnle 1981a). Development of universal programmes can later on also be interpreted as a result of piecemeal, pragmatic learning from experience of policies and their shortcomings. But, and this may be important, some early institutional solutions for social security programmes may have been more conducive to being transformed into universal programmes than other early solutions, e.g. early means-tested pension programmes were easier to transform into universal citizenship-based programmes than pension schemes based on work merit or employment record (cf. Palme 1999; Hatland 1992). Thus, early institutional solutions and structures, make some later reforms, adjustments and extensions easier than other kind of reforms, and help explain strains of 'Nordic exceptionalism'.

- *Egalitarian pre-industrial society.* The Nordic countries are marked by relatively egalitarian pre-industrial social structures; early predominance of independent or relatively independent peasants; historically early enfranchisement of peasants; and the formation of separate agrarian political parties creating party systems distinct from those of other European countries and giving such parties a key role in the power-play and horse-trading about public policies in general, including welfare/social policies. Peasants gained a relatively stronger political role, and a more important role as taxpayers and potential beneficiaries of public policies. Peasants were critical of public outlays in general, and particularly of outlays or programmes from which they would be excluded as beneficiaries, thus it was more difficult to outline social security policies covering only industrial workers. The socialist or social democratic forces were weak at the time of the industrial take-off and the political setting was more conducive to searching for and defining universal solidaristic welfare solutions rather than class solidaristic solutions.
- *Cultural homogeneity.* The combination of relatively egalitarian social structures, small and relatively homogenous populations in terms of ethnicity, religion and language, and a long historical tradition of public/communal responsibility for welfare issues, made universal social programmes more likely than in inegalitarian, culturally heterogeneous and fragmented societies. But over time, the idea of universalism gained strength also beyond the Nordic countries, circumstances changed, lessons from historical/foreign examples could be learnt.
- *Extraordinary crises.* Although the idea of universal social security programmes to some extent was vented in the late 1800s, and was promoted in ILO documents and in parliamentary committee reform proposals in Norway in the 1930s, it was only after the Second World War that universal programmes were actively and comprehensively introduced in Scandinavia (and also in Britain, see p. 20). The war experience itself has been mentioned by many (e.g. Titmuss 1968; Seip 1986; Goodin and Dryzek 1987) as an important driving force for solidaristic, universal social policy solutions, meaning that the devastating war brought leading political opponents closer together in their fight against Nazism and occupation and being conducive for forming a broader common value platform for the prospective peace era.

Welfare reforms of the 1990s: quo vadis universalism?

In 1945, no Norwegian social benefits had universal coverage (Hatland 1992: 78). As of the early 1970s all Nordic countries had established universal coverage of old age pension systems, sickness insurance, occupational injury insurance, child allowance and parental leave schemes. The unemployment insurance was in principle universal and compulsory in Norway only, while merely union members were selectively covered in the other countries. The same overall institutional pattern existed at the time of the international recession around 1990, and at the end of the 1990s, although with some modifications. The introduction of a partial income-test of the 'pension-supplement' – part of the basic old age pension in Denmark in 1994 can be seen as a potentially significant change towards some element of means-testing of the amount of pension benefits, but in this case, means-testing at the top of the income scale, not means-testing of the low- or no-income members of the population. A similar means-testing of the top range of income-earners has been introduced as part of the new pension reform in Sweden, passed in 1998, and in the Finnish reform of 1996–1997: the hitherto universal minimum national pension is offered only to pensioners with employment-derived (earnings-dependent) pensions below a certain income limit (which is set high) or to people beyond pensionable age who have not been employed (Kuhnle 2000: 388).[13] These are interesting novel examples of tendencies towards introducing selectivity in the allocation of benefits in universal membership schemes in Nordic welfare states – interesting exactly because the very few on top of the income pyramid are excluded from some benefits. Simultaneously, the insurance or reciprocity principle has been strengthened in the Swedish and Finnish pension reforms by establishing a closer link between what is paid into the system and what can be taken out. In the Norwegian case, this link has been weakened during the 1990s in the national pension scheme. However, this trend has created more space for other important tiers of pension provision in Norway, such as occupational and individual pension schemes and other forms of savings and sources of income in old age. Reforms within these tiers of pension provision have opened up for less socially redistributive elements within the occupational schemes and increased the pure market logic and risk exposure within the private pension schemes. Both rhetorically and empirically, when considering the whole pension provision system, it can be claimed that the insurance principle has been strengthened in Norwegian pension policy (see Chapter 10, this volume, by Rune Ervik). Proposals to retract on the principle of universalism in the allocation of benefits have been discussed, but not implemented, in the field of child allowances, according to a similar method of means-testing as for pensions. The normative development in the health care sector displays though a somewhat different picture: during the 1990s, patient rights gradually achieved more attention, which resulted in a law on patients' rights in 1999 (effectuated in 2001). Yet most of the welfare services are de facto rationed i.e. through queuing.

An important arena for changes in the thinking and reforms of the western and Nordic welfare states has been employment policies. Unemployment or the problem of 'non-work' has been given much political attention, even in countries with little experience of high unemployment rates, such as Norway. General trends in European welfare policy reforms in this area are towards *active measures* rather than passive, negative *sanctions* rather than positive *incentives, duties* rather than rights, *selectivity* rather than *universal social rights.* The leading theme is the idea of a 'new welfare contract' between the citizen and the state (Ferrera and Rhodes 2000; White 2003). In this area, at least, a kind of convergence seems to be evolving: both in terms of the interpretation of political challenges and in terms of political answers, irrespective of national institutional preconditions and the political colour of the government.

The primacy of work has always been central to Scandinavian welfare legislation, characteristic for these welfare states is the close relation between the institutions of welfare and work; the Scandinavian countries stand out as both 'strong work societies' and 'strong welfare states'. Thus, an 'active labour market policy' and the 'work approach' have been cornerstones of welfare policy since the Second World War, especially in Norway and Sweden. Yet, during the 1990s, the new 'work' and 'activity approaches' emerged that tightened eligibility criteria and reduced periods and levels of support (Kildal 2001). Yet the most distinctive difference between the 'new' and 'old' work approaches is the introduction of a 'work-for-your-welfare' requirement: an immediate 'duty to work' *in return* for benefits in the lowest tier of the income maintenance system, which has been described as a 'new trajectory' different from the former 'income security' policy in terms of social rights (Goul Andersen 2000: 80).[14]

In assessments of the last decade's welfare political developments, it is sometimes stressed that neither Norway nor other Nordic countries have moved towards convergence with a 'neo-liberal' model of social protection (e.g. Swank 2002: 152). By the mid-1990s, at least, Norway has enjoyed more continuity of welfare state programmes than other Nordic countries. Some non-market related benefits have been introduced during the 1990s, such as cash support measures for parents with small children in Norway (since 1998).

Yet, several trends in Norwegian welfare policy development suggest at least some modifications of its basic principles, not least the new 'work approach', which consists of various initiatives to increase labour market participation by strengthening the link between *contributions* and *benefits,* that is, strengthens the norm of reciprocity at the cost of the principle of universalism. The consequence is that more people are directed into the means-testing social assistance system, which is another move towards selectivism.[15] That the issue of targeting in welfare reforms has become a key concept both in Norwegian and international debates confirms this interpretation, together with trends towards greater use of user charges in the public system as well as towards more private providers of social and health services.

Concluding remarks

In this chapter we have primarily been concerned with the normative basis of Nordic welfare policy, mostly with Norwegian references. More precisely, we have been concerned with the definition and justifications of one of its characterizing traits, the principle of universalism: what is the meaning of this principle; what is the origin of it; why did it gain a foothold in our welfare states – which values and ideas are expressed though universal arrangements; what significance do reasons for universalism have in current Scandinavian welfare policies? Relating to the current convergence debates, the question in focus is whether the inherent norms of recent western welfare reforms, for one reason or another, are becoming more alike, and if so, what consequences these shared norms may have for future development of national welfare reforms. However, for us the basic issue has been to reconstruct the types of arguments that prepared the ground for universal welfare policies and to reassess the status of these arguments in current welfare debates.

In our conceptual and historical analysis, the preliminary conclusion is, first, that the arguments that supported the introduction of the principle of universalism were more indirect and pragmatic than current conventional political and academic wisdom tell us. It was rather a question of moving away from a social policy that had become normatively unjustifiable and economically inefficient than a vision and aim of expanding the risk-pool from particular classes to embracing all citizens, although such visions were not at all absent. Thus, the principle of universalism seems to be a result of a kind of 'overlapping consensus' rather than a result of a unified vision and aim (of one or many parties). Second, the frequently heard claim that the social democratic movement was the driving force for the adoption of a principle of universalism has not been corroborated. Many social policies developed before social democratic parties reached power, and other parties often, for various reasons, advanced the idea and practise of universalism of one kind or another. Finally, a peculiar observation seems to be that the arguments that are used to support more targeting and means-testing policies today are similar to arguments once used – 50–70 years ago – to support the introduction or adoption of universal policies (e.g. human dignity, efficiency and incentives).

Notes

1 An early version of this chapter was presented at the 9th International Congress of Basic Income European Network, Geneva, September 12–14, 2002. We thank in particular Anders Molander, Einar Øverbye and Axel West Pedersen for their careful reading of a draft and for their constructive criticism and suggestions.

2 Strange as it may seem, most political rights are attributed by virtue of citizenship while social rights, which sometimes incur substantial public expenditures, more often are attached to residence.

3 The main principle in the Norwegian National Insurance Scheme – *Folketrygden* – is residence. Resident is a person who has resided 12 months or more in Norway; citizenship, work participation or ability to pay has no significance in the attribution of rights and duties (§ 1–3). Yet, according to the EEA agreement that came into force in 1994, only *employed citizens* may bring with them pension rights when moving to another EEA country. This means that both citizens from a third country (a non-EEA country) as well as non-working citizens of EEA countries are not recognized as members when moving between EEA countries. Another group, which is denied membership in the Norwegian pension system, is asylum seekers, as granted political asylum or residence permission is required for pension rights.

4 Obviously, from a normative perspective, there is a significant difference between the allocation of benefits based on objective, standard criteria – and welfare allocations based on professional discretion of individual needs. While a just allocation of benefits requires *impartial* treatment of everyone, elements of arbitrariness, unpredictability and uncertainty are brought into the process of allocation wherever the professionals act as the welfare state's gatekeepers. Hence, justly designed welfare institutions that aim at compensating people for individual brute bad luck, may very well conflict with a fair *implementation* of the welfare policies.

5 Tim Knudsen (2000) has searched for the genesis of the Scandinavian universalistic welfare state. He repudiates the common social democratic explanation, or explanation by other political groups for that matter, and concentrates on *the state's* importance for the development of the Scandinavian welfare state. A main focus is the state's capacity to perform a welfare policy. This was built up by the Protestant church, which became the kingdom's instrument in its new caring duties for the poor and sick after the Reformation.

6 Based on works of Palme (1990) and Goodin and Le Grand (1987), Hatland discusses the development of the pension system according to the allocation principles of 'need', 'work merit' or 'citizenship', and reports that no European states provided universal benefits in their first social security legislation (1992: 104–8). Moreover, he states that universalism is first of all developed in countries that initially legislated means-tested benefits and services – seldom in countries with initial legislation based on work merits.

7 Bismarck very much favoured compulsory social insurance for workers, and that scheme(s) should be financed by the state and not by worker premiums, which came to be an element of the legislation passed in *der Reichstag* in 1883. He argued, on practical Christianity and conservative paternalism, for a social reform that assigned a greater responsibility to the state for the protection of the working class. He favoured compulsory insurance because he considered it unrealistic and out of touch with real life to require that the workers should insure themselves against needs caused by illness, invalidity and failing capacity for work in old age (Svenstrup 2000: 115).

8 Finland passed legislation for a fully funded system in 1937, but no benefits were paid before the Second World War and, after the war, it was transformed into a means-tested system similar to what the other Nordic countries had ended up with (Palme 1999: 32).

9 Not widely known, Iceland was first among the Nordic countries to introduce an old age (and disability) relief or pension law: already in 1890 the parliament enacted a means-tested scheme for old and weak persons outside the poor

relief system. This law has also been seen as a model for the Danish law of 1891 (Berner 1894). See also Chapter 12 in this volume.

10 New Zealand was also the first country to introduce a family allowance scheme in 1926 (Kaim-Caudle 1973).

11 A maturing of the nation-building argument is in recent years extended to reach beyond the borders of the national communities, especially in western Europe where a 'European identity' is consciously being nurtured in the headquarters of the European Union. Already in the mid-1950s a Nordic social union was established, among other things to promote a Nordic identity, but also for the pragmatic reason of promoting a common Nordic labour market.

12 Lowe (1994) claims that, contrary to conventional historical accounts, the report's success was in fact only short-lived, both in Europe and in Britain; a remarkable disparity exists between the report's ideal of a welfare system where ordinary people could experience freedom of poverty guaranteed as a right to adequate resources without means-testing, and its practical implementation. The new social security system's six main pillars (Beveridge 1942: para. 17) were never implemented (the 'adequacy of benefit' and 'the unification of administrative responsibility'), soon abandoned (flat-rate contributions and benefits) or heavily qualified (comprehensiveness and classification) (Lowe 1994: 120–3). Why it never became a practical blueprint for the postwar British welfare state, is a complex question that is most interesting, but beside the issue of this chapter. Although the rejection or failure of implementation of many of the report's recommendations may be sought in the inconsistencies of the report itself, a not unimportant reason may also be of a structural kind relating to the normative basis of the British society; the lack of a cultural 'soundboard' which may have existed in Scandinavia where Beveridgean ideas, more or less openly referred to, gained stronger support in practice.

13 Einar Øverbye has in a comment to the authors made the point that the new Swedish basic pension supplement is only price-indexed, while the new earnings-related component is indexed according to wages. This may cause the Swedish system to gradually slide towards contribution-based pensions for workers and means-tested supplements for the 'lumpenproletariat' – unless the same happens as in the 1960s, that the centre parties (including the agrarians) lobby to introduce a new pension supplement to keep up a high basic pension (Øverbye, private correspondence 2003).

14 'Workfare workers' are priced lower than other workers, they neither have any bargaining power, nor labour rights to sickness or unemployment benefits, vacation etc.

15 This development is in concordance with Lawrence Mead's description of current western welfare policies as a change from a notion of 'rights', to ideas of 'social contract' and reciprocity: 'the needy should receive aid, but *only in return for some contribution to the society*' (Mead 1997: 221, *our italics*).

References

Baldwin, P. (1990) *The Politics of Social Solidarity; Class Bases of the European Welfare States 1875–1975*, Cambridge: Cambridge University Press.

Bergh, T. (1987) *Storhetstid. 1945–65. Arbeiderbevegelsens historie i Norge*, vol. 5, Oslo: Tiden.

Berner, H. E. (1894) 'Arbeiderforsørgelsen i de nordiske lande', *Statsøkonomisk tidsskrift*: 115–39.

Beveridge, Sir W. H. (1942) *Social Insurance and Allied Services*, London: Cmd 6404, HMSO.

—— (1943) *The Pillars of Security*, London: Allen & Unwin.

Bull, E. (1982) 'Velferdsstaten i historisk perspektiv', in S. Stjernö (ed.) *Velferd eller nöd?*, Oslo: Pax.

Dworkin, R. (1977) *Taking Rights Seriously*, London: Duckworth.

Esping-Andersen, G. (1985) *Politics against Markets: The Social Democratic Road to Power*, Princeton: Princeton University Press.

Esping-Andersen, G. and Korpi, W. (1987) 'From poor relief to institutional welfare states: the development of Scandinavian social policy', in R. Erikson, E. J. Hansen, S. Ringen and H. Uusitalo. (eds) *The Scandinavian Model: Welfare States and Welfare Research*, New York: M. E. Sharpe.

Ferrera, M. and Rhodes, M. (2000) 'Recasting European welfare states: an introduction', in M. Ferrera and M. Rhodes (eds) *Recasting European Welfare States*, London: Frank Cass.

Flora, P., Alber, J., Eichenberg, R., Kohl, J., Kraus, F., Pfenning, W. and Seebohm, K. (1983) *State, Economy, and Society in Western Europe 1815–1975. A Data Handbook, Volume I: The Growth of Mass Democracies and Welfare States*, Frankfurt: Campus Verlag.

Goodin, R. E. and Dryzek, J. S. (1987) 'Risk-sharing and social justice: the motivational foundations of the post-war welfare state', in R. Goodin and J. Le Grand (eds) *Not Only the Poor*, London: Allen and Unwin.

Goodin, R. E. and Le Grand, J. (eds) (1987) *Not Only the Poor. The Middle Classes and the Welfare State*, London: Allen & Unwin.

Goul Andersen, J. (1999) 'Den universelle velferdsstat', *Grus* nr 56/57: 40–62.

—— (2000) 'Welfare crisis and beyond: Danish welfare policies in the 1980s and 1990s', in S. Kuhnle (ed.) *Survival of the European Welfare State*, London and New York: Routledge.

Harris, J. (1994) 'Beveridge's social and political thought', in J. Hills, J. Ditch and H. Glennester (eds) *Beveridge and Social Security*, Oxford: Clarendon Press.

Hatland, A. (1992) *Til dem som trenger det mest? Økonomisk behovsprøving i norsk sosialpolitikk*, Oslo: Universitetsforlaget.

—— (2001) 'Mer målrettet velferdspolitikk?' NHO, *Horisont* nr. 4.

Kaim-Caudle, P. R. (1973) *Comparative Social Policy and Social Security*, New York: Dunellen Company.

Kildal, N. (2001) *Workfare Tendencies in Scandinavian Welfare Policies*, Genéve: ILO InFocus Programme on Socio-Economic Security paper series.

Knudsen, T. (ed.) (2000) *Den nordiske protestantisme og velfærdsstaten*, Århus: Aarhus Universitetsforlag.

Kuhnle, S. (1981a) 'The growth of social insurance programmes in Scandinavia: outside influences and internal forces', in P. Flora and A. J. Heidenheimer (eds) *The Development of Welfare States in Europe and America*, New Brunswick and London: Transaction Books.

—— (1981b) 'Welfare and the quality of life', in E. Allardt, N. Andrén, E. J. Friis, G. Gislason, S. S. Nilson, H. Valen, F. Wendt and F. Wisti (eds) *Nordic Democracy*, Copenhagen: Det Danske Selskab.

—— (1983) *Velferdsstatens utvikling: Norge i komparativt perspektiv*, Bergen/Oslo: Universitetsforlaget.

—— (1990) 'Den skandinaviske velferdsmodellen – skandinavisk? velferd?

modell?', in A. R. Hovdum, S. Kuhnle and L. Stokke (eds) *Visjoner om velferdssamfunnet*, Bergen: Alma Mater.

—— (1996) 'International modeling, states and statistics: Scandinavian social security solutions in the 1890s', in D. Rueschemeyer and T. Skocpol (eds) *States, Social Knowledge, and the Origins of Modern Social Policies*, Princeton: Princeton University Press.

—— (2000) 'The Nordic welfare state in a European context: dealing with new economic and ideological challenges in the 1990s', *European Review*, 8 (3) July: 379–98.

Leichter, H. M. (1979) *A Comparative Approach to Policy Analysis. Health Care Policy in Four Nations*, Cambridge: Cambridge University Press.

Lowe, R. (1994) 'A prophet dishonoured in his own country? The rejection of Beveridge in Britain (1945–1970)', in J. Hills, J. Ditch and H. Glennester (eds) *Beveridge and Social Security*, Oxford: Clarendon Press.

Marklund, S. (1988) *Paradise Lost? The Nordic Welfare States and the Recession 1975–85*, Lund: Arkiv.

Mead, L. M. (1997) 'Citizenship and social policy: T. H. Marshall and poverty', *Social Philosophy and Policy*, 14 (2): 197–230.

Olsson, S. E. (1990) *Social Policy and Welfare State in Sweden*, Lund: Arkiv.

Palme, J. (1990) *Pension Rights in Welfare Capitalism. The Development of Old-age Pensions in 18 OECD Countries 1930 to 1985*, Stockholm: Swedish Institute for Social Research, Dissertation Series 14.

—— (1999) *The Nordic Model and the Modernization of Social Protection in Europe*, Copenhagen: Nordic Council of Ministers.

Rawls, J. (1993) *Political Liberalism*, New York: Columbia University Press.

Rothstein, B. (1998) *Just Institutions Matter. The Moral and Political Logic of the Universal Welfare State*, Cambridge: Cambridge University Press.

Sejersted, F. (1984) *Høyres historie 3: Opposisjon og posisjon 1940–1984*, Oslo: Cappelen.

Seip, A.-L. (1981) *Om velferdsstatens fremvekst*, Oslo: Universitetsforlaget.

—— (1986) 'Velferdsstaten Norge', in L. Alldén, N. Ramsöy and M. Vaa (eds) *Det norske samfunn*, Oslo: Gyldendal.

—— (1994) *Veiene til velferdsstaten*, Oslo: Gyldendal.

Sosialdemokrati 2000 (2000): 'Arbeiderpartiets programdebatt. Tema Velferdspolitikk', Oslo: Arbeiderbevegelsens Utredningssekretariat.

Svenstrup, T. (2000) 'Den etiske socialisme. Biskop Martensens samfundssyn i 1870'erne', in T. Knudsen (ed.) *Den nordiske protestantisme og velfærdsstaten*, Århus: Aarhus Universitetsforlag.

Swank, D. (2002) *Global Capital, Political Institutions, and Policy Change in Developed Welfare States*, Cambridge: Cambridge University Press.

Sysiharju, A.-L. (1981) 'Primary education and secondary schools', in E. Allardt, N. Andrén, E. J. Friis, G. Gíslason, S. Sparre Nilson, H. Valen, F. Wendt and F. Wisti (eds) *Nordic Democracy*, Copenhagen: Det Danske Selskab.

Titmuss, R. M. (1968) *Commitment to Welfare*, London: Allen & Unwin.

White, S. (2003) *The Civic Minimum: On the Rights and Obligations of Economic Citizenship*, Oxford: Oxford University Press.

3 The normative foundations of the Scandinavian welfare states in historical perspective

Bo Stråth

Introduction: the concepts of *folk* and *folkhemmet*

In the introduction to the new (1981) edition of *The Crisis of German Ideologies*, George Mosse noted that while his book appeared to have left the impression among some readers that *völkisch* thought must inevitably lead to Nazism, this was not his intention. Not only were 'moderate', mainstream conservatives in pre-1933 Germany deeply infected with *völkisch* thoughts, but there also existed the non-authoritarian *völkische* socialism of Gustav Landauer which drew on the ideal of the *Volk* as a democratic community of equals (Mosse 1981). Eugene Lunn has suggested that Landauer's *völkische* socialism could provide an antidote to the tendency among historians to teleologically link *völkische* romanticism with the triumph of Hitler's version of *völkische* ideology (Lunn 1973).[1]

Mosse contended that socialists of all countries made efforts to combine *völkisch* and socialist thought and speculated that if such a blend had been successful, National Socialism might not have triumphed so easily. Lars Trägårdh has taken up and developed this idea in a comparison of *völkische* ideologies in two 'Germanic' countries, Sweden and Germany, taking 1933 as point of departure for the analysis. The same year as Germans voted their way to *völkische* Nazi dictatorship, a new coalition government headed by the social democrats came to power in Sweden. Founded by men inspired by Lassalle, Marx, Kautsky and other luminaries of the German socialist movement, the Swedish party was in many ways modelled on the German SPD. However, by the end of the 1920s the Swedish social democrats began to integrate *völkische* and socialist themes. They defined their party from a workers' class-based party to a people's party, bent upon the idea of a *folkhem*, a home for the people. Class alliances replaced the class struggle as the dominant strategy for achieving the socialist dream of the classless society (Trägårdh 1999).

The Swedish social democrats appropriated the political priority of interpretation of the *folk* concept after a protracted discursive struggle with the conservatives who, at the beginning of the twentieth century, activated the concept in a strategy of what one of the protagonists in the debate on modernization, the professor in political science ('*statsvetenskap*') Rudolf Kjellén (well-known later on for his geopolitical theories) labelled 'national socialism' as an ideological instrument to ward off the threats of class-struggle socialism. Rudolf Kjellén opposed class struggle socialism as a point of departure for the political discourse. He argued from his conservative point of departure for national socialism, where the country was seen as a whole which involved all the people in political work and gave them responsibility. The country was supposed to be a home for the whole people. The integrative idea of the '*folkhemmet*', in which society was organized as a family, with the home as a metaphor, subordinated the class struggle to the national welfare.

When Kjellén talked about the concept of *folkhemmet*, *folk* had a different connotation from *Volk* in Germany. *Volk* went much more than *folk* in a holistic direction inspired by Herder's philosophy and Romanticism. *Folk* rather connoted the empirically derived view on the composition of all social classes. Both varieties of the concept contained dimensions of a future potential as well as past achievements, but *Volk* transmitted a more utopian and *folk* a more empirical value charge (Jansen 1993).

The Swedish social democrats were early on attracted by the *folkhemmet* concept, although they wanted to give it another content. The conservative version they rejected as 'the fortified poor-house' with a reference to the biased distribution between military and social state expenditures in the conservative programme. They gradually found themselves involved in a discursive struggle about the definition of the *folk* concept. When the social democrats somewhat later took over the *folkhemmet* metaphor and made it their symbol, they argued that the happiness of the lower classes, of which the working class was just one part, was based on their efforts to contribute to the *folkhemmet*. *Folk* and *folkhem* as expressions of traditional values were mobilized as linguistic instruments for modernization (Stråth 1996).

At the end of the 1920s, a decisive debate on the concepts of *folk* and class was underway in the Social Democratic Party. In 1929 the party leader, Per-Albin Hansson summed it up: 'Behind the words are realities. It is by no means unimportant whether we consider the party a representative of class interests or a bearer of the interests of the whole *folk*' (Stråth 1996: 91).

From its very start the party had been a *folk* party, Hansson continued, in order to legitimize the reformulation historically. When the first party congress, in 1889, made a statement on the suffrage question, the argument had been that the *folk* must be the master of the house. Kautsky's argument in Germany in the same year, that it would be misleading to regard the concepts of 'people' and 'proletariat' as synonymous, had provoked protests from influential intellectuals in the Swedish party, Hansson argued. Although the Swedish Social Democratic Party was still very much a party of the industrial working class in terms of membership composition at the turn of the century, it changed in this respect during its first two decades, he continued. In 1907 the party leader, Hjalmar Branting, had argued that the party was a '*folk* party in the best sense of the word'.

The political attraction of the *folk* concept was strong by 1930. One expression of this attraction was the fact that the two liberal parties, when they merged in 1934, chose *folkpartiet* as their new name. This did not help them much in their fight for votes, however. By 1930, the social democrats had clearly appropriated the concept and its interpretation.

In the nineteenth century Germany and Sweden shared fundamental social and cultural values, which Lars Trägårdh has described as a tendency to extol the organic *Gemeinschaft* in comparison to the *Gesellschaft* of citizens ('community' against 'society') – in English: to take the collective rather than the individual as the basic unit from which society should be constructed. Given this tendency, Trägårdh asks whether the divergent trajectories of Swedish and German histories express varieties of an underlying Germanic ideology, embracing mutations and variations diverse enough as to include both Hitler's Third Reich and the Swedish welfare state (Trägårdh 1990: 26).

An elaboration on Trägårdh's question shows important differences rather than similarities between the *Gemeinschaft* and the *Gesellschaft* concepts in Germany and Sweden, however. Ferdinand Tönnies developed in 1887 a view on the difference between the two concepts in German (Tönnies 1991; Jansen 1993). *Gemeinschaft* connotes utopian dreams of an archaic past, which he nostalgically pitted against the atomistic *Gesellschaft*, which described the division of labour and lack of cohesion in the emerging industrial society. *Gemeinschaft* contained, in the influential version of Tönnies, the same holistic Romanticist dimension as *Volk*. These two concepts were politically exploited and overstretched in the 1930s.

There was not the same tension or opposition between the concepts in Sweden as in Germany. They were less dichotomic. The politically important concept in Sweden is *Gesellschaft*, *samhälle*, from the verb *hålla samman*, meaning 'keep together'. It connotes both *Gemeinschaft*, community and political organization/administration. *Samhälle*, *Gesellschaft*, society, *societas* even became synonymous with the state in the twentieth century. When the social democrats argued for the welfare state they talked about the need for a strong society. *Samhälle* was never in opposition to the state or seen as something between market (or family: Hegel) on the one side and the state on the other. When the English and American neo-liberal language was translated into Swedish in the 1980s the Anglocism *civilsamhälle* was invented and incorporated to express such opposition.

Gemenskap was never so holistically overstretched as *Gemeinschaft*. *Gemenskap* has much less political power than *samhälle* in Swedish and than *Gemeinschaft* in a comparison with the German language area. The concept connotes rather private relationships, such as in *arbetsgemenskap*, *familjegemenskap* or the religious *församlingsgemenskap*. The politically potential concept is the Latinized form *kommun*. A concept like *folkgemenskap* is almost without political potency, while *Volksgemeinschaft* in Germany was loaded with explosive content. In Sweden one could talk about a continuity between the concepts of state, society and community. The semantic field around these three concepts expresses overlapping rather than disconnection. In Sweden there was a tension between corporatist/collectivist and individualist ideas of social organization, but it was a tension which rather provoked political pragmatism.

The transformation of the *folk* concept was similar in Denmark and Norway. The social protest in Scandinavia had its origin in broad popular coalitions, which never became populist. The labour movement became the driving force in these coalitions, but under inclusion rather than exclusion of the others. The farmers constituted an integrative element of the coalitions. In all three countries red–green coalitions took over the governments in the early 1930s in response to the Great Depression. The social conflict was not exclusively between labour and capital, between the working class and the bourgeoisie, but had a less polarized and more complex cultural and discursive framing around the *folk* concept.

Also the overlapping between the concepts of state and society, *stat* and *samfund*, was as obvious in Norway and Denmark as in Sweden. A good illustration is the argument brought forward by Nicolai Wergeland at the constitutive Norwegian assembly at Eidsvoll in 1814 when he, drawing on both Rousseau and Locke, discussed what constitutes the state. The aim of the state which he defines as 'a state, a civil society', was the unification of the individual wills and forces into one common will and force (Midgaard 2003).

The impression of a Scandinavian similarity in the organization of society around the *folk* concept is strong, but there were interesting differences. *Folk* and 'nation' were concepts, which in Norway were appropriated early by the political left, for instance. The Norwegian nationalism emerged in the 1880s as a left project against the union with Sweden. *Folk* was pitted against union where *folk* stood for left and union for the political right. Another important difference is that the state view is less organic and less based on corporatist ideas in Denmark and Norway than in Sweden. Wergeland's argument of 1814, cited above, is a case in point. One reflection of this difference is that Sweden had a Four Estate Diet until 1865, which, in turn, can be referred to the fact that Sweden had a much stronger nobility. The nobility hardly existed in Norway and in Denmark its political role was cut short in 1660. The social organization was based on a more immediate king–people relationship whereas in Sweden various coalition patterns between the king, the nobility and the 'people', i.e. the peasants/the farmers and the burghers, emerged promoting corporatist views on society.

In Sweden, as opposed to Norway, the collapse of the union in 1905 did promote conservative reform policies under the motto domestic consolidation rather than revanchism. It was in this context that Kjellén and his fellows activated the *folk* concept. A language emerged around the concept of people, which per se attracted the social democrats, although they wanted to fill the key concept with an alternative content. A discursive struggle between reform conservatives, who since 1905 energetically affirmed modernization and industrialization, and the social democratic-social liberal coalition of workers, small farmers and petty bourgeoisie about the shape and the content of the *folk* concept worked despite different alternatives in a unifying, nationally consolidating direction. There was a considerable continuity when, in the 1930s, the social democrats took over the setting of the political agenda and the interpretative priority in the debate on society.

The argument in this chapter is clear: the social democratic appropriation of the interpretative power of the *folk* concept and the semantic field around it was crucial for the way in which society was organized in the north. The occupation of this semantic field by the left political spectrum is a shared element in the value transformation in all the three Scandinavian countries. There is one shared element in the historically-shaped preconditions in all three countries. Social protest and claims for more democracy originated in a broader popular coalition in which the labour movement was, or rather, became, the driving force, though not to the exclusion of others. Farmers also formed an integral part of this coalition. The lines of division and conflict, in the construction of community and the demarcation between 'Us' and 'Them', were detected *within* the 'bourgeoisie' and *within* the farmer class, between high and low bourgeoisie, large and small farmers or crofters.[2] This pattern increased the potential for the formation of coalitions with the labour movement (Stråth 1988a, 1988b, 1990). This cultural construction of social community resulted in a less polarized society with a higher capacity for communication than one which follows a Marxian scheme that opposes capital and labour.

Three dimensions of 'folk'

There are three important dimensions in the *folk* discourse:

1 the role of the farmers and the way they solved the tension between the concepts of 'equal' and 'free', a tension evident ever since the unity of these two concepts was proclaimed in the French Revolution;
2 the individualization and de-hierarchization of the religious dimension through the revivalist movement and the free churches, which transformed the Lutheran state churches in the direction of people's churches and prevented the emergence of throne–altar compacts. The emphasis on individual responsibility withdrew the basis for holistic worldviews and promoted pragmatism rather than fundamentalism;

3 the emphasis on *bildning/dannelse*, self-education, in *folkrörelserna/folkbevegelserne*, the popular movements, which made them non-elitarian and prevented the hi-jacking of them by populists.

These three dimensions shed light on the decisive differences between German and Scandinavian varieties of the concept of *völkisch*, and also on Romanticist, socialist and social democratic traditions. The Scandinavian social democratic versions were less holistic and more empirically and pragmatically oriented.

The national question set the frame of how these three dimensions were intertwined more precisely in the three countries. The national question was crucial in Norway and Sweden, although it oriented action in very different directions. In Denmark, this question had been removed from the national agenda after the defeat to Prussia in 1864. In Norway the national question became the symbol of a popular mobilization against union with Sweden which involved farmers, large parts of the 'bourgeoisie', and the labour movement. In Sweden, the break-up of the union with Norway in 1905 promoted a conservative reform strategy with the purpose of unifying the nation as has already been said.

Legitimacy was provided not only through the national question, but also through the specific Protestant ethic that permeated popular movements composed of a pietistic value orientation which emphasized individual freedom in combination with radical claims for equality.[3] The fact that political legitimacy was provided by this kind of value-orientation meant that political elites were forced to adjust. This pattern was more pronounced in Norway and, to a certain extent in Sweden, than in Denmark, where the heritage of Grundtvig (see below) meant a different kind of popular pietism with the large farmers at its core and following less ascetic guidelines than in Norway and Sweden.

The puritan dimension was reflected in the social legitimacy of economic power, which in Norway was based on a low degree of economic concentration. The degree of economic concentration was much higher in Sweden, but through a skilfully developed image of thrift, diligence, industry and assiduity, and with the Wallenberg family as a model, the economic elite still managed to comply with the pietistic criteria for legitimacy. In Denmark, as opposed to Norway, but similar to Sweden, a system of large commercial banks emerged. Although most of the banks were regional or local, at least four operated nationally. The biggest name in the Danish financial world up to the 1890s was C. F. Tietgen. This astute businessman had built up his *Privatbanken* during the 1870s and the 1880s, first establishing a steam shipping company which targeted the emigration to America as its key market. He invested in tramways, railways, telephone communications and lime-works, amalgamated a considerable proportion of the Danish alcohol production in *De Danske Spritfabriker*, and merged a great number of Copenhagen breweries to *De Forenede Bryggerier*, which was later joined by Tuborg. He also demonstrated great audacity and foresight in his investments by allocating capital to enterprises which only offered the prospect of a long-term yield.

At first glance Tietgen resembles a Danish Wallenberg. However, appearances can be deceiving. Tietgen never managed to build industrial development blocs of strategic importance for the Danish economy as a whole as Wallenberg had for Sweden. A large proportion of financial outflows from Danish banks had gone to trade and shipping whereas Tietgen had a weakness for beer breweries. A number of less successful investments meant that he failed to accumulate a private fortune. He also had a weakness for keeping up appearances by throwing big parties and banquets with himself as the principle protagonist. In fact, his control over the enterprises where he had placed capital was not very tight. He delegated much of his owner responsibility to the company management. The Wallenberg family was very different on most of these points. The Wallenberg family made a point of seeing but of not being seen. They held a firm grip over their investments through the loyal managers they placed to oversee their capital who were expected to make the most of their talent. The family was discrete rather than ostentatious in its behaviour. Although they accumulated an overwhelming wealth they did not flaunt it, preferring to radiate virtues such as moderation and responsibility. This attitude penetrated the management style of their entire empire and coloured their relations to the Social Democrats and trade unions.

Tietgen was no Wallenberg and would probably have failed in a Swedish context. In Sweden the same degree of egalitarian moralism as in Norway did not work as an obstacle against the development of a modern banking system. The puritan framework of the popular movement was there, however, and the key to economic success was to understand how to cope within the dictates of this morality. In Denmark the same type of moralistic barriers against economic concentration as in Norway, or against spectacular manifestations of economic power as in Sweden, did not exist. In his own Danish environment Tietgen was nevertheless one of the people, one of 'Us', in a culture where the burghers had represented a popular force joined with the king against the nobility since the seventeenth century. The normative basis of the legitimatization of economic power varied in all three of the Scandinavian countries (Stråth 2001: 76–8, 82–3).

There were not only crucial differences as to the issue of legitimacy to capital ownership. The value transformation in the wake of industrialization and modernization in the north was never a smooth and unchallenged teleological development towards social democratic welfare states. The value transformation occurred under heated debates and political conflicts in discursive struggles over the problem definition and the interpretative priority of key concepts. Legitimacy was never stable over longer periods of time but was repeatedly challenged. The first massive challenge in all four of the countries was the general radicalization of the political language around 1920. The second challenge was the Great Depression in the 1930s, where red–green coalition governments re-established confidence and legitimacy through state intervention and state responsibility for crisis management. After the Second World War the next challenge to legitimacy occurred when the Social Democrats in Sweden and Norway wanted a tighter political and trade union control over the economy in order to guarantee investments and full employment. Legitimacy was restored after the Social Democrats renounced many of their claims. Compromises were negotiated in the framework of the emerging Cold War, which did not allow for political polarization. Social Democrats guaranteed legitimacy and industry guaranteed economic growth for political redistribution. However, this new equilibrium was also fragile since the Social Democratic guarantee was repeatedly challenged from the left. This was obvious in Sweden, Norway and Denmark, when the protests against economic concentration and economic power grew dramatically in the 1960s. The fact that the economic elite, riding on the back of the Social Democratic guarantee of the market economy, acquired a high degree of legitimacy in Scandinavia during certain periods did not imply that they became Social Democrats. The previous has also demonstrated, however, that the degree of legitimacy for private economic concentration, within this Scandinavian pattern, varied considerably, being strongest in Sweden and weakest in Norway. The economic elites did maintain their own substantial norms and value-orientations and the political debate was occasionally polarized by the constant presentation of competing alternatives. The concept of consensus, in this respect, is not very relevant when considering Scandinavian political culture. A high degree of successful compromise achieved over and above opposing positions is more characteristic.

There is a Scandinavian pattern of recurrent challenges to legitimacy and democracy. When, at the end of the 1960s, there was a challenge through rapidly growing criticism from the left something new occurred. The employers re-established legitimacy themselves during the 1980s in the framework of a neo-liberal rhetoric emphasizing values and characteristics such as nearness, smallness, flexibility and individualism. A key concept in this new language was 'co-worker'. The concept of *civil* society, *civilsamhälle*, was an invention taken over from the Anglo-American neoliberal discourse and introduced as an instrument to express distinction between society and state, where earlier at least a high degree of overlapping, if not synonymity, had existed.

The farmer figure: equality and freedom

The Enlightenment was not retarded in the Nordic peasant communities, as sometimes has been argued. However, there was a specific kind of

Enlightenment. In Scandinavia the tension between freedom and equality in the political culture was more easily contained than elsewhere. The Enlightenment tradition in the north contained a pragmatic dimension, which sometimes in its modern and bureaucratic version seems to come close to Max Weber's idea of permanent disenchantment. There emerged in the pragmatic bargaining cultures a paradoxical positivist quest for perfection in a search for public welfare. A science-based belief in classification, ordering and social engineering went hand-in-hand with both religious revivalism and political pragmatism in a contradictory but consistent way. There was a belief in progress towards higher stages of social organization, but the eugenics in Sweden in the 1930s demonstrate how ambiguous this process was.

The peasant figure which the intellectuals and the clergy created in *Norden* was not just a romantic construction with no relation to real world but an increasingly active participant in economic and political processes. In most other parts of Europe he was basically a rhetorical, even utopian figure. There he was eliminated from the political processes. He was rendered harmless and then revitalized through rhetoric. The inherent tension between the concepts of freedom and equality was better controlled in the north by means of the peasant myth. The Nordic peasant was too conservative to be radical but too radical to be conservative (Witoszek 1997). The peasant icon neither led to peasant populism as it did in Central Europe. Nationalism and the construction of a *folk* community, when the class community was launched as an alternative community and as an identity category of the industrial workers at the end of the nineteenth century, is another example of the fact that social criticism in the wake of Enlightenment not was transformed into the antithesis of Enlightenment. The conservative integration of the class into the nation in Sweden around 1900, when the conservatives suggested national socialism as an alternative to class struggle socialism, was a careful response to popular protests under the metaphoric symbol of *folkhemmet*, the people's home, a response which in the long run transformed both the conservatives and the social democrats. In Norway there was more of a merger between popular nationalism and class struggle.

The nineteenth century as both modernization and a permanent peasant revolt is no doubt an alternative development both to the French, British and American standard of Enlightenment modernization and to what Theodor Adorno and Max Horkheimer, in the mirror of the German and Soviet developments, called the dialectics of Enlightenment. The peasant was not only a historically derived construct. He was also a political actor and provided cohesive mortar in the processes of national integration. The core of the peasant myth is a figure which is difficult to conceptualize with the term of peasant which connotes subordination in a feudal order. The Nordic peasant is rather somebody between a yeoman and a freeholder in an English context, moving towards farmer around 1900.

The politically negotiating peasant was not utopian but actually existed. His *bildning/dannelse* was the basis of politics, not *Blut und Boden* mysticism based on a mythical peasant figure. Politics was based on the disputes and quarrels of the parish assembly and the Diet about who should pay for the poor relief, for instance. There is a constant odour of dunghill, cow-house and cow trade (as opposed to the more macho-oriented stable and the horse trade of the Wild West), which in the political culture is expressed with concepts as *lagom*, compromise and consideration. However, as has been mentioned above, there was also, amidst the quest for improvement, a fundamentalist element of positivist perfection.

The emerging welfare state at the end of the nineteenth century had early on a universalistic dimension in the sense that the social insurance systems were considered as rights belonging to all citizens. A case in point is the Swedish pension system introduced in 1913 after almost 30 years of negotiations since 1884. This case illustrates another aspect of the preconditions of the Scandinavian value production. There is a communicative nearness between social democrats, social liberals and reform conservatives far from polarization, but with the effect that the social bargaining process is often a lengthy one. In the same year as Bismarck in Germany introduced a new social insurance scheme for the workers with a simple imperial decree, the outdrawn pension negotiations began in Sweden. The emerging welfare state was in this respect the opposite of Bismarck's concessions *von oben* to the working class. Constituent elements in most European nineteenth and twentieth century welfare projects were a mixture of self-defined needs among the lower classes and the fear of social and political revolt among the ruling classes. In Scandinavia the gravitation point of this mixture was closer to the former pole. The solidarity patterns which developed in the nineteenth century, and which later on were transformed into the modern welfare state, were only in the latest phase a social democratic project from the 1930s onwards when they began to design a more definite *folk* concept for the rest of the century. The reforms during the decades around 1900 involved civil servant elites, liberal intellectuals and, particularly, the peasants (Baldwin 1990; Rotholz 1997).

The religious dimension: community without holism

There was in Scandinavia a tension between corporatist/collectivist and individualist ideas of social organization, but it was a tension, which rather provoked political pragmatism. A good illustration is the transformation of the Lutheran state churches in the direction of *folk* churches by the social democrats in the 1930s under impression of the revivalist free church movement, which since the end of the nineteenth century had claimed religious de-hierarchization and individual responsibility for the transcendental dimension (Belzén 1973; Stråth 1993a, 1993b). Another example is the political implementation of liberalism, which never developed a real opposition to the state, at least not before the 1980s.

The anti-clerical message came from the revivalist movement which enforced the established churches in Scandinavia around 1850 to define themselves as *state* churches as opposed to the revivalist *free* churches (Thorkildsen 1997). As a consequence of this attack the tendencies to redefine the state churches as *folk* churches grew in order to canalize the protests. Although this transformation was even more palpable in Denmark and Norway it was also observable in Sweden. This was an alternative scenario to the divorce between the church and the state in Catholic countries like France and Italy.

This was also an alternative scenario to the German merger of the *Rechtsstaat* and the *Kulturstaat* in the framework of the *Machtstaat*. The Lutheran churches in Germany fulfilled little of the potential inherent in Luther's thoughts. *Pietismus* in Germany challenged the Orthodoxy in many ways but never the *landesherrliche Kirchenregiment*. The enlightened absolutism regarded the church as well as the schools as state institutions. The churches became departments of the government in the merger of *Thron und Altar*. In several respects the organization of religion in the north was from a superficial point of view reminiscent of the German one. The very concept of state church indicates a parallel. The decisive difference was that pietism and popular protest eroded the compact throne and altar much more in the north. Wichern and the Inner Mission in Germany never developed the same power as the popular movements, *folkrörelserna/folkbevegelserne*, which were exactly popular not populist movements, in the north, far from the *völkerlische Bewegungen* in Germany.

The German subordination of the church to the state has interestingly enough not only been referred to as the state power but also as the role of German idealism (Holborn 1952: 359–84). The revival of religious feeling in Germany in the nineteenth century gained strength from the idealism and its transgression of rationalism. Schleiermacher and the whole Romantic school is a case in point. The German idealism assigned the church only a limited and well demarcated space. This stands in clear contrast to the pragmatic penetration of the whole society by the revivalist movements in the north. In this respect Great Britain is much more adjacent than Germany. In a contradictory but consistent way religious penetration meant at the same time the emergence of a demarcation between the sacred and the profane.

This development of the religious reflection in a 'de-hierarchizing', individualizing, non-holistic direction had an impact on the shape of the semantic field around the concepts of *folk*, *gemenskap*, *samhälle*, *stat* and *kyrka*, which is difficult to overestimate. This framework of the political debate had crucial impact on the definition of problems and the search for solutions.

The popular movements, *folkrörelserna/folkbevegelserne*, are crucial in a chain of events which goes from Enlightenment as a reaction to Lutheran state church orthodoxy via eighteenth century pietism to popular revivalist movements within or in opposition to the state churches. This specific Nordic Protestant ethic was a cultural genre which preserved a principle not only different from the Catholic cultures but was openly hostile to them, the principle of unconditional personal freedom and the supreme value of the individual. In a contradictory way, pietist revivalist individualism was quite compatible with a homogenization of mental and intellectual structures. Knowledge was experienced to be based on reason, rational humanity and pragmatism instead of dogmas. The Christian idea of equality before God never provoked a democratization where the peasants could be put to an improper use (Rotholz 1997). The peasants were subjects rather than objects in the modernization of the north; subjects in the sense of voluntarily-acting, not subjugated, individuals.

The Lutheran and popular chain in political culture merged and formed a parish community, which later in the nineteenth century became the nucleus of the secular communes. Here the Kantian self-realization took on a popular and pragmatic dimension. Kant regarded the society as based on reason and human conventions among individuals as a dynamic unit, the elements of which worked not only with but also against each other. The conflicts urged the individuals to form societies. The endeavour towards societies governed by conventions and collective organization provoked resistance, however. The threat of social dissolution was always there. Kant came close to the Scottish moral philosophers Adam Smith, David Hume and Adam Ferguson in this view. However, the moral theory of Kant met with critique from more organically oriented thinkers, who argued that the point of departure that all individuals were free and equal and acted rationally was impossible. Reason was not situated in the individual but with the people. The moral rather than reason keeps the organism together which constitutes the people, according to Hegel, for instance. The German difference between Kant and Hegel also mediates a difference between Scandinavia and Germany.

One expression of the Kantian view is the tight connection between the central state and the local community. They confronted one another in pragmatic bargaining which Eva Österberg has referred to as the 'negotiating state' (Österberg 1989, 1992; Aronsson 1997).

The popular movements are difficult to imagine without their revivalist element. The popular movements were much more than the labour movements and the rising working class. The labour movements took form and content from this religious ambience and were lastingly influenced by them. This is similar to the case of Britain. The difference between the two lies in the fact that the protest in Scandinavia was to a considerable extent early on canalized through independent labour parties, while in Britain the political affiliation of the protest with the conservative and liberal parties lasted much longer.

The Scandinavian individualism was so contaminated by the Christian element that it effectively put off Nietzsche and the whole *fin de siècle* pessimism. The religious protest against the absolutization of doctrines collided with the imperatives of nationalism and functioned as a braking mechanism in the process of wide, national mobilization (Witoszek 1997). It was also important that this de- and re-institutionalization of faith took place without any significant assault on the established church per se. The state churches, transformed in the direction of *folk* churches particularly in Norway and, even more, Denmark, survived (Thorkildsen 1997).

'*Bildning*'/'*dannelse*' as instruments of self-realization

The penetration of the Enlightenment in the north must be seen in the context of the social communication capacity developed through the popular movements. Education (*bildning/dannelse*) was a key instrument for self-realization and created from below as opposed to e.g. the German *Bildungsbürgertum*. Here we must draw attention to the development of a communicative skill of the peasantry, whose training ground was the parish meetings and which later on paved the way for the communicative capacity between social democracy and a liberalism with a social rather than economic emphasis. The growing articulateness and the ability of the peasant freeholders to negotiate their agenda provided a school of politics and education.

The peasants were not only carriers of freedom and equality but also of education. They were the core in the ambitious enlightenment programme of Danish clergyman N. F. S. Grundtvig in the nineteenth century. It is difficult to exaggerate his influence not only in Denmark but all over Scandinavia. His programme must be seen in the framework of a Danish popular mobilization against an experienced threat of a militarily and culturally expansive Germany. Grundtvig's programme of education, moulding ('*dannelse*'), was both far-reaching and wide spread. From a point of departure in an imagined Christian community based on the Holy Communion and baptism his scheme embraced the establishment of farmers' producers' cooperatives and a farmers' political party for political reforms. Against the artificial Latin-based scholarship at the universities he put the 'real' *dannelse* as an emancipative instrument in the hands of the peasants. *Folkehøjskolen*, the people's high school, became a veritable movement which spread from Denmark to the other Nordic countries. They became formation and education centres, where the popular thirst for knowledge was satisfied. The peasants as carriers of education is no doubt an alternative role as opposed to most stereotypes.

A comparison between Grundtvig and the father of the modern university, Wilhelm von Humboldt, is instructive. Both were influenced by English liberalism and utilitarian ideas. They embraced both enlightenment and romanticist ideas. They considered education (*dannelse/*

Bildung) as an emancipative instrument. Education and freedom were closely interrelated in their perspective. However, with freedom they did not mean the same thing. While von Humboldt required that the state both guaranteed the academic freedom and paid for it, Grundtvig regarded that education had to be organized independently of the state and in conscious opposition to the mandarins of the universities. Humboldt's academic freedom paved the way for the emergence of the German *Bildungsbürgertum* under the state control which never emerged as a social formation in Norden. There the concept of *dannelse/bildning* connoted much more the popular (revivalist, temperance, labour), not populist movements which all had study circles and local libraries as organizational corner stones. The role of the peasants and the popular movements as carriers of education gave the modernization of the north its specific shape. This is particularly valid for the way in which national romanticism developed in a much more common sense and Enlightenment-oriented direction than, for example, in Germany. It is true that the civil servants and the bourgeois society were sceptical about cultural and political maturity of the peasants but this scepticism never resulted in the emergence of a bourgeois education alternative such as the German *Bildungsbürgertum* (Sørensen and Stråth 1997).

Here two opposite patterns of the role of education in processes of social integration from above and from below respectively emerge. These alternative integrative processes were not in a simple way *caused* by the different approaches to the education issue, of course. The different solutions to the question of *dannelse/bildning/Bildung* reflect deeper cultural differences between the Scandinavian/Nordic and the German societies. Not least the role and the social self-esteem of the peasants are important in this connection (Sørensen and Stråth 1997).

Social democracy as a continuation/transformation of Lutheranism and parochial political culture, and of social liberalism, yes, indeed, even reform conservatism, could be seen as an expression of how differently the inherent tension contained in the freedom and equality ideals was handled in Scandinavia. However, there was amidst the pragmatism a germ of puritanism and fundamentalism which was visible in, for instance, the revivalist movements, but not only there. Amidst the empiricism and the positivist ideals of the education movement there was a quest for social perfection. The belief emerged that collective welfare could be organized through social engineering. Public ordering of private life would perfect the *folkhemmet.* This quest for social engineering was most evident in Sweden (Hirdman 1989). However, everywhere in Norden, as well as elsewhere, the national idea of the nations as selected peoples phrased in a biologistic race language was a general dimension of the interpretative framework until the 1950s. There was in Norden a racial discourse connected to the idea of Protestant progression (Hirdman 1989).

The Swedish State Institute for Race Biology founded in 1921 with

Herman Lundborg as its founding director is a case in point. He was a race biologist, medical doctor and professor. He examined military conscripts and the same population in the North and published several books. *Rasbiologi och rashygien* in 1914 was important for the establishment of the government institute. In this book Lundborg tried to demonstrate the superiority of the Nordic race. He had excellent connections to the German academic community and was awarded a honorary doctorate at the Heidelberg University in 1936. Although the demarcation to the increasingly overstretched German race-biological discourse became more distinct among Swedish political and intellectual elites, from the 1930s race-biological theories continued to inform ideas of public welfare.

The total separation between race-biological theories and social democratic welfare politics occurred after the Second World War in the wake of the insights that the German horror had given. The compulsory sterilization in Sweden in the 1930s is a case in point. The discourse on modernity, enlightenment and welfare informed by a Darwinian development language in several academic disciplines, perhaps did not determine, but facilitated, the sterilizations. It was indeed the visions to create a new and better society that motivated the sterilizations. The Swedish sterilizations should not be called genocide because they did not aim at a specific group. Neither had the sterilizations much to do with ethnical racism. The biological logic behind them makes it more justified to talk about eugenic racism. The idea was to get rid of unborn people who potentially were a burden to the new welfare society as it was designed in the 1930s, and unfit or unwilling to partake in that project. The idea was not to get rid of a certain race but to reinforce one (Banke 1999, 2001; Arvidsson *et al.* 1994).

The thin edge between what in retrospect emerges as widely different alternatives is characteristic for all developments. There are no paths of dependencies, which guarantee that the developments follow certain directions. The paths become visible only in retrospect when they are constructed as instruments to understand the problems of the present. This is the meaning implicit in George Mosse's question quoted at the beginning of this chapter. Discursive struggles are always open and without guarantees. There was nothing inherent in specific Scandinavian social structures as opposed to inherent elements in corresponding German structures that drove the developments in so many different directions. The conservative occupation of the *folk* semantics in Sweden around 1900 contained in the German case at that time a rather strong socialist element propagated by Gustav Landauer. Between then and the 1930s the developments in the two countries crossed each other.

The racial language in biological terms disappeared from Scandinavia after the experiences of the 1930s. However, historical experiences can always be reactivated and transformed in order to fit in problem solutions of the present. There are considerable continuities when again at the beginning of the twenty-first century the demarcation between 'Us' and 'Them' is getting sharper in Scandinavia. New views on immigration and on the integration of immigrants as well as growing signs of right extremism and political populism demonstrate that the present is always a balancing act on the edge. In Norway a populist right party is bigger than the Labour Party. The collective experiences provide certain guidance, but in periods of great change, often experienced as crises, the problems of the present can scarcely be modelled on the past experiences. The way to cope with them is rather to construct another history in order to legitimatize steps that are taken (Frykman 2000; Hirdman 1989).

What is the historically constructed Scandinavian value pattern as it has been outlined here – with all its variety – based on manufacturing industry and economic growth worth today? Although cultural patterns and value orientations are relatively stable, it is worthy to remember that economies – and economics – have changed dramatically since the 1970s with a decrease in political control over economies and much larger opportunities for capital evasion from state control. After all, speculation in portfolios and in foreign currencies with managers compensating themselves for bad performance through 'parachute agreements' with capital owners, whether it be a state or private owner, do not provide the same kind of legitimacy for economic concentration as the ownership of a manufacturing enterprise with thousands of employees. Political control of the economy was a precondition for the political guarantee of legitimacy. This control is no longer as it was. It has become more difficult to attach legitimacy to economic power, and to combine economic concentration with democratization. Both political and economic legitimacy are under erosion today and it is not that easy to find the value criteria on which a new legitimacy can be built. The more visible are the signs of the value crisis.

Notes

1 For a discussion of the concept of *völkisch* in a comparative European perspective, see Hettling (2003).

2 'Bourgeoisie' is put within quotation marks, because *borgerlighet* is a much vaguer concept in the North and more diluted with agrarian elements than bourgeoisie or *Bürgertum* in Germany, for instance. The verbatim translation of the German concept would be *borgardöme*, and this word does not exist in the Scandinavian languages.

3 For a development of this point, see several of the contributions in Sørensen and Stråth (1997).

References

Aronsson, P. (1997) 'Local politics – the invisible political culture', in Ø. Sørensen and B. Stråth (eds) *The Cultural Construction of Norden*, Oslo: Scandinavian University Press.

Arvidsson, H., Berntsson, L. and Decik, L. (1994) *Modernisering och välfärd*, Stockholm: City University Press.

Baldwin, P. (1990) *The Politics of Social Solidarity. Class Bases of the European Welfare State 1875–1975*, Cambridge: Cambridge University Press.

Banke, C. F. S. (1999) 'Den sociale ingeniörkunst i Danmark. Familie, stat og politik fra 1900 til 1945', Ph.D. dissertation, Roskilde University.

—— (ed.) (2001) *Folk og fælleskab*, Working Report No. 2, Dansk Center for Holocaust – og Folkedrabsstudier, Copenhagen.

Belzén, N. and Belzén, A. (1973) *Arthur Engberg – publicist och politiker*, Stockholm: Prisma.

Frykman, E. (2000) 'The cutting edge: a sterilisation campaign in Sweden', in J. Kaye and B. Stråth (eds) *Enlightenment and Genocide. Contradictions of Modernity*, Brussels: PIE-Peter Lang.

Hettling, M. (2003) *Volksgeschichten im Europa der Zwischenkriegsszeit*, Göttingen: Vandenhoeck & Ruprecht.

Hirdman, Y. (1989) *Att lägga livet til rätta. Studier i svensk folkhemspolitik*, Stockholm: Carlsson.

Holborn, H. (1952) 'Der deutsche Idealismus in sozialgeschichtlicher Beleuchtung', *Historische Zeitschrift*, (174): 359–84.

Jansen, C. (1993) '"Deutsches Wesen", "deutsche Seele", "deutscher Geist". Der Volkskarakter als nationales Identifikationsmuster im Gelehrtenmilieu', in H. Kuzmics, R. Blumert and A. Treibel (eds) *Transformationen des Wir-Gefühls. Studien zum national Habitus*, Frankfurt/Main: Suhrkamp.

Lunn, E. (1973) *Prophet of Community: The Romantic Socialism of Gustav Landauer*, Berkeley: California University Press.

Midgaard, K. (2003) 'Fra autoritært til liberalt styre: Forfatningsspørsmål og forfatningspolitikk i 1814 som historisk eksempel', unpublished manuscript, University of Oslo.

Mosse, G. L. (1981) *The Crisis of German Ideology: Intellectual Origins of the Third Reich*, New York: Howard Fertig.

Österberg, E. (1989) 'Bönder och centralmakt i det tidigmoderna Sverige. Konflikt-kompromiss-politisk kultur', *Scandia* (Lund) No. 1.

—— (1992) 'Folklig mentalitet och statlig makt. Perspektiv på 1500- och 1600-talens Sverige', *Scandia* (Lund), No. 2.

Rotholz, W. (1997) 'Das kriterium der nationale Identität und die Nationenbuildung: der skandinavische Fall', Arbeitspapiere 'Gemeinschaften', No. 6, Humboldt University, Berlin and European University Institute, Florence.

Sørensen, Ø. and Stråth, B. (eds) (1997) *The Cultural Construction of Norden*, Oslo: Scandinavian University Press.

Stråth, B. (1988a) 'Die bürgerliche Gesellschaft Schwedens im 19.Jahrhundert. Soziale Strukur und politischer Wandel', in J. Kocka (ed.) *Bürgertum im 19.Jahrhundert.*, Band 1, Munich: Dtv.

—— (1988b) 'Continuity and discontinuity in passing front I and II. Swedish 19th century civil society: culture, social formations and political change', in B. Stråth (ed.) *Democratisation in Scandinavia in Comparison*, Gothenburg University.

—— (1990) 'Introduction. Production of meaning, construction of class identities and social change', in B. Stråth (ed.) *Language and the Construction of Class Identities. The Struggle for Discursive Power in Social Organisation: Scandinavia and Germany after 1800*, Gothenburg University.

—— (1993a) 'Kungliga salighetsverket? Socialdemokratisk kyrkopolitik i Sverige före 1940', in *Arbetarhistoria*. Meddelanden från Arbetarrörelsens Arkiv och Bibliotek, Nos 66–67, Stockholm.

—— (1993b) *Folkhemmet mot Europa*, Stockholm: Tiden.

—— (1996) *The Organisation of Labour Markets. Modernity, Culture and Governance in Germany, Sweden, Britain and Japan*, London: Routledge.

—— (ed.) (2000) *Myth and Memory in the Construction of Community. Historical Patterns in Europe and Beyond*, Brussels: PIE-Peter Lang.

—— (2001) 'Nordic capitalism and democratisation', in H. Byrkjeflot, F. Sejersted, S. Myklebust and C. Myrvang (eds) *The Democratic Challenge to Capitalism. Management and Democracy in the Nordic Countries*, Oslo: Fagbokforlaget.

Thorkildsen, D. (1997) 'Religious identity and Nordic identity', in Ø. Sørensen and B. Stråth (eds) *The Cultural Construction of Norden*, Oslo: Scandinavian University Press.

Tönnies, F. (1991 [1887]) *Gemeinschaft und Gesellschaft. Grundbegriffe der Reinen Soziologie*, Darmstadt: Wissenschaftliche Buchgesellschaft.

Trägårdh, L. C. (1990) 'Varieties of volkish ideologies. Sweden and Germany 1848–1933', in B. Stråth (ed.) *Language and the Construction of Class Identities. The Struggle for Discursive Power in Social Organisation: Scandinavia and Germany after 1800*, Gothenburg University.

—— (1999) 'The concept of the people and the construction of popular political culture in Germany and Sweden: 1848–1933', dissertation 1993, Ann Arbor: University Microfilms International.

Witoszek, N. (1997) 'Fugitives from utopia: The Scandinavian Enlightenment reconsidered', in Ø. Sørensen and B. Stråth (eds) *The Cultural Construction of Norden*, Oslo: Scandinavian University Press.

4 The origin, development, consolidation and transformation of the Danish welfare state

Lars Bo Kaspersen

Introduction

What is the normative foundation of the Danish welfare state? Has it developed as a consequence of conflicts and negotiations between political parties, economic classes, organized interests and key persons? Or is the normative foundation embedded in a moral–religious discourse? What are the norms and from where do they originate?

This chapter takes an alternative path and shall attempt to answer the question about the origin and development of the normative foundation of the Danish welfare state using a slightly different approach. I shall argue that the normative foundation does not originate in norms but in 'exceptions' – situations in which norms are abandoned (Schmitt 1988 [1934], 1996 [1932]). The normative and legal foundation is set in a 'state of exceptions' in which norms are either disappearing or undergoing radical change. These 'states of exceptions' are most often situations in which the survival of the state is at stake. During the last two centuries Denmark has experienced these 'states of exceptions' several times, often in relation to wars. Thus the conflicts with the British Empire 1801 and 1807, the wars against Prussia in 1848 and 1864, World War One in 1914, the Second World War and the German Occupation 1940–1945 and the 1945–1949 period with a new world order emerging are all examples of different 'states of exceptions'. Also the external shock to the foundation of the agricultural structure when cheap grain was imported from USA, Russia and Australia can be seen as a 'state of exception' where action was needed.

This chapter shall illustrate with some examples how the normative foundation of the Danish welfare state must be seen in the light of specific 'moments' or periods in which the survival of the Danish state has been at stake and in which the state has been forced to demonstrate a strong political will. I shall point out certain periods and 'breakpoints' or 'state of exceptions' in which Denmark has been vulnerable and in which decisions have become crucial in the short and long run to secure autonomy and sovereignty with deep implications for the development of the welfare state. The rationality of survival has overruled any other political ideology whether social democratic, social liberal or conservative at crucial moments. In other words, I claim that besides the internal political struggles and social mobilizations driven by certain political ideologies, the Danish welfare state must also be conceived as a response to an external pressure in a struggle of survival as a sovereign state. Consequently, the distinctive character of the Danish welfare state is also a distinctive form of defence. To put it in its must acute form: the welfare state in Denmark can be seen a defence mode in the widest sense of the word. More precisely, as we shall see, the welfare society became the means of defending the state.[1] Moreover, the development of the welfare state and a welfare society went hand-in-hand with the consolidation of Denmark as a nation state. A specific welfare ideology merged with a form of nationalism.

The structure of the chapter is the following: the point of departure is a conceptual effort to clarify my use of the concepts of state and welfare state. It is crucial for the argument to understand that the definitions of state and welfare state applied in this chapter differ from conventional uses of the concepts. The next section analyses the first part of the history of the Danish welfare state from the mid-nineteenth century onwards. Most important is the friend–enemy relation with Germany and the impact on the political and social structure of the Danish state and society. After this the third and fourth sections take us into the twentieth century in which the shift from Germany to the USSR as the principal enemy is of importance. The last part of the chapter focuses on the last ten years and questions if we are undergoing a process of change from a welfare state to a security state.

The normative foundations of the Danish welfare state

When we have to address the question concerning the normative foundation of the Danish welfare state we often tend to look into the area of political ideologies. Often we approach the problem by examining which political ideologies were crucial to the driving political actors in shaping the welfare state and its institutions during the foundational years of the welfare state. Over the years historians and social scientists have discussed which political parties, interest groups and social movements can be pointed out as the major driving force in the development of the welfare state in Denmark. Several scholars argue that the Danish welfare state can be seen as an outcome of a struggle between the political powers of social democracy and the economic powers of capital (Esping-Andersen 1990). Others argue that the Danish welfare state has strong bourgeois roots (Nørgaard 2000) or that class alliances and ideologies changed over time (Baldwin 1990). These various accounts differ in which political ideologies have been most influential at a given time in the course of the development of the Danish welfare state. Thus it is often contested if Denmark is a social democratic or a social liberal welfare state or how influential liberalism and conservatism as political ideologies have been on the Danish 'model'. Another aspect of the normative foundation of the welfare state has been discussed in recent years: the role of religion and the church. Sørensen (1998) and Knudsen *et al.* (2000) claim that the Danish Protestant church and its ethics have played a major role in the development of the welfare state. In other words, the normative foundation has to be found in a religious–moral discourse rather than in a political–ideological one.

This chapter attempts to step along another path than these otherwise interesting and important discussions of the normative foundation suggest. Instead I shall argue that any political ideology which becomes a ruling ideology, i.e. an ideology which is a part of the normative basis of the ruling political parties and political actors, is constrained and framed by another rationality embedded in any state, notwithstanding state form or regime type. Any political party or movement embedded in a specific political ideology that becomes a ruling political ideology most often realizes that ruling a state is somewhat different from seeking power and influence as an opposition party. A state is a political entity with its own agenda. It is not merely a reflection of the interest of powerful actors in society. A state has a life of its own. In theory a state must always possess a rationality which directs its activities towards reproduction and survival. Without some form of willingness to survival a state will wither away. A state must possess some form of locus or centre with the ability to formulate a political will and make decisions in order to survive as an independent entity. The political will emanating from such a centre whether it is a king, a state council, a government or a dictator must successfully attempt to direct as many 'elements' of a state (citizens, political parties, state institutions, companies, local political institutions, trade unions and many other interest organizations) as possible towards a common will to survive. In order to survive a state must always seek to remain as a sovereign entity in a system of states. At given moments in history the will to survive totally overrides and determines any political ideology or any other rationality.[2] To survive as a state is not only a military security issue. To remain sovereign, to continue to be recognized by other states, to survive as a state entity implies a continuous orientation of several areas and activities of state and society towards this goal. A strong defence can, apart from military strength, involve several other matters: education level, the state of health, the size of population, the strength of the economy, the access to raw materials, the avoidance of extremist ideologies which otherwise could cause tensions and divisions in society, legitimate political institutions, some consensus and social cohesion. All these elements can be seen as important from the point of view of the defence of the state. In other words, the normative foundation of any state – welfare state or any other state form – is not only based upon norms stemming from a political ideology but a normative foundation is also embedded in decisions about survival and recognition. At times these decisions can overrule and undermine the official political party ideology. Moreover, these moments tend to have a more lasting impact structuring the state, society and state-society relations with important implications for citizenship, rights and obligations.

Concepts and frameworks

Research on the welfare state, its origin, development, character, effects and apparent crisis has exploded over the last two or three decades. Within welfare state studies the term welfare state is rarely clearly defined. The term welfare state consists of two elements: *welfare* and *state*. When we find a definition of the term it is almost always the *welfare* part of the term we find defined.[3] The state is not defined but welfare becomes the key to conceptualize the welfare state. Much of welfare state research has a strong emphasis on social policy. Often welfare equates with social policy.

The focus on social policy leads to a development towards three types of welfare state regimes or models. Esping-Andersen's three regime-types of welfare states are looming large in the debate.[4]

Although this 'welfare modelling business' can be quite useful in some cases, especially when we need to specify some distinctive characteristics of different types of designing and implementing social policies in different welfare states, it does not provide us with a distinctive characterization or definition of a welfare state in contrast to other state forms. If we take a closer look at most political organizations, which can be called states, they can be characterized as welfare states since most of these entities provide some form of welfare either by the state itself or by market or family. So what do we do in order to specify the state form to be called a welfare state? A first and necessary step is a conceptualization of the state. My conceptualization of the modern state can be condensed into the following propositions:

- The state is constituted in its relationship with other states – in a mutual struggle of recognition. The state is essentially and existentially defined by its relationship to other states.
- The modern state emerges slowly in the early modern Europe as a consequence of interplay between external warfare and an internal centralization, territorialization and hierachicalization and often with war as an important driving force.
- A central government and administration characterize the modern state.
- The modern state is demarcated and territorialized. The domain of sovereignty is demarcated.
- The modern state tends to have monopoly of the means of violence and taxation.

- The modern state emerges in most western European countries during the eighteenth century in which most states create a (civil-) society (a market). The French Revolution marks the fulfilment of this endeavour. The civil and political rights, the right of property and the market is in place. Here we have a '*Rechtsstaat*' with a state–society separation. This is the first time in world history we have seen a state developing a market society and it is the first time these two entities are separated.
- In the following centuries we see the welfare state or more precisely the *Sozialstaat*/welfare state developing. The welfare state is characterized by state intervention in society. In other words, a welfare state is a state form characterized by the state intervening in society to mitigate the social question and increase its strength by optimizing its resource base and strengthening the social cohesion.
- The modern state is confronted with the 'social question'.

These propositions are very general but I claim they are common denominators for all states in western Europe. Why, then, are states different? States are very different because they, among other things, are situated in very different geopolitical spaces, they have different social structures and different resource bases (natural resources, raw materials, ethnic composition and size, and different size of population etc.). Thus, to specify the distinct character of the Danish welfare state requires a detailed study of Denmark, its history, its geopolitical location, social structure etc.

The modern state emerges slowly from the late fifteenth century (Machiavelli's *stato*) to the seventeenth century (Hobbes' *Leviathan*) but it was not until the late eighteenth century we find the demarcated territorial sovereign state with its dual monopoly and with a state–society separation – the state often described by Weber. In many places in Europe the territorial sovereign state form develops into a nation state during the nineteenth and twentieth centuries. It is beyond the scope of this chapter to deal at any length with a more theoretical discussion of the nation state. The nation state as a state form is, however, characterized by a correspondence between:

- The defence of the state with a monopoly of the means of violence.
- A domain of sovereignty (a territory).
- A government, administration and legal system covering this domain.
- A national economy.
- A national identity.
- National citizenship and some loyalty between state and citizen.

The transformation of the citizen to a national citizen contributed to the development of a nation state as a strong state form. For the first time in history the whole population became involved in the struggle of the state for survival. Each citizen now became participant in the nation state project and each citizen was in the last instance willing to sacrifice health and life in order to protect the state and secure the survival of the nation. Almost everybody realized that it was now a matter of defending one's own conditions of life – a defence of one's own rights, identity and right of property. The nation state became further consolidated during the nineteenth century and right up to the period after the Second World War. As already indicated the Danish nation-building project later merged with the welfare state/society project.

The French Revolution and the Bourgeois Revolution can be seen as the establishment of the *Rechtsstaat* with civil and political rights. The key element of the Rechtsstaat was 'provision and safeguarding of legal equality, universal freedom of acquisition and contract, freedom of movement and settlement, and the guarantee of acquired property' (Böckenförde 1991: 152). During the nineteenth and twentieth centuries a transition is taking place from the Rechtsstaat with its separation between state and society to a *Sozialstaat* or, in a post 1945 term, a *welfare state* in which the state increasingly intervenes in society. The Rechtsstaat contains a contradiction. The state underwrites the basic principles of equality before the law, freedom of employment and the guarantee of acquired property. The problem is, of course, that the realization of these principles generates social problems. Social inequality based upon property emerges. A consequence of the legal consolidation and perpetuation of that inequality through the property guarantee is an increasing class antagonism. The social question becomes a reality.

> If this development, which is inherent in society as a result of the way in which it is constituted, is given free rein, unrestrained by the state, then the state's guarantee and protection of legal liberty and equality becomes a meaningless formality for an ever-increasing number of people. What ought in principles to be the freest society, founded on the equality of law, exudes material unfreedom. So the state, in line with its original relationship to society and in accordance with its function as guarantor of the free society and its basic constitution, is bound to intervene by making selective use of its sovereign regulatory power in order to keep society from destroying itself ... The state must counter the social inequality continuously spawned within society out of the dialectic of liberty and equality; it must modify it through the medium of social conciliation and social services in order effectively to maintain the reality of individual and social liberty and equality before the law.
>
> (Böckenförde 1991: 166–7)

Böckenförde argues that state intervention is taking place in order to avoid society destroying itself. The argument must, however, be extended.

The state intervenes to prevent society from destroying itself and, consequently, also preventing the state from undermining itself. State-society is mutually conditioned in the modern state and the existence of society is crucial to the state in order to survive in a struggle of recognition with other states in the state system. The state needs a society from which resources can be extracted.

In other words, the welfare state – or in Böckenfördes terms 'the Sozialstaat' – can be defined as a state form developing in western Europe and America where the state intervenes in society to protect society from itself and to strengthen the state and its resources in order to be able to remain recognized as an independent sovereign state. As a consequence of this definition welfare state means more than social policy even in its broadest sense. Therefore the welfare state intervention must be seen in the light of two interrelated processes. The state intervenes partly in order to strengthen its own position towards other states and partly in order to mitigate and reduce the 'social question'. Poverty, malnutrition, poor living conditions, a poor health standard and low level of education are all matters which can weaken the defence capability of a country.

Concerning the social question different actors have, of course, different motives to intervene but from a statist perspective the social question is not only important because it ethically seems to be important. It can be crucial to remove incentives for rebelling riots and civil disorder that can weaken the state towards other states and weaken the power position of the state elite.

In other words, a welfare state is a state form, which develops during the nineteenth century as a response to a beginning crisis of the liberal state. The liberal state that emerged in different variants in the eighteenth and nineteenth centuries was characterized by a state separated from the market (society) but where the state preconditioned the market. When market forces expanded with poverty and other problems a social question arose as a consequence. In some states such as Denmark the attempt to solve the social question led to a specific variant of a welfare state. Due to the character of its geopolitical situation Denmark developed a distinctive national welfare society in which national welfare institutions constituted the defence of the Danish people.

The onset of the Danish welfare state

The development of the Danish welfare state must be seen in relation to the 1660 Revolution. In 1660 Absolutism was introduced in Denmark and the period from 1660 to the mid-nineteenth century can be characterized as a long reform process which unintentionally ended up with a territorialized demarcated nation state in 1864 with the loss of the German-speaking territories. The state expanded and centralized and a (civil-) society (the market) gradually emerged generated by the state. The fulfilment of a society (market) and as a corollary the state–society separation was achieved with the liberal-democratic Constitution (June 1849) and the Freedom of Trade Act (1857). The emergence of the liberal-democratic constitution can be seen as:

1 being a part of a context of Europeanization processes with changes in the relations between states;
2 a war against Prussia in 1848; and
3 a social mobilization in Denmark with inspiration from the processes of nationalism, and political and economic liberalism.

The years 1848/1849 were crucial to the development of the Danish state. The problem of the duchies (Holstein and Sleswig) and Prussia led to radical reforms and reorganization of the Danish state now based upon a liberal-democratic constitution which limited the King's capacity to form the political will (Skovgaard-Petersen 1985: 74–94, 218–49; Bjørn 1990: 338–46). The liberal democracy places the individual in the centre and, finally, with the Act of Freedom of Trade in 1857 the individual had finally become liberated from the old medieval guild structures. The liberal-democratic constitution heralds the atomized society celebrating the individual and individualism. It did not last in its pure form since a new organization of the various political interests already took place from the late 1860s (Hvidt 1990: 145–60; Rerup 1989: 163–77). Denmark was already on its way to become a national organizational society in the late 1860s.

From the mid-1860s a new situation emerged which had a deep impact on the Danish state and society. In order to unify Germany Bismarck's strategy involved wars against Denmark (1864), Austria (1866) and France (1871). The defeat to Prussia in 1864 came as a deep shock to Denmark. Denmark lost the southern part of Jutland and the two duchies of Schleswig and Holstein (Hvidt 1990: 127–40). Again Denmark had to reorganize herself. Among other things a revision of the constitution took place in 1866 (Rerup 1989: 149–55). The most important consequence of the defeat was that Denmark now realized the fact that Germany was now a great power and a threat to Danish sovereignty and independence. Germany was the principal enemy.

From 1864 up to the First World War Germany/Prussia was the enemy, which led to various measures and alliances internally in Denmark. First it resulted in a major conflict between left and right concerning the constitution and the defence of the country. I shall return to this conflict and its 'solution' later. Second, it reinforced nationalism which already had taken off in the early nineteenth century but which now became extremely strong. Third, the defeat also led to a shift towards Britain, which was now regarded as the coming key trading partner. Thus, a major development of the Danish infrastructure taking place after 1864 was oriented towards a new international political situation. The railway to Esbjerg (West

Denmark), railway ferries over the Belt (Little Belt) and the construction and extension of the harbour in Esbjerg were all measures taken to enable Denmark to redirect its export from Germany to Britain (Hvidt 1990: 253–6). These developments were crucial to the evolution of the Danish state and society when the rapid internationalization of the economy changed the conditions of the Danish economy in the 1870s and 1880s. The cheap grain from the 'new' states of the USA, Australia and Russia was sailed into Europe with the new steam ships and this undermined the Danish agricultural export. The Danish agricultural structure transformed itself almost within a decade and the farmers established co-operatives and went from vegetable production to animal production. The new produce (bacon, eggs and butter) was sold in England. This structural change of the agricultural sector and reorientation of the export market from Germany to Britain could only take place because Denmark had invested enormously in infrastructure in the aftermath of the 1864 defeat and, moreover, directed railways, ferries and harbours towards the west. In other words, it was crucial to the success of the co-operative movement and the agricultural 'revolution' that a political, military and ideological new orientation took place after 1864. Only this enabled the Danish 'co-operative miracle'. It is, however, important to stress that other decisions could have been made with a better or worse result. At least, in retrospect we can see that this amalgam of decisions taken in a specific period of the history of the Danish state had a character and strength that enabled Denmark to survive.

The latter half of the nineteenth century is a clear example of how new external circumstances forced the state to make decisions. The German problem after 1864 and the internationalization of the economy beginning in the 1870s and 1880s confronted Denmark with new difficult circumstances. It compelled Denmark to respond in order to survive politically, militarily and economically and the response was among others a revision of the constitution, an agricultural structural change, infrastructural changes, and a shift from Germany to Britain as major trading partner.

The problem of Germany and the revision of the constitution had a number of implications. First and foremost the problem of defence was heavily discussed throughout the last four decades of the nineteenth century, and it was a key point in the disputes between right (the conservatives, landowners, civil servants, bourgeoisie) and left (the farmers). This conflict becomes even more tense after the revision of the constitution in 1866. The farmers and others saw this revision as a major deterioration and a weakening of the democratic basis of the constitution. The 1866 constitution strengthened the right and the landowners and it increased the problem of reconciliation between the two houses of the parliament. The wide gap between right and left was a huge problem. Partly due to this the country faced an unsolved problem of defence. Partly, it faced an intensifying social problem caused by the fact that more and more young people left the countryside for the towns and cities leaving the old people behind without any income. With a constitution without a solution to the problem of reconciliation of the two houses of the parliament it was difficult to find sustainable solutions to the problem of defence as well as the social problems.

The Conservative government outplayed the opposition between 1875–1894 under the leadership of Prime Minister J. B. S. Estrup. He managed to keep the opposition – despite the majority in the Folketing (the House of Commons) – out of influence by governing through provisional finance acts. The first act was passed in 1877 and during the Period of the Provisional Laws between 1877–1894, Estrup and the Conservatives forced through a measure for the building of the fortifications around Copenhagen. However, the conflict between government and opposition never took a character that paralyzed the country. Underlying this conflict a common project existed generating some level of consensus – the national project (Hornemann-Møller 1992: 62). The defeat to Germany in 1864, the loss of the Danish-speaking North Slesvig and a general fear for the new Germany created nationalism. This, again, generated an ideological and to some extent military mobilization and contributed to reproduce the consensus.

Daily politics was, however, characterized by a policy of obstruction from the left but internally the left was too weak to bring about a change of the system. Consequently, the moderate part of the opposition began to co-operate and negotiate with the Conservative government, and in 1891 a majority in the Rigsdag passed a number of social acts and in 1894 the two parties came to an agreement, which brought about a political stabilization. The series of social acts introduced from 1891 inaugurated a new period in Danish history. For the first time the state budget contained an account of social expenses next to the expenses of the King, the Church, the navy and the fleet. In other words, the state intervened for the first time in society at a larger scale. It can seem odd that Estrup and the right started an intervention in societal matters to solve a social question. It would hardly have had happened if Bismarck had not set the example in Germany some years prior to Estrup's intervention. The inspiration from Bismarck is very conspicuous. In contrast to Bismarck the social acts passed in Denmark did not target the working class but the old and poor left in the countryside as a result of the migration to the towns and cities.

Crucial to the inception of these welfare elements were a number of decisions taken by Estrup and the state apparatus which, again, had been driven by an underlying rationality: to sustain sovereignty and to remain in power. Decisions related to the survival of the state overrode ideologies of the left and the right at that time. State intervention at this scale was not the norm but an outcome of decisions to survive as a state and, of course, to remain in power as a party.

The idea of a 'welfare society': the alliance between the Social Liberal Party and the Social Democratic Party 1905–1947

During the last part of the nineteenth century and early part of the twentieth century the behaviour of the German neighbour led to increasing tensions between the two countries especially because Germany annexed the whole of Slesvig. The threat became more real to Denmark, but most politicians realized that an armed conflict with Germany would only cause pain and defeat. The leader of the small Social Liberal Party founded in 1905 (Det Radikale Venstre) and the later Minister of Foreign Affairs, Peter Munch, took the stance that Denmark should avoid military conflicts with Germany. A defeat would be inevitable. Munch argued that the Danish state as a sovereign entity would disappear in a military confrontation with Germany. Denmark should remain neutral and, consequently, stay out of any great power conflict. The politics of neutrality was not new but it was strongly emphasized during the years of governments that included the Social Liberals and later Social Democratic–Social Liberal coalition governments. In particular, a strong emphasis on disarmament policy was new. Up to 1870s Denmark was one of the most militarized countries in Europe.

These circumstances led Munch to rethink the relationship between state and people. He argued that state and the people are not a unity. The state might come under severe threat – it might even disappear for some time, but the people can continue its existence as a people. By strengthening society or more precisely 'peoples' community' Denmark might survive. Therefore the only strategy for Denmark was the development of a strong national community or society which could resist the external enemy. By referring to the fate of Poland Munch argued that the state might wither away but the people will remain a national people and survive as a unity. It required, however, that a responsible government provided the conditions of growth of a strong national community. Here, according to Munch, it was important to remove class inequality and huge class differences in general. Thus Munch stated that:

> The state and the people are not a unity. If the unlike accident would overtake the Danish people – to be subsumed by a foreign state, then the People shall exist anyway . . . And the people will live stronger and more secure with a more developed spiritual and material culture when there is no class boundaries which split and divide a people in contending parties with different worldviews.
>
> (Munch 1905: 55, *author's translation*)[5]

He goes even further in 1908:

> we can no more defend the Danish state with culture than with fortifications. Culture can, however, forge the Danish People in to a spiritual

> protection. If the sad situation occurred that the Danish state was conquered – it is fitting to realize the truth that it could happen – then a unique and highly developed Danish culture as far removed from the militaristic culture of the conqueror state as possible, guarantee that the Danish People would be able to preserve its own national life until the external independence will be returned.
>
> (Munch 1905, the quotation is from Lidegaard 1998a, *author's translation*)[6]

These quotations demonstrate that Munch's vision and political ideology were embedded in a worldview in which the lines between international and domestic issues were blurred. Domestic politics are the crucial element in the survival of the Danish state. In the short run the state can wither away but in the long run it will survive if the Danish society and community proves to be strong and coherent enough. The aim was a protection of Danish sovereignty, but the means was a development of national institutions – welfare institutions or welfare society to put it in modern terms. It required among other things a strong national health system, and systems of social protection and an education. Building such institutions could unite the people in a strong national project.

Thus we find a close connection between Denmark's international situation, its geopolitical location and the domestic political circumstances. Munch's social vision stressing a strengthening of the nation fitted well into an alliance with the Social Democrats. The leader of the Social Democrats, the later Prime Minister Th. Stauning and his ideas about the welfare state corresponded in a number of ways with Munch's vision about the necessary internal armament process as a response to external threats. To Munch it was crucial that the Danish people not only were well educated and morally rearmed but also existed in an environment without serious class conflicts and tensions. Consequently, the people would not become susceptible to totalitarian ideologies and, moreover, one would feel more responsible towards one's own society and nation.[7] Munch juxtaposes the external defence strategy of the state and the internal construction of society. 'The defence consists of an internal organization of society – developing education and culture levelling out social differences' (Lidegaard 1998b).

This enabled the Social Liberal party to build a bridge to the Social Democrats. This alliance has been a key element in the construction of the Danish welfare state throughout the twentieth century. Where the welfare society was a goal for the Social Democrats – to create a society for the working class from cradle to grave – the welfare society and its institutions were merely a means for the Social Liberals. If not the party as such then at least the leader, Munch, was more concerned about the state and society as a whole and not so much particular class interests. The goal for Munch was to secure an autonomous and sovereign Danish People.

Every step towards a welfare society was not in the first case an intended project with clear goals. It was rather an outcome of new external conditions, an underlying rationality to stay sovereign combined with various ideologies taking part in the development. The response from Munch and Stauning to the new external situation and the internal social problems was a welfare society.

One could argue that April 9 1940 tested Munch's policy. He hoped that Denmark would avoid German occupation, but as we know it did not happen. But Munch's policy passed the test in another respect. The internal defence of the nation proved to be very efficient. The policy of co-operation with Germany became 'despite the humiliations, tragedies, and compromises which necessarily follows from a foreign occupation, a spectacular success' (Lidegaard 1998b). The Danish nation was never threatened during the occupation. But the increasing struggle of resistance against Germany led to a hard critique of the politics of neutrality. This break with the policy of neutrality inaugurated a new phase in Danish history and the development of the welfare state.

The welfare society as a means against communism 1947–1970s

After the Second World War a new international situation emerged. After the victory of the Allied forces Denmark became a part of the American sphere of interest. Denmark's geopolitical position was important. Denmark's location at the entrance to the Baltic, as well as its possession of Greenland in the North Atlantic, made it vital to US strategy (Villaume 1999: 22). It became crucial to USA – and the Danish government/social democrats – to keep the Russians and communism out of the way. In Denmark the Communist Party gained an enormous support and many seats in the parliament in the first election after the war. The social democrats feared that a continuation of this development would in the long run undermine the position of the social democrats and the whole country (Gravesen *et al.* 1999: 3). Despite conflicting views on many issues between the social democrats and the Americans the communist problem made it more acceptable for the Danish social democracy to become an American ally. This situation, combined with the general shortage of resources after the war, led to the acceptance of the American offer about the Marshall Aid in 1947 and as a corollary membership of NATO in 1949 (Sørensen 2001; Villaume 1999; Lidegaard 1996, 1999). It was a difficult and contested decision (Lidegaard 1996: 549–60).

This was a fundamental break with Danish foreign policy – the most decisive break since the end of the Napoleonic Wars. The first part of the twentieth century implied a policy which kept Denmark out of all conflicts and alliances. This position now changed radically. If the Danish welfare state wanted to survive under these new conditions of existence, it required:

1 security – not at least from the external and internal communist threat;
2 the best possible opportunities for trade and economic stability.

In order to solve the security issues it became vital to find a strategy that could deal with the external as well as the internal threat from communism. One of the 'solutions' to this problem became a development of a 'strategic alliance' between the Social Democratic Party as the leading party and the USA (Lidegaard 1996: 578–88). In order to diminish the communist threat in the east the Americans saw clearly that they had to prevent the communists from establishing fifth column activity in Denmark (and other Scandinavian countries). This could facilitate a Russian invasion. Consequently, the best strategy from an American point of view was support of a welfare state project that minimized the number of social problems and therefore prevented the spread of communism. Therefore the most important American ally in Denmark became the Social Democrats and not the bourgeois parties. The Social Democrats were ready with their welfare project and the Social Democrats themselves regarded the communists as the principal enemy. The USA had another strategic interest in Denmark, which was Greenland. During the Second World War Greenland became crucial to the USA and the control of the North Atlantic. After the war this interest increased and air bases became vital to the defence of the USA. Since Denmark used to be a neutral country Greenland became a problem for Denmark. It was a very sensitive and difficult issue to handle for the Danish government but, eventually, the Social Democratic Prime Minister Hans Hedtoft realized that Greenland was not only a problem but also an asset for Denmark. Thus it became important in solving the Danish defence problem that led to participation in the US-led NATO alliance (Lidegaard 1996: 551).

A strengthening of the social democratic–social liberal welfare state with extended social rights to secure the poorest was the best means to undermine the strong communist position in Denmark. Thus the welfare state was a fusion of a social project and a defence project. Joining NATO had the implication that Denmark became subjected to American dominance in a military sense, but at the same time it led to a situation where the US paid the Danish defence bill while it developed a stable welfare society!

The postwar welfare state was a defence project intertwined with an attempt to solve 'the social problem'. To remove the problem of unemployment was important because it reduced the incentive of the working class to support the communists. Welfare policies and unemployment became a means to immunize the working class against communism.

Despite the strong impact of social democratic policies the structure of the Danish welfare state in the postwar years were still based upon an alliance between the Social Democrats and the Social Liberal Party, but often in vital issues with support from the bourgeois parties. The Cold

War and its frozen friend–foe picture was some sort of obstacle for the social democratic vision about the welfare state as a society based upon universalism and individual social rights. For some decades it was still a welfare state that supported a class-based welfare state structure. The state protected the major four classes and tried to keep a balance between these classes. The strong Anglo-American influence was evident but the Marshall-type of individual rights-based welfare did not become the basis structural principle of organizing welfare services until the 1970s (with some clear exception such as the pension reform from 1956) (Bernild 2001).

A precondition of the evolution and consolidation of the Danish welfare state was, besides the previously mentioned security problem, a further development of trade and industry. Denmark needed access to the world market and it was in the interest of Denmark to have an open market especially for agricultural products and a stable monetary regime. The two key trading partners, Germany and Britain, were both, for different reasons, in very difficult situations. Thus neither of the two countries were ready to import Danish products to the extent needed to create a better economy and, as a result, living conditions of the working class.

One step to improve the European and the Danish situation was the Marshall Plan. Most European states feared American dominance in Europe but eventually most countries accepted the plan and the American conditions (Lidegaard 1999: 40; Jensen 1989: 62). In 1947 Denmark had no reserves of foreign currency and no prospect of obtaining credit in the near future. Moreover, the country had developed a large deficit of the balance of payment in just two years. Consequently, the $278 million Denmark received from 1948 to 1953 was an important injection to the economy and its future prosperity. The country literally needed a process of industrialization. The only opportunity to develop more jobs lay in a new and modern industry. It required coal, iron, chemicals, metals and other resources, but in order to finance these resources Denmark needed an increase in export. A higher income from export – foreign currency (dollars) – could only come from agricultural products and an opening of the market was desirable in the big countries, especially Britain and Germany who protected their own agricultural sector (Schmidt 1993: 267–8). After difficult negotiations in the OEEC Denmark found some obligingness from the other countries.

The costs of receiving the financial injection were basically an acceptance of an American economic and political architecture. The Americans had several demands such as an organization with the purpose of organizing the Marshall aid (OEEC), and new policies within areas of customs, trade, currency and technology. The period from 1948 to 1953 was crucial in the development of new structures within these areas and thus, again, new external conditions almost determined certain aspects of a new economic and social structure in Denmark. A former key civil servant, Erik Ib

Schmidt, reminds us that Denmark was even forced to raise taxes as a consequence of its new membership of OEEC and NATO – a step which has not even been taken by EU (Schmidt 1993: 272–89).

The acceptance of the Marshall Aid and the membership of NATO took Denmark into the Alliance. It was a definitive abandonment of neutrality and non-bloc policy. It was a very difficult step for the Social Democrats that throughout the first half of the twentieth century had argued for neutrality and to stay out of any bloc and alliances. The approval of the Marshall aid was seen as a necessary economic decision to continue the already started welfare policy (Lidegaard 2002: 286). The NATO-decision was on the other hand a clear political decision to join the Alliance and leave the non-bloc ideal.

Two other important aspects of the postwar development with relevance for Denmark need to be mentioned. First of all, the US policies structuring the western world also included an evolution of a monetary and exchange rate regime which could be characterized as a 'semi-fixed rate dollar standard' – the Bretton Woods system (Hirst and Thompson 1999: 33). This monetary system was a key element in Denmark's quite remarkable growth and increasing wealth during the late 1950s and throughout the 1960s. It provided the necessary stability and combined with opening of markets, Denmark could flourish as a trading nation.

The other element of major importance was access to markets. The changing Danish governments knew very well that free trade and opening of markets were a key to the further development of the welfare state. Again export of agricultural products was crucial to Danish welfare but also the increasing expansion of small- and medium-scale industries with a huge potential for export was important. First of all the European Coal and Steel Union and the EEC were important developments. Denmark was here in a dilemma. A strong majority of the grass roots in the social democracy and the Trade Unions opposed the idea of joining the EEC. Moreover, Britain, the largest market for Danish agricultural products, was not a member. Consequently, Denmark stayed outside until Britain joined in 1972. Among leading Social Democrats, most notably the Prime Minister Jens Otto Krag, membership of the EEC was a necessary political and economic decision. Already from the early 1960s the industry export had overtaken the agricultural export and Denmark was no longer a 'farm nation' but dependent on industrial growth. Krag saw it as his mission to take Denmark into the EEC to provide the foundation of a future development and expansion of the welfare state (Lidegaard 2002: 568–85). When Britain decided to apply in October 1971, Krag wanted to follow. More than 25 per cent of the Danish export went to the EEC countries and more than 20 per cent to Britain. According to Krag and his welfare state strategy it would have disastrous consequences for Denmark to stay outside the EEC. Krag succeeded in taking Denmark into the EEC in 1972 supported by voters from the bourgeois parties and a minority of his own party voters. A Denmark outside Europe would mean no future prospect of the welfare state.

The period from the early 1950s to the early 1970s provided to a large extent a fairly stable and favourable set of conditions of existence for the Danish welfare state. A rapid increase in social expenditure and expansion of the public sector facilitated by economic growth contributed to a further development and consolidation of the welfare state. In the late 1960s and early 1970s changing governments and the leading civil servants elaborated more policies and institutional changes in order to strengthen the welfare dimension. A fundamental administrative reform at municipal level was introduced in the 1970s, and this new municipal structure provided better conditions of the set of social reforms, which followed shortly. A number of these reforms was seen as the creation of the 'world's best welfare state'.

This quite remarkable expansion of the welfare state was based upon continuous growth and a full employment policy. Consequently, several events in the early 1970s had severe implications for the Danish as well as other welfare states. A conjunction of events from the late 1960s, but mainly 1971 and onwards, caused a completely new situation. A radical change in US foreign policy and economic policy combined with the oil crisis gave rise to a political, ideological and fiscal crisis of the welfare state. The 1969 Nixon-doctrine was the first significant shift in US foreign policy. It terminated the global containment of communism policy (Reifer and Sudler 1996: 28). This policy shift led to the pursuit of a détente with the USSR and a dramatic change in the relationship to China. When Kissinger in July 1971, and later Nixon in 1972, shook hands with Chairman Mao the world was taken by surprise, not at least Japan (Calvocoressi 1991: 78). Simultaneously, this policy shift meant a signal to the western allies that they to larger extent had to look after themselves. The restructuring of the alliance implied a new prioritization of its aims: internal communist revolts were no longer seen as a real threat. This signal was repeated by the US decision to close the gold window. On 15 August 1971 Nixon declared the end of the dollar-gold convertibility and it was the collapse of Bretton Woods System.[8] It was, however, not only a signal, but also a new economic policy with new priorities. The key priority was now to reduce inflation by all means including the acceptance of a higher level of unemployment. The Keynesian economic policy was replaced by Friedman monetarism. In other words, the employment policy, which to some extent was the key to welfare, collapsed. These political and economic changes had severe consequences for the welfare states and it coincided with the 1973 and 1979 OPEC oil crises (Hirst and Thompson 1999: 5). The oil shock was more consequential for the USA's main competitors, especially the European countries, because oil was paid in US dollars. The dollar surplus accumulated in Europe and Japan during the 1960s disappeared and the trade balances went into deficit. Also, the rise of oil prices involved higher production costs (Reifer and Sudler 1996: 28).

A change in US policies, the collapse of the Bretton Woods System, the two oil shocks, some domestic failures and the general instability in the international economy brought Denmark in a difficult situation. Politicians and civil servants in Denmark thought that the peak of the welfare state was close to being reached and the true welfare society based upon genuine universalistic principles now had to be implemented. Major social and administrative reforms were introduced and everything was ready, when the model due to these mainly external events ran into major problems: higher production costs, deterioration of the trade balance, currency problems, higher inflation and a rapid increasing unemployment which again became a major financial burden. These developments sucked dry the treasury and stunted the further development of social policies in years to come.

The 1970s entailed a new situation that placed Denmark in a set of new conditions. It is beyond the scope of this chapter to examine how Denmark responded to these new circumstances. It is, however, a well-known story that it took several Danish governments and more than 20 years to return to a situation with low unemployment, trade balance surplus and inflation under control. The Danish state has survived as a welfare state, but changes and modifications have taken place.

Today

The welfare state and the welfare society as a defence mode is now, however, under pressure. The importance of the anti-communist struggle diminished from the 1970s and from 1989 it disappeared. The Americans had no longer any strong geo-political interest in Denmark. Without an external enemy, the state – the welfare state as well as the nation state – loses a part of its basis of legitimization. After the end of the Cold War Denmark is out of the shadow cast first by Germany, and then by the USSR. These countries functioned as external enemies and motivated a mobilization of Denmark.

The welfare project as an inner fortification against the external threat has also changed character. Even today we find a division in Danish political life between those arguing for a strengthening of the national welfare project as an internal fortification and a countermeasure against increased European integration. Moreover, a part of this strategy is a total mobilization of Danish values as an attempt to protect against the 'increasing Europeanization devoid of identity'. In contrast to these opinions another wing argues that the survival of the welfare state depends upon a development of increased active participation in the European project. A development of the common European market as a means to a strengthening of Denmark is seen as central to the survival of the Danish welfare state.

The picture has become even more complex since September 11, 2001 when Denmark, again, has strengthened its involvement in fighting terrorism and Denmark has demonstrated a surprisingly strong will to send troops in support of America's war. A new external enemy is looming large – an enemy which has to be fought both externally and internally (terrorism and Islamic fundamentalism). Can the welfare state become a means to prevent potentially disillusioned people living in Denmark from turning to supporting terrorism? Or must the welfare state change itself into a security state to protect its population? These questions need to be explored further in the coming years.

Conclusion

The normative foundation of the welfare state can be explored from different angles. Here I have paid attention to the importance of the decisions taken by the state in order to survive (or more precisely by the centre or locus of the state in which the political will to survive has been formulated). My claim is that we tend to neglect that the state has its own agenda – to remain independent and sovereign – which is always there notwithstanding the political ideologies dominating the current debate in the country among parties and interest groups. At crucial moments mostly when new external conditions of existence emerges this rationality tends to override any other agendas brought forward by the political parties. Any state must struggle for survival as a state and thus many welfare aspects must also be viewed in this light.

To claim that the state is an actor with its own autonomy and rationality has often been criticized by various scholars who find it methodologically or theoretically unacceptable. I argue, however, that certain developments can best be understood from a statist perspective as long as we keep in mind that it is only a limited – but neglected – view of the processes leading to a welfare state we see from this angle. Here I emphasize that the development of the Danish state during the last 150 years can be conceived as a process in which the nation-building project merges with the welfare project as a response to developments in the international environment. The welfare state developed a welfare society as a strategy to survive in the international environment – the welfare society became a defence mode.

Notes

1 This chapter and the thesis of the welfare state as a defence mode is an outcome of a research project 'Life-modes and welfare state at a crossroad' (Livsformer og velfærdsstat ved en korsvej?) sponsored by the Danish Research Council (humanities). For further reading see T. Højrup (2003).

2 We cannot necessarily assume that a state or a state elite make the best decision or develops the best strategy. Therefore, many states during history have been punished. The wrong decisions and a poor strategy lead to a weakening of a

state and society. In the worst cases states have withered away such as Poland did four times.

3 More recent examples are Pierson (1998: 6–7) and Esping-Andersen (1990: 21–3).

4 Esping-Andersen distinguishes between the 'liberal' welfare state regime (USA, Canada and UK) based upon the principle of means-tested assistance, modest universal transfer or modest social insurance plans, the conservative, corporatist welfare state regimes (Germany, Italy, France) based upon social insurance schemes and traditional familyhood and, finally, the social democratic regime-type (Scandinavia) based upon extended universalism and decommodification of social rights (Esping-Andersen 1990: 26–9).

5

> Staten og Folket er ikke eet. Skulle den usandsynlige Ulykke ramme det danske Folk, at blive lagt ind under en fremmed stat, saa lever Folket alligevel . . . Og Folket lever stærkere og sikrere jo mere udviklet dets aandelige og materielle Kultur er, jo mindre der er tilbage af de Klassegrænser, som splitter og deler et Folk i stridende lejre med forskelligartet Tænkevis.
>
> (Det ny Aarhundrede, 2. Aarg., 2. Bd., 1905: 55)

6

> vi kan lige så lidt forsvare den danske Stat med Kultur som med Festningsværker. Derimod kan Kulturen skabe det danske Folk et aandeligt Værn . . . Hvis Forholdene skulde stille sig saa ulykkeligt at den danske Stat blev erobret – det sømmer sig at se i Øjnene den Sandhed at dette kan ske – da vil en ejendommelig, højt udviklet dansk Kultur saa fjern fra Erobrerstatens militaristiske Kultur som muligt betyde Sikkerhed for, at det danske Folk kan bevare sit eget nationale Liv, indtil det faar ogsaa sin ydre Selvstændighed tilbage.
>
> (Munch 1905, the quotation is from Lidegaard 1998b)

7 The attempt by the Social Liberals to reduce tensions and inequalities in the Danish society and at the same time strengthen the common cultural and spiritual dimension of the population appears clearly in the first party programme from 1905 (Odense-programmet 21 May 1905).

8 The closing of the gold window was an unintended consequence of the Vietnam War. The enormous trade surplus changed in 1971 to a huge deficit. As a consequence the USA printed more dollars to pay for the war. This led to inflation and therefore the other countries preferred gold rather than dollars (Reifer and Sudler 1996: 26).

References

Baldwin, P. (1990) *The Politics of Social Solidarity: Class Bases of the European Welfare State, 1875–1975*, Cambridge: Cambridge University Press.

Bernild, O. (2001) 'Velfærdsstaten og det livsformsorganiserede danske folk frem til 2. verdenskrig', Working paper, Lov-project (mimeo).

Bjørn, C. (1990) *Fra reaktion til grundlov*, Gyldendal og Politikens Danmarkshistorie, Copenhagen: Gyldendal/Politiken.

Böckenförde, E.-W. (1991) *State, Society and Liberty*, Oxford: Berg Publishers.

Calvocoressi, P. (1991) *World Politics since 1945*, London: Longman.

Esping-Andersen, G. (1990) *The Three Worlds of Welfare Capitalism*, Cambridge: Polity Press.

Gravesen, B., Nielsen, N. J. and Mariager, R. (1999) 'Arbejderbevægelsen og udenrigspolitikken', *Arbejderhistorie*, (4).

Hirst, P. and Thompson, G. (1999) *Globalization in Question* (second revised edition), Cambridge: Polity Press.

Højrup, T. (2003) *Livsformer og velfærdsstat ved en korsvej?*, Copenhagen: Museum Tusculanums Forlag.

Hornemann-Møller, I. (1992) *Den danske velfærdsstats tilblivelse*, Copenhagen: Samfundslitteratur.

Hvidt, K. (1990) *Det folkelige gennembrud og dets mænd*, Gyldendal og Politikkens Danmarkshistorie, Copenhagen: Gyldendal/Politiken.

Jensen, L. D. (1989) 'Denmark and the Marshall Plan, 1947–48: the decision to participate', *Scandinavian Journal of History*, 14.

Knudsen, T. (ed.) (2000) *Den nordiske protestantisme og velfærdsstaten*, Aarhus: Aarhus Universitetsforlag.

Lidegaard, B. (1996) *I Kongens navn*, Copenhagen: Samlerens forlag.

—— (1998a) 'Vi opnaaede da, at København ikke blev bombarderet...', in H. Dethlefsen and H. Lundbak (eds) *Fra mellemkrigstid til efterkrigstid*, Copenhagen: Museum Tusculanum.

—— (1998b) 'Systemet Munch – 50 år efter', *Radikal Politik*, (9), 17 June.

—— (1999) 'Danmarks overlevelsesstrategi i den kolde krigs første år', *Arbejderhistorie*, (4): 35–46.

—— (2001/2002) *Jens Otto Krag*, 2 volumes, Copenhagen: Gyldendal.

Munch, P. (1905) *Det ny Aarhundrede*, 2: 2, Copenhagen.

Nørgaard, A. S. (2000) 'Party politics and the organization of the Danish welfare state, 1890–1920: the bourgois roots of the modern welfare state', *Scandinavian Political Studies*, 23 (3): 183–215.

Pierson, C. (1998) *Beyond the Welfare State*, Cambridge: Polity Press.

Reifer, T. and Sudler, J. (1996) 'The interstate system', in T. K. Hopkins and I. Wallerstein (eds) *The Age of Transition*, London: Zed Books.

Rerup, L. (1989) *Danmarks historie*. Bd. 6, Tiden 1864–1914. Copenhagen: Gyldendal.

Schmidt, E. I. (1993) *Fra psykopatklubben*, Copenhagen: Gyldendal.

Schmitt, C. (1988 [1934]) *Political Theology*, Cambridge: The MIT Press.

—— (1996 [1932]) *The Concept of the Political*, Chicago: University of Chicago Press.

Skovgaard-Petersen, V. (1985) *Danmarks historie*. Bd. 5, Copenhagen: Gyldendal.

Sørensen, A. B. (1998) 'On kings, pietism and rent-seeking in Scandinavian welfare states', *Acta Sociologica*, 41 (4): 363–75.

Sørensen, V. (2001) *Denmark's Social Democratic Government and the Marshall Plan 1947–50*, København: Museum Tusculanum.

Villaume, P. (1999) 'Fra antimilitarisme til atlantisk aktivisme', *Arbejderhistorie*, (4).

5 Nordic social politics in the late twentieth century

An analysis of the political reform agenda

Anders Nordlund

Introduction

During the last several decades, it has often been suggested that comprehensive and interventionist welfare states will be reduced to a bare minimum due to a number of challenges (e.g. Castells 1997; Greider 1997). Undoubtedly, policy makers in the Nordic countries were under severe pressure during the 1980s and 1990s. All Nordic countries experienced difficult economic problems, although problems in Norway were moderated by income from the oil industry. In particular, policy makers in Finland and Sweden had to deal with the worst recession of the postwar period. Furthermore, many politicians, political advisors and participants in the political debate assumed increased globalization would fundamentally alter conditions for national policy-making.

Nordic social policy was not unchanged during the 1980s and 1990s. However, a great deal of empirical research suggests that changes in Nordic welfare states were in fact relatively limited during this period (e.g. Eitrheim and Kuhnle 2000; Heikkilä *et al.* 1999; Lehto *et al.* 1999; Pierson 2001; Ploug 1999). Why has economic and political pressure for radical changes not resulted in a profound change in the Nordic welfare states? Analysis of political parties' reform agendas appears to be key to an improved understanding of the obvious discrepancy between pressures for policy changes and actual policy outcomes. This chapter attempts to contribute to an improved understanding of the normative foundation of Nordic social policy-making by an analysis of interviews conducted in late 1990s with high-level representatives of Nordic political parties.

Analytical and methodological considerations

All parties with seats in Nordic parliaments at the time of data collection were asked to participate in this study. Table 5.1 shows the 28 parties that consented to participate. The parties included in the study cover almost all the major parties in Nordic countries and a number of smaller parties. The only missing cases that might influence the analysis are the

Table 5.1 Participating political parties in the study

	Denmark	*Finland*	*Norway*	*Sweden*
Communists and left socialists	Unity List, Socialist People's Party	Left Wing League	Red Electoral Alliance, Socialist Left Party	Left Party
Social democrats	Social Democratic Party	Social Democratic Party	Labour Party	Social Democratic Party
Centrist and agrarian parties	Liberal Party	Centre Party		Centre Party
Liberal parties	Social Liberal Party	Swedish People's Party	Liberal Party	Liberal People's Party
Christian parties		Christian Democratic Party	Christian Democratic Party	Christian Democratic Party
Other centrist parties	Centre Democratic Party			
Conservative parties		National Coalition Party	Conservative Party	Moderate Party
Protest parties	Progress Party	Young Finnish Party	Progress Party	
Environmental parties				Green Party

Note
Classification of parties is taken from Petersson (1994), with the exception of Unity List (Denmark), Young Finnish Party and Red Electoral Alliance (Norway).

Conservative Party in Denmark and the Centre Party in Norway. In arranging for participation in the study, we explicitly requested an interview with a party official or a politician at the highest level in each party.[1] Interviews with the parties were conducted in 1997, with the exception of one Swedish party interviewed in early 1998.[2]

The following analysis and discussion are based on semi-structured interviews. At the beginning of the interviews, respondents were reminded to answer as representatives of their respective parties rather than expressing personal opinions. Each interview lasted about one hour. All the interviews were recorded and subsequently transcribed word for word. For clarity, a few quotations used in this chapter are not translated word for word. However, care has been exercised to keep the meaning of the respondents' accounts intact.

A thematic content analysis was carried out on the data generated by the interviews (cf. Baxter 1994). The analysis began with several readings of each interview with the objective of forming a preliminary understanding of the content. The next step of analysis followed the 'meaning condensation' approach described by Kvale (1996). Four themes were salient in the data:

1 policy towards the welfare state as a whole;
2 policy regarding the relationship between labour market participation and social security benefits;
3 policy regarding care of disabled individuals;
4 policy regarding production of welfare services.

In order to increase the reliability of this study, a presentation is made in the following section of research on Nordic social policy development, and in the subsequent sections findings from the interviews are triangulated with this research.

Nordic welfare state development in the late twentieth century

Pierson (2001) argues that cost containment and recalibration in the form of rationalization were salient elements of Nordic reform agendas in the late twentieth century. By *cost containment*, Pierson refers to attempts to contain spending on social programmes. *Recalibration* refers to reforms aimed at making social programmes consistent with current goals and demands for social provision. According to Pierson, recalibration may in turn be divided into two types: rationalization and updating. According to Pierson, an example of *rationalization* is when modification of a programme is in line with new ideas about how to achieve established goals. Pierson also states that rationalization includes reforms of service systems with the objective of improving the efficiency of provision or responsiveness to consumer needs and demands. *Updating* in Pierson's terminology refers to initiation of new programmes or modification of existing programmes in response to newly recognized social needs.

Several researchers on Nordic social policy have pointed to the fact that activation of beneficiaries of public income maintenance programmes was increasingly emphasized during the 1990s (e.g. Boje and Åberg 1999; Drøpping *et al.* 1999; Ploug 1999; Kildal 2001). In the Nordic countries, a broad range of different measures has been used to encourage activation, e.g. education, vocational training and re-training, etc. The term *work approach* has often been used by politicians as well as researchers to describe the intentions of the increased emphasis on beneficiaries' activity. Drøpping *et al.* describe the work approach in the following way:

> According to [the work approach], there should be a direct link between the social security system and labor market service, in the

> sense that it is an official task of the income maintenance scheme to maximize labor market participation. No person should be granted long-term public income support until all possibility of making the person self-sufficient through employment had been exhausted.
>
> (Drøpping *et al.* 1999: 135, 136)

However, the objective of maximizing labour market participation is not a novel objective of postwar Nordic social policy (cf. Hvinden 1994; Kosonen 2000; Lindqvist and Marklund 1995; Olsson 1993). Thus, it is possible to argue that the work approach reflects a policy objective compatible with postwar Nordic social policy, albeit the strength and content of this policy have varied over time and between countries.

Privatization was a common theme in political rhetoric during the 1980s and 1990s. The privatization rhetoric was undoubtedly loud during the 1980s, but actual privatization of welfare state services was quite modest (cf. Olsson 1993; Lehto *et al.* 1999). The privatization debate in the Nordic countries continued during the 1990s and a number of reliable indications pointed in the direction of an increased role of privately provided health and social care services (cf. Lehto *et al.* 1999; Rostgaard and Fridberg 1998; Rostgaard and Lehto 2001; Trydegård 2001).

A salient trend in many western countries in the late twentieth century was the de-institutionalization of health and social care. The Nordic countries were not an exception to this trend, and institutions for care of the disabled and mentally ill were successively closed down during the 1980s and 1990s (cf. Rostgaard and Lehto 2001; Hanssen *et al.* 1996). Associated with this trend was an increased emphasis on provision of care in regular housing or smaller residential homes within the community (ibid.). Furthermore, decentralization of authority to municipalities was also a clear trend in the Nordic countries during the 1980s and 1990s (Hanssen *et al.* 1996).

Denmark

With the exception of the populist Progress Party, non-socialist parties did not indicate deep-seated dissatisfaction with the Danish welfare state. For example, there existed no consensus among non-socialist parties that the Danish welfare state was a main cause of economic problems during the 1980s and 1990s. For example, the Liberal Party representative stated the following:

> problems had been much more severe if we had implemented drastic cuts in social programmes ... the welfare state is not to blame for [economic problems during the 1980s] ... It is not the size of the benefits that are the problem.
>
> (Liberal Party, Denmark)

Thus, an examination of the social policy objectives of various Danish parties in the late 1990s, with the exception of the Progress Party, provided no indications of a desire to move towards a major reform of the Danish welfare state. Even though the interviews did not reveal any potential for significant downsizing of the welfare state, neither did they provide indications of a significant potential for major expansion. For example, the Centre Democrats emphasized the limits to further increases in public expenditure. The SDP stated that Denmark had reached a maximum tax level and future social policy was mainly a question of prioritization within the current size of the welfare state. The Socialist People's Party endorsed a similar position:

> We are concerned if individual taxation increases greatly over the current level. This is possibly caused by the fact that we had an anti-tax party in 1972, which became the second-largest party under the leadership of Mogens Glistrup.
>
> (Socialist People's Party, Denmark)

Thus, the interviews with the Danish party representatives indicated strong support for cost containment of public expenditure. A secure majority of the Danish parties did not express any support for downsizing of the welfare state. Equally significant is that the SDP and the Socialist People's Party did not see increased taxes as a viable response to raising costs.

However, representatives of non-socialist parties believed that benefit levels in cash benefit programmes could in some cases cause incentive problems. Non-socialist parties, with the exception of the Progress Party, regarded such disincentives as a relatively minor problem. The SDP representative acknowledged that incentive problems might occur at some point, but argued that Denmark had not yet reached that point. Nonetheless, the SDP and the non-socialist parties agreed that the design of unemployment and social assistance programmes *before* the changes implemented during the 1990s were to a great extent to blame for problems of high unemployment. The unemployment problem was explained as a result of social programmes' lack of expectations for individual activity.

There was a consensus across parties that Danish social policy had emphasized expectation of individual activity among beneficiaries of public income support during the 1990s, especially among young people. The Unity List and the Socialist People's Party were critical of these activation measures. These two parties described the activation measures as a violation of the individual's right to negotiate wages and conditions of employment, and to be a member of a union. Other parties expressed a positive attitude towards increased emphasis on individual activity. The representative for SDP, for example, stressed two reasons why an increased emphasis on duties had been necessary. First, that activation measures provide the unemployed a chance to become self-supporting. Second, that it is important to be able to assure that 'no one gets anything that they do not have a right or need for'. Otherwise, according to the SDP representative, the legitimacy of the welfare system would be in question and citizens' acceptance of taxes would decline. Since the SDP and the non-socialist parties agreed to the same policy, there is no question that activation of beneficiaries occupied a central position on the Danish political agenda during the 1990s.

The definition of the work approach suggested by Drøpping *et al.* (1999) appears to have a good fit with policy-making in Denmark during the 1990s. Agreement was present among non-socialist parties and the SDP concerning the importance of a tight link between labour market services and public provision of income support. These parties also agreed that no individual should be granted long-term income support until all options of returning to the labour market have been exhausted. Rationalization also appears to be an accurate description of the political intentions expressed by most of the parties in support of changes to Danish unemployment protection benefits. A common argument among parties that saw the need for changes regarded implemented changes as necessary on the grounds that the former unemployment benefit system had not produced outcomes compatible with initial intentions.

The need for a policy to handle consequences of de-institutionalization of psychiatric care was an issue in the interviews with the Liberal Party and the SDP. Furthermore, increased freedom of choice between private and public service providers was a popular theme among the non-socialist parties. For example, the representative for the Liberal Party stated the following regarding important policy issues for the party:

> [It is important that] all our service areas provide citizens with a freedom of choice between public solutions, private solutions and own solutions. In particular, this is important regarding childcare and elderly care ... The social services should consist of a plurality of offers.
>
> (Liberal Party, Denmark)

Although with different arguments, the Progress Party and the Centre Democrats also indicated a positive attitude to privately produced welfare services. The Social Liberals emphasized their support for voluntary organizations. The representative for the SDP stated that the party had contributed to increased freedom of choice between providers of elderly care and childcare. However, the representative for the SDP readily agreed that the issue of privately produced services had created internal conflicts within the party, and that this had resulted in a very diffuse party policy.

Finland

In the early 1990s, Finland was struck by the worst economic crisis since the war. The Finnish parties agreed that this crisis had resulted in cuts in social programmes. Even though parties agreed that the 1990s had been characterized by cuts, none of the parties argued that retrenchment politics had resulted in a fundamental change in the Finnish welfare state as it evolved up to the beginning of the 1990s. For example, the Left Wing League stated that no welfare programmes had been abolished, but that:

> benefit levels were reduced ... We are back to the benefit levels of [the late 1980s]. It is not a question of major cuts ... savings were not conducted in panic ... the systems have remained relatively stable.
>
> (Left Wing League, Finland)

The parties, with the exception of the tiny neo-liberal Young Finnish Party, denied that the expansion of the Finnish welfare state during the 1980s was a cause of the recession in the early 1990s. Instead, socialist parties and most non-socialist parties regarded the welfare state as a set of institutions that had saved Finland from potentially devastating social consequences during the recession. The representative of the SDP expressed this attitude in the following way:

> [The welfare state did not cause the recession in the beginning of the 1990s.] However, the recession meant that we could not hold on to the same benefit levels as before. We did not change the service system or the cash benefit system, but benefit levels were lowered ... but the Finnish welfare state has helped individuals to bridge over the recession.
>
> (Social Democratic Party, Finland)

The representative for the Centre Party, an opposition party at the time of the interviews, stated the following regarding their rationale for being involved in decisions for retrenchments:

> the welfare state was tremendously important for avoiding much greater problems ... Private industry's employer organizations put forward ideological reasons to cut the welfare state. But from the viewpoint of the Centre Party, the answer is no! Our involvement in retrenchments was strictly guided by practical reasons since the severe economic situation could not be solved in any other way.
>
> (Centre Party, Finland)

The conservative Coalition Party explained cuts in the welfare state as follows:

> When it was decided to cut the budget, all ministries had to review their expenditures. We were forced to cut most in areas with the highest expenditure ... However, when we think of the situation in Finland during this mass unemployment, our generous unemployment benefits saved Finland from civil unrest.
>
> (Coalition Party, Finland)

The following statement made by the representative for the Christian Democratic Party indicates the broad consensus behind the welfare state endorsed by all major Finnish parties:

> [The welfare state] has contributed to a feeling of security ... and parties have been united regarding [the welfare state]. No party has questioned the welfare state and it has united political parties. It has been an area in which parties have found one another.
>
> (Christian Democratic Party, Finland)

Thus, parties which were members of the government or had been members of government agreed that the principal objective for cuts was not to downsize the Finnish welfare state. Instead, they described their involvement in retrenchments as guided by the objective of balancing the budget in a situation when government finances deteriorated sharply due to a severe recession. Consequently, the interviews indicated a strong presence of a cost containment dimension in Finnish social policy-making during the 1990s.

The SDP, the Swedish People's Party, the Centre Party, the Christian Democratic Party and the Coalition Party stressed the need for measures to encourage beneficiaries to enter the labour market. Non-socialist parties emphasized the need to coordinate benefit levels, fees for social services and the tax system in order to reduce incentive problems. The SDP stressed the need to increase beneficiaries' labour market participation through education and rehabilitation. Thus, only the representative for the SDP put forward arguments for a work approach compatible with the definition provided by Drøpping *et al.* (1999).

The interview with the Coalition Party indicated that care of disabled had occupied a high place on the political agenda during the 1980s and 1990s. The interviews also indicated that the role of publicly produced services and freedom of choice regarding services were on the political agenda. In the 1980s, the SDP and the Centre Party reached an agreement to offer parents the alternative of placing children under the age of three in public childcare or receiving money for home care. Both the SDP and the Centre Party described this reform as valuable. The Coalition Party emphasized the need to decrease the dominance of publicly produced services and to increase choice between private and public service providers. Other Finnish parties did not put forward these issues as clearly as the Coalition Party. Moreover, the representative for the SDP expressed concern for sparsely populated areas if privately produced services were increased at the expense of public services.

Norway

None of the Norwegian parties blamed the welfare state directly for economic problems. The Red Electoral Alliance, the Socialist Left Party and the Labour Party expressed a solid position that the welfare state was not associated with any problems for Norwegian society. The Christian Democratic Party respondent, the prime minister's party at the time of interviews, expressed the following:

> we wish to maintain welfare programmes and as far as we can afford they should not be decreased. We have argued that it is possible to tighten up the sickness benefit system so that employees should pay some during sickness. However, that is not something that this government will push particularly hard for.
>
> (Christian Democratic Party, Norway)

However, the Christian Democratic Party's representative also noted that that:

> [Oil has made] the Norwegian state's finances very solid. Thus, the problem is not the lack of money. But we have to be cautious with how money is spent, since it can put too great pressure on the economy and result in inflation . . . it is also important to realize that we have great economic commitments in the future and that revenues from oil will decrease. Thus, it is important to think about future generations in this context.
>
> (Christian Democratic Party, Norway)

The other non-socialist parties were slightly more critical of the Norwegian welfare state as compared to the Christian Democratic Party. Although critical, the representatives emphasized the importance of the state as a provider of social protection. The following statement by the representative for the Conservative Party indicates this:

> The Social Democratic Party tries to spread a myth that the Conservative Party has 'state fright'; that we are against a strong public sector. That is *not* correct! We have for the last hundred years had the same approach: we need a strong state, but a restricted state; a state that first of all prioritizes the most important tasks and solves them better. According to our view, resources are currently spread thinly over everything and everybody, which means that the most important tasks such as health care, school, education are not solved satisfactorily.
>
> (Conservative Party, Norway)

However, the representative of the Conservative Party also stated that:

> Too much of the economy is allocated through the public sector and we would like to give more of these resources back. That is to say, an increased freedom of choice in the sense that the individual can keep more of the income and take care of oneself instead of paying high taxes that are then paid back to the individual or the family. This is a system change that we would like to see.
>
> (Conservative Party, Norway)

Furthermore, the Conservative Party, the Liberal Party and the Progress Party all argued that the Norwegian welfare state bore indirect responsibility for problems during the 1980s and the early 1990s. Their main criticism was that the comprehensive Norwegian welfare state had reduced individual responsibility.

Despite critical remarks from some of the non-socialist parties, no significant potential for a major reduction in the Norwegian welfare state was indicated in the interviews. The representatives of the Liberal Party, the Conservative Party and the Progress Party returned several times during the interviews to the issue of lower taxes. However, these expressions of support for tax cuts were not connected to any explicit suggestions for drastic cuts in social programmes. Nevertheless, a large majority of the Norwegian political parties subscribed to an understanding that a sharp increase in the welfare state would be damaging to the public economy. The Labour Party described their own political approach in the following way:

> our biggest political challenge for the moment is to convince people that in order to take care of the welfare society in the future, we cannot expand and expand and expand. This is a pedagogic challenge. In order to safeguard the welfare society we cannot simply expand the welfare state. It is necessary to prioritize. We must conduct skilful distribution politics, and not only conduct politics of handouts. And *that* is a pedagogic challenge when income from oil is increasing and when we have stated that in solidarity with future generations we must develop an oil fund and not use up the money pumped up from the North Sea.
>
> (Labour Party, Norway)

The only parties that argued for a radical expansion of the welfare state were the small Red Electoral Alliance, which lost representation in the election of 1997, and the Socialist Left Party, which attracted 6 to 8 per cent of the votes during the 1990s. Consequently, a consensus was present between the Labour Party and non-socialist parties on the question of saving profits from the offshore sector for the future. This consensus seems to be the main explanation for the cautious expansion of the Norwegian welfare state – relative to the country's oil wealth – during the 1990s (cf. NOSOSCO 2001: 187). Thus, the interviews indicated that cost containment was a prevalent dimension of Norwegian policy-making during the 1990s.

The interviews indicated that the work approach was a distinctive trend in Norwegian social policy during the 1990s. Several parties stated that income maintenance programmes had been modified during the 1990s in order to increase labour market participation among beneficiaries. The representative of the Labour Party was very positive towards measures aimed at increasing labour market participation among beneficiaries:

> The work approach is about trying to stimulate those who are outside the labour market to get training or reduce barriers to the labour market ... The work approach is more than reduced benefits ... It is also about making clear that individuals must accept available jobs ... The work approach must be understood in a broader sense than only to give incentives ... it is also to improve labour market programmes in order to make them more goal-oriented, to understand that people may have other problems than getting a job ... measures must to a greater extent be individually tailored.
>
> (Labour Party, Norway)

This statement indicates a slightly broader definition of the work approach than the definition suggested by Drøpping *et al.* (1999). Although the Labour Party representative put training and requirements for beneficiaries to search for employment in the forefront, the representative acknowledged that the work approach might also include measures to strengthen economic incentives to participate in the labour market. In contrast, the two parties to the left of the Labour Party were critical of the work approach. The representatives for the Christian Democratic Party did not clearly indicate the party's position, but argued that the work approach had gone too far in some cases, e.g. in early-retirement programmes.

Reforms in care of the disabled were discussed by several Norwegian parties. Representatives of the Christian Democratic Party, the Liberal Party, the Progress Party and the Socialist Left Party all mentioned deinstitutionalization of care of the intellectually disabled as important and valuable. However, the parties also expressed concerns that reforms had meant a decreased quality of life for a number of the disabled due, for example, to increased isolation or problems for the municipalities to finance high-quality care.

The Norwegian parties underscored the idea of the state as the main provider of health and social care. For example, the Conservative Party and the Progress Party argued that the state should take over the responsibility for health care from the counties. Nevertheless, the non-socialist parties argued for decreased dominance of publicly produced services and increased freedom of choice between private and public service providers. The representatives of the Conservative Party and the Progress Party stressed that their parties wanted an increased role of private suppliers of health care. The representatives of the Christian Democratic Party and the Liberal Party argued for the importance of cash benefits for parents that do not choose to use a place in a public kindergarten. The Red Electoral Alliance and the Socialist Left Party were the only parties that explicitly argued against an increased role of private service providers.

Sweden

The SDP and the Left Party distinguished themselves from other Swedish political parties in their emphasis on the welfare state's positive contribution to the economy. Non-socialist parties did not single out the welfare state as a prime cause for economic problems. However, the non-socialist parties had a tendency to argue that the current welfare state serves a humanitarian purpose solely, without any positive contribution to, for example, labour market participation and economic growth. Of the non-socialist parties, the Centre Party expressed less criticism of the welfare state. According to the representative for the Centre Party, the welfare state had only temporarily caused problems for public finances during the 1990s, while increased fees and changes of the financing system for social programmes had returned the system to economic balance. The Christian Democratic Party expressed relatively cautious criticism of the welfare state. According to the party representative, the welfare state has provided citizens with a necessary security net. However, the representative also argued that the welfare state has lessened individual responsibility. The Liberal Party and the Moderate Party were the only parties explicitly arguing that the conditions of the Swedish welfare state had changed in the late twentieth century. The representative of the Liberal Party did not regard the welfare state as the prime cause of economic problems during the 1990s, but argued that the conditions for the welfare state had changed significantly during the 1980s and 1990s. According to the Moderate Party representative, Sweden's crisis in early 1990s was caused by a system failure. Although social policies pursued over the years were not directly responsible for the severe economic crisis of the early 1990s, the representative argued that since the social policies pursued were part of a broader public policy that was not compatible with a market economy, the welfare state was partly responsible for the crisis. The Moderate Party in particular regarded high taxes and an oversized public sector as the main problems for Sweden's economy. The representative for the Moderate Party stated the following regarding the relation between taxes and social policy:

> Low- and middle-income earners in Sweden pay the highest taxes in the world which means individuals dispose very little of their own income and own resources . . . It is important to make sure that individuals are given the opportunity to live on their own incomes and to have the security that is implied by having control over own resources . . . We also know that individuals and families are good at managing their own recourses efficiently; better than politicians are. That is why taxes are such an important social policy issue, because it relates to the basic security of people's lives.
>
> (The Moderate Party, Sweden)

Although the Green Party described themselves as defenders of the welfare state and opponents of the social policies advocated by the Moderate Party, the representative for the Green Party argued that the welfare state has undermined solidarity between individuals.

The interviews indicated that the political potential for a systemic change and a radical downsizing of the Swedish welfare state was insufficient. However, the interviews provided several pieces of evidence that, particularly during the 1990s, cost containment was a salient dimension in Swedish social policy-making. For example, the Centre Party mentioned reform of the pension system as a major event in Swedish social policy-making during the 1990s – a reform fully compatible with the implementation of the ATP-system, according to the representative:

> we have strived after a synthesis that unites the parties and generates a trustworthiness to a new pension system for forthcoming generations . . . a system that is economically stable and that has an intrinsic force that benefits economic development, which in turn decides the solvency in the pension system.
>
> (Centre Party, Sweden)

The representative for the SDP described the need for containing costs in the following way:

> [the economy for the welfare state] must be connected to the financial situation of the state in general. [The state's financial situation was in the 1990s] a black hole if the state's total finances was considered . . . the objective [for changes of social programmes] was to strengthen the state's finances in general.
>
> (Social Democratic Party, Sweden)

The representative of the SDP argued strongly that the work approach was an extant main feature of Swedish social policy:

> All systems have had the objective to push individuals to work . . . [the work approach] has been tremendously important for economic

> growth ... that the labour force have been at the right place at the right time, in good shape, well trained ... but have also been important for individuals ... to have a job, receive a pay-cheque, have been important for individuals' freedom.
>
> (Social Democratic Party, Sweden)

Furthermore, the representative of the SDP argued that Swedish social programmes had suffered from problems. For example, the representative described problems with sickness benefits in the following way:

> [In some cases sickness benefits could before the corrections] reach 105 per cent of previous income ... and then the incentive to work vanishes. [That is not compatible with the work approach.]
>
> (Social Democratic Party, Sweden)

Thus, the SDP emphasized the work approach in social programmes as a feature of the Swedish welfare state that contributed positively to the economy, albeit that labour market problems during the 1990s had created problems. Furthermore, the intention behind changes of sickness benefits expressed by the representative of the SDP bears great resemblance to the concept of rationalization suggested by Pierson (2001), i.e. that the intention was to restore sick pay to its originally intended role. However, the interview also showed the presence inside the Social Democratic Party of a broader definition of the work approach than suggested by Drøpping *et al.* (1999). As the above quotation shows, the representative for the SDP also cited the effect of benefit levels on beneficiaries' incentive to work.

The Centre Party advocated a policy that at least partially resembles the work approach as defined by Drøpping *et al.* (ibid.). The representative for the Centre Party stated that they wanted:

> a reformation of social programmes that puts welfare goals in the forefront instead of a materialistic goal. The goal should be that people should return to an ordinary life, health, labour market, etc.... but it is more than about work. It is also about a full worthy life for the individual, self-realization. It is too crude to only regard it as a work approach.
>
> (Centre Party, Sweden)

The interviews indicated that disability care was on the Swedish reform agenda. The Christian Democratic Party and the Left Party argued that reform measures in the care of the disabled were a significant advancement. The Liberal Party emphasized the need for further reform in order to increase empowerment among the disabled. Furthermore, the representative of the Green Party expressed concerns that reforms of psychiatric care had led to a situation in which many former institutionalized patients did not receive enough support after discharge. The Liberal Party and, in particular, the Moderate Party were advocates for lessening the dominance of publicly produced services and for increasing freedom of choice between service providers. The Christian Democratic Party placed especially great emphasis on the importance of the family's role in the care of children. The Left Party argued sharply against political attempts to reduce the role of the public sector.

Nordic reform agendas in the late twentieth century

The interviews indicated that Nordic political parties were generally reluctant to express any support for drastic cuts in the welfare state. Whether this finding is a result of party ideologies or a strategy to avoid being associated with unpopular cuts is difficult to determine. Interviews with professional politicians and officials must, of necessity, be interpreted with caution. However, previous research and official statistics indicate that the Nordic welfare states had in fact not been economically downsized or radically changed during the 1980s and 1990s. Thus, it appears safe to conclude that Nordic political parties during the last decades tried to avoid being involved in major cuts if other solutions were at hand. Nevertheless, findings from the interviews did not provide indications of any strong movement towards expansion of the four countries' welfare states. Consequently, cost containment had a salient position on the Nordic policy agenda in the late twentieth century (cf. Pierson 2001).

The interviews indicated that several Nordic political parties had subscribed to policies aimed at increasing labour market participation by tightening the link between cash benefit programmes and labour market services. Thus, the definition of the work approach suggested by Drøpping *et al.* (1999) makes a good fit with many statements put forward in the interviews. However, statements made by the representatives of the SDP in Norway and Sweden imply a broader understanding of the work approach than suggested by Drøpping *et al.* (ibid.), since the two party representatives also included in the concept the effect of benefits on incentives to participate in the labour market.

Pierson (2001) argues that besides cost containment, recalibration in the form of rationalization had an important position on Nordic policy agendas in the late twentieth century, i.e. modification of programmes in line with new ideas of how to achieve established goals. Pierson's term *rationalization* and the understandings of the term the *work approach* expressed in the interviews appear to be closely related. Maximizing labour market participation has been a prevalent goal in Nordic social policy during the postwar period. Thus, it appears reasonable to regard statements supporting changes in line with the definition of the work approach suggested by Drøpping *et al.* (1999) as equivalent to support for rationalizing cash benefit programmes.

However, the interviews also revealed aspects of Nordic policy-making that do not appear consistent with cost containment and recalibration in the form of rationalization. For example, de-institutionalization of care is difficult to characterize as an example of the dimensions proposed by Pierson. The reason is that the goal of abolishing institutional care in favour of provision of care in smaller residential homes or regular housing, represented a totally new policy approach. Thus, to argue that de-institutionalization of care during the 1980s and 1990s is an example of rationalization appears to be inaccurate.

The interviews indicated that greater choice between private and public service providers was an important issue for several Nordic parties. It is questionable to argue that policies pursuing an increased role for privately produced services fit into the concept of rationalization. According to Esping-Andersen and Korpi (1984: 53), a distinct feature of Nordic social policy in the late 1970s was that social citizenship was taken more literally compared to other countries in the sense that policy makers deliberately attempted to ensure that all citizens were treated on equal terms. An increased role for privately produced services may jeopardize the goal of equal treatment of citizens for at least two reasons. First, citizens in different parts of the Nordic countries will have access to different supply-mixes of services, especially since the number of private service providers is likely to be greater in densely populated areas than in sparsely populated areas (cf. Lehto *et al.* 1999: 114; Blomqvist and Rothstein 2000: 165, 166, 196, 198). Second, *if* a greater role for privately produced services implies a more efficient utilization of economic resources, municipalities in different parts of the Nordic countries will have different opportunities to organize their service systems efficiently. For example, competition between potential service providers will vary sharply between densely and sparsely populated regions. Such differences may in turn contribute to increased differences between municipalities in terms of attendant variations in both the quantity and quality of service providers. Consequently, allowing an increased role for privately produced services appears not to be an effective policy to reach the goal that all citizens should be treated on equal terms and thus fits Pierson's definition of rationalization poorly, if we take Pierson at his word that changes should represent a new way of reaching previously established goals. Thus, the dimensions of cost containment and recalibration in the form of rationalization do not alone sufficiently explain the variation in social policy-making in the Nordic countries. An accurate description of Nordic social policy-making during the 1980s and 1990s must also include reformation of the organization of welfare services.

Due to the methodological design of this study, it would be presumptuous to argue that each Nordic party's reform agenda has been exhaustively identified. However, the data provided by the interviews and previous research makes it possible to formulate – for analytical purposes – three ideal types of Nordic reform agendas. Table 5.2 shows these three ideal types of reform agendas.

Agenda A is an ideal type of reform agenda that does not regard the welfare state as it evolved during the postwar period up to late 1970s as a problem at all. The postwar welfare state is seen as beneficial for the society in general, its economy and its citizens. This view implies that there are no inherent obstacles to continued economic expansion of the welfare state. Moreover, it implies that expansion of programmes should occupy a central position on the political agenda. Cash benefit programmes established before the 1980s are not regarded as problematic and programmes that were subject to retrenchments during the 1980s and 1990s should be restored to their original condition. In addition, public production of welfare services is regarded as superior to private production. Finally, in similar fashion to the other two agendas, Agenda A reflects support for de-institutionalization of care.

Agenda B is an ideal type of reform agenda that reflects a moderate concern regarding trends in the postwar welfare state. Social programmes that were established prior to the 1980s are regarded as occasionally creating various types of disincentives for labour market participation. Agenda B reflects the opinion that taxes cannot be raised further, which implies that cost expansion of social programmes must be curtailed, i.e. cost containment enjoys a central position on the agenda. However, major cuts are not on the agenda. Instead, the preferred reform option is recalibration. Also on the agenda is increased freedom of choice between public and private service providers. However, the state is nonetheless assumed to have the main responsibility for financing and regulation of services.

Agenda C is an ideal type of agenda that stands for a radical change of

Table 5.2 Three ideal types of reform agendas

	Agenda A	*Agenda B*	*Agenda C*
Understanding of existing welfare state	Not problematic	Partly problematic	Problematic
Social expenditure	Cost expansion	Cost containment	Cost reduction
Change of cash benefit programmes	Restoration	Recalibration	Reorientation
Organization of service production	Public production, de-institutionalization	Service plurality, de-institutionalization	Privatization, de-institutionalization

the welfare state. The current welfare state is regarded as a severe obstacle to economic performance and individual liberty. The high taxes demanded by the Nordic welfare states are regarded as incompatible with a healthy market economy. Furthermore, economic efficiency is assumed to be possible only by undisturbed market processes and not by allocation of resources in accordance with political decisions. Consequently, the welfare state must be downsized and taxes must be drastically reduced, i.e. cost reduction is high on the political agenda. Moreover, cash benefit programmes must be significantly re-orientated. In particular, it is regarded as essential that individuals themselves should to a large degree both pay for social protection themselves and decide what social protection is appropriate. Finally, public production of services is regarded as inefficient and an obstacle to maximizing the freedom of choice between different service providers.

The interviews indicated that most left-wing socialist parties promoted a reform agenda that fit Agenda A's very closely. The only exceptions were the Socialist People's Party in Denmark and the Left Wing League in Finland. The Socialist People's Party strongly defended programmes implemented prior to the 1980s and was in particular critical towards reforms in line with the work approach. However, the representative for the Socialist People's Party acknowledged that Denmark had reached a maximum tax level. Although statements expressed by the representative for the Left Wing League in Finland had a close fit with Agenda A, the party must be regarded as a slightly deviant case. During the 1990s, the Left Wing League was a member of a government that pursued a tough cost containment policy, which implies that the party has been prepared to compromise with parties with agendas that resemble Agenda B.

Statements made by representatives for social democratic parties in the Nordic countries did not have a close fit to only one of the ideal types described above. The social democrats maintained a strong defence of the idea of a comprehensive welfare state. Furthermore, they portrayed the current welfare state as beneficial for the economy and its citizens. Nevertheless, the representatives for the social democratic parties acknowledged that some social programmes established prior the 1980s had created incentive problems and that economic conditions during the 1990s had required adjustments. In particular, social democratic parties in Denmark, Norway and Sweden all agreed that it had been necessary to change social programmes in line with the work approach. Furthermore, all Nordic social democratic parties appeared to recognize the need for a cost containment policy. However, service production seemed to be a delicate question for social democratic parties, since the interviews either indicated an ambiguous policy or the absence of a policy regarding privately produced services. Consequently, the reform agendas of Nordic social democratic parties were a mix between Agenda A and B, but with a bias towards Agenda B.

Representatives of Nordic centre parties did not indicate a common reform agenda. Nevertheless, Nordic centre parties clearly subscribed to reform agendas which either closely or approximately fit Agenda B. The parties did not regard the welfare state as a major problem for the economy or the society in general. Nevertheless, the centre parties expressed sentiments that were in line with a cost containment policy. The Liberal Party in Denmark distinguished themselves from other centre parties by strongly arguing in favour of recalibration of social programmes in line with the work approach, and for the need for increased freedom of choice between privately and publicly produced services.

Nordic liberal parties, with the exception of the Swedish People's Party in Finland, expressed relatively sharp criticisms of their respective welfare states. However, interviews indicated support for cost containment rather than for a cost reduction policy. Furthermore, none of the liberal parties provided any explicit suggestions for re-orientation of social programmes. The reform agendas of the Nordic liberal parties are not easy to put into one of the three ideal types suggested above. However, liberal parties' agendas appear to fit more closely with Agenda B than Agenda C.

Christian parties in Finland, Norway and Sweden articulated reform agendas with a close resemblance to Agenda B. The representatives made few remarks critical of the welfare state. However, all Christian parties saw it necessary to apply a cost containment policy, and their proposals for changes in social programmes were in line with the concept of recalibration. In addition, the Christian democratic parties distinguished themselves by emphasizing the importance of the family as a central provider of care.

The reform agendas of the Nordic conservative parties differed substantially from each other. The Coalition Party in Finland expressed milder criticism of the welfare state than the conservative parties in Norway and Sweden. In contrast, the Moderate Party in Sweden aimed harsh criticism at the welfare state. The Moderate Party representative, argued sharply for the necessity for a cost reduction of social expenditure. The Norwegian Conservative Party also argued that the welfare state was too large vis-à-vis the economy, but the representative simultaneously defended the idea of a strong state taking responsibility for a broad set of social programmes. Although the Norwegian and the Swedish conservative parties did not present any explicit suggestions for reorientation of cash benefit programmes, it is difficult to make sense of the two parties' agendas without significant reorientation. The reason is that both interviews indicated the objectives of major tax cuts in order to increase individuals' freedom of choice regarding social protection. Furthermore, there appears to be a contradiction in the views expressed by the representatives of the Norwegian and the Swedish conservative parties. On the one hand, they did not explicitly provide examples of current public services to be privatized; the Norwegian Conservative Party even argued that the state should take over responsibility for health care from the counties. On the other hand, it is difficult to find the two parties' agendas consistent without a concomitant intention to pursue significant privatization of public service production. Although not entirely clear-cut, the reform agendas of the conservative parties in Norway and Sweden are probably best categorized as closest to Agenda C.

Several statements in the interviews with the Progress Party in Denmark and Norway and the small Young Finnish Party in Finland fitted into Agenda C. However, only the reform agenda of the Young Finnish Party had a close fit to Agenda C. The representative of the Progress Party in Denmark provided a very unclear picture of the party's own policies, which made it difficult to distinguish the reform agenda for the party. The representative of Norwegian Progress Party mixed suggestions of radical changes of principles for Norwegian social programmes with statements close to Agenda B.

For obvious reasons, political parties' reform agendas are difficult to place into the ideal model presented in Table 5.2. However, the above analysis of Nordic political parties' reform agendas provides evidence that the support for a reformation of the Nordic welfare states in accordance suggested in Agenda C was, in the late twentieth century, clearly insufficient. Furthermore, the interviews indicated support for cost containment and recalibration of cash benefit programmes, in particular since the social democratic parties supported these reform strategies. However, the social democratic parties also indicated an ambivalence regarding service plurality. The Nordic health and social care systems are significantly decentralized, which means that local governments have a strong say regarding choice of service providers. This might be one possible explanation for the increased role of private service providers that emerged in the Nordic countries during the 1990s, despite ambiguous support among social democratic parties at the national level.

Acknowledgements

The author gratefully acknowledges the financial support of the Swedish Council for Social Research, and support and criticism from Richard M. Coughlin, Björn Halleröd, Sven Hort, Staffan Marklund and Antti Miettinen.

Notes

1 In Sweden we asked to interview party secretaries, due to their unique insight into the party's activities. However, one party secretary in Sweden was unable to participate in the study and we accepted an interview with a member of the presidency of the party. The parties in Denmark, Finland and Norway do not share the uniformity of the Swedish party organization, which resulted in a mix between politicians and party officials. In Denmark, Finland and Norway repre-

sentatives were either party secretaries, party leaders, officials close to the prime minister or vice-chairs of the party. In some cases, however, we accepted the parties' wishes to be represented by a social policy spokesman or an official close to the party leader or the party secretary.

2 The author of this chapter conducted all interviews. Several of the interviews with Finnish respondents were conducted together with Antti Miettinen (a Finnish native speaker).

References

Baxter, L. A. (1994) 'Content analysis', in B. M. Montgomery and S. Duck (eds) *Studying Interpersonal Interaction*, New York and London: The Guilford Press.

Blomqvist, P. and Rothstein, B. (2000) *Välfärdsstatens nya ansikte: Demokrati och marknadsreformer inom den offentliga sektorn*, Stockholm: Agora.

Boje, T. P. and Åberg, R. (1999) 'Den nya danska arbetsmarknadspolitiken – rättigheter såväl som skyldigheter', *Arbetsmarknad & Arbetsliv* 5 (1): 5–26.

Castells, M. (1997) *The Information Age: Economy, Society and Culture. Vol. II: The Power of Identity*, Oxford: Blackwell Publishers.

Drøpping, J. A., Hvinden, B. and Vik, K. (1999) 'Activation policies in the Nordic countries', in M. Kautto, M. Heikkilä, B. Hvinden, S. Marklund and N. Ploug (eds) *Nordic Social Policy: Changing Welfare States*, London: Routledge.

Eitrheim, P. and Kuhnle, S. (2000) 'Nordic welfare states in the 1990s: institutional stability, signs of divergence', in S. Kuhnle (ed.) *Survival of the European Welfare State*, London and New York: Routledge.

Esping-Andersen, G. and Korpi, W. (1984) 'From poor relief towards institutional welfare states: the development of Scandinavian social policy', Stockholm: Institutet för social forskning.

Greider, W. (1997) *One World, Ready or Not: The Manic Logic of Global Capitalism*, New York: Simon & Schuster.

Hanssen, J.-I., Sandvin, J. T. and Söder, M. (1996) 'The Nordic welfare states in transition', in J. Tøssebro, A. Gustavsson and G. Dyrendahl (eds) *Intellectual Disabilities in the Nordic Welfare States: Policies and Everyday Life*, Kristiansand: Norwegian Academic Press.

Heikkilä, M., Hvinden, B., Kautto, M., Marklund, S. and Ploug, N. (1999) 'Conclusion: the Nordic model stands stable but on shaky ground', in M. Kautto, M. Heikkilä, B. Hvinden, S. Marklund and N. Ploug (eds) *Nordic Social Policy: Changing Welfare States*, London: Routledge.

Hvinden, B. (1994) *Divided Against Itself: A Study of Integration in Welfare Bureaucracy*, Oslo: Scandinavian University Press.

Kildal, N. (2001) *Workfare Tendencies in Scandinavian Welfare Policies*, Genève: ILO InFocus Programme on Socio-Economic Security Paper Series.

Kosonen, P. (2000) 'Activation, incentives and workfare in four Nordic countries', in *Comparing Social Welfare Systems in Nordic Europe and France*, Paris: MiRe/Drees.

Kvale, S. (1996) *InterViews: An Introduction to Qualitative Research Interviewing*, Thousand Oaks: Sage Publications, Inc.

Lehto, J., Moss, N. and Rostgaard, T. (1999) 'Universal public social care and health services?', in M. Kautto, M. Heikkilä, B. Hvinden, S. Marklund and N. Ploug (eds) *Nordic Social Policy: Changing Welfare States*, London: Routledge.

Lindqvist, R. and Marklund, S. (1995) 'Forced to work and liberated from work.

A historical perspective on work and welfare in Sweden', *Scandinavian Journal of Social Welfare*, 4: 224–37.

NOSOSCO (2001) *Social Protection in the Nordic Countries 2000. Scope, Expenditure and Financing*, Copenhagen: Nordic Social-Statistical Committee.

Olsson, S. E. (1993) *Social Policy and Welfare State in Sweden*, Lund: Arkiv.

Petersson, O. (1994) *The Government and Politics of the Nordic Countries*, Stockholm: Publica.

Pierson, P. (2001) 'Coping with permanent austerity: welfare state restructuring in affluent democracies', in P. Pierson (ed.) *The New Politics of the Welfare State*, Oxford: Oxford University Press.

Ploug, N. (1999) 'Cuts in and reform of the Nordic cash benefit systems', in M. Kautto, M. Heikkilä, B. Hvinden, S. Marklund and N. Ploug (eds) *Nordic Social Policy: Changing Welfare States*, London: Routledge.

Rostgaard, T. and Fridberg, T. (1998) 'Caring for children and older people – a comparison of European policies and practices', *Social Security in Europe 6*, Copenhagen: The Danish National Institute of Social Research.

Rostgaard, T. and Lehto, J. (2001) 'Health and social care systems: how different is the Nordic model?', in M. Kautto, J. Fritzell, B. Hvinden, J. Kvist and H. Uusitalo (eds), *Nordic Welfare States in the European Context*, London: Routledge.

Trydegård, G.-B. (2001) 'Välfärdstjänster till salu – privatisering och alternativa driftformer under 1990-talet', in SOU 2001: 52, *Välfärdstjänster i omvandling*, Stockholm: Fritzes.

Part II

Normative tensions

6 The women-friendly welfare states revisited[1]

Birte Siim and Anette Borchorst

Introduction

The Norwegian political scientist Helga Maria Hernes conceptualized in her book *Welfare State and Women Power. Essays in State Feminism* the Scandinavian countries as potentially women-friendly societies. She argued that this was a result of the combined impact of a broad political mobilization of women from below and the institutionalization of gender equality from above. She defined a woman-friendly state as a state which 'would not force harder choices on women than on men, or permit unjust treatment on the basis of sex' (Hernes 1987: 15).

Hernes' argument marked a break with the previous rather pessimistic view among feminist scholars that had stressed women's marginalization and their dependency on the patriarchal state. This change towards a focus on the empowerment and inclusion of women was stimulated by the increasing presence of women in politics, especially in Norway and Sweden. At the same time, feminist theory took a comparative turn, similar to the development in mainstream welfare state theory. During the following decade a number of scholars engaged in designating typologies of western welfare states that were gender sensitive and served as a point of departure for the growing body of empirical studies (Orloff 1993; Lewis and Ostner 1994).

The notion that 'politics matter' became very powerful in the comparative welfare state tradition, and the most influential typologies were based on political–ideological differences in governmental power. The notion was above all advocated and demonstrated by the Swedish–Danish sociologist Gøsta Esping-Andersen, and the so-called power resource school (1990). This approach emphasized the relatively high decommodifying impact of the Scandinavian welfare states that rendered the well-being of individuals independent of market forces. The tradition was criticized by feminist scholars, because its emphasis on class made it gender blind and ignored the role of the family and social services. A number of feminist studies developed an alternative approach analysing the gendered impact of the interaction between the state, the market and the family in different welfare models. Since the late 1990s the mainstream literature has, however, increasingly focused on the impact of welfare policies on family structures and on the position of women and children. In this way, feminist and mainstream welfare state traditions have converged in the contention that the Nordic social democratic welfare states should be regarded as an ideal for western countries. It is still a controversial question, whether the Scandinavian route to gender equality is possible and desirable in other countries, and whether the logic of gender segregation and gender hierarchy has indeed been challenged to such an extent that the model may be adequately termed as women-friendly.

This chapter explores the underlying normative assumptions of the concept of the women-friendliness of the Nordic welfare states. We claim, first, that there is an analytical distinction between women-friendly social policies and policies that contribute to enhance gender equality. Second, the goal of gender equality is ambiguous, because we have seen that policies that increase gender equality for some women may also increase inequality between women. We argue that the concept needs reformulation in order to be applied analytically to welfare state traditions and contexts different from the social democratic and Nordic societies. One main point is that it should be possible to distinguish between different dimensions of welfare, and between strategies that stress equality and strategies that stress diversity and difference. Another point is that it should be possible to distinguish analytically between the civil, social and political dimensions of citizenship. There are different interpretations of the norms of gender equality, and the comparative turn has illuminated the tension between the universal principle of gender equality and its particular interpretation in different contexts. Finally, feminist constructivism and postmodernism has challenged 'false universalisms' and emphasized diversity and difference. The question is then, whether it is possible to link the normative principle of gender equality with contextual political research and with the poststructuralist/postmodern emphasis on diversity and difference.

The normative foundation of the women-friendly welfare state

The notion of women-friendliness, introduced by Hernes, inspired Nordic feminist debates about the characteristics of Nordic welfare states and democracies (Siim 1988; Skjeie 1992; Borchorst 1994). Hernes' analysis of the political changes of the Nordic democracies during the 1970s and 1980s from a male worker paradigm to 'state feminism' also represented a paradigmatic shift in feminist understandings of the state as a potential ally (Skjeie and Siim 2000). The claim that the Nordic democracies embody a state form that makes it possible to transform them into women-friendly societies rests upon assumptions about the needs and interests of women that are not uncontroversial. The term 'women-friendly welfare states' has both analytical and normative aspects. It is explicitly based upon the political culture and institutions of the Nordic countries that value social equality. Hernes' vision is a country 'where injustice on the basis of gender would largely be eliminated without an increase in other forms of inequality, such as among groups of women' (1987: 15). This is an ambiguous ideal that is to some extent premised on an idea of common and collective interests of women, which are different from the interests of men.

One of the analytical potentials of the concept is that it challenges universal theories and conclusions about women's marginalization in the modern welfare state based upon Anglo-American theory and research. The concept has thus contributed to highlight the specific Scandinavian and Nordic context focusing on the political culture, democratic institutions and understanding of citizenship that has made women's presence in politics possible (Phillips 1995). Hernes' observation that the exceptionalism of Scandinavia related to a specific interplay between women's agitation from below and their political inclusion from above was central. She argued that women had become empowered as political subjects by the institutionalization of gender equality, and she claimed that the welfare state might be an instrument for the improvement of women's situation as workers, mothers and citizens. This empowerment hypothesis challenged the marginalization thesis, which had dominated feminist welfare state research so far, stressing the oppression of women by the patriarchal state.

Hernes' approach was founded upon a grand vision of gender equality, which combines social rights for women with their political inclusion. From an analytical point of view, it is, however, important to distinguish between social and political dimensions of women-friendliness. These two dimensions of citizenship – social rights and political inclusion – have different characteristics, history and dynamics. It is an empirical question to what extent women's political rights have been strengthened by the development of extensive social rights, or whether the Nordic tradition for active citizenship has influenced women-friendly social policies. Comparative research has shown the cross-national variations in the interplay between women's civil, political and social rights, and this has been the basis for the construction of different citizenship models (Bussemaker and Voert 1998; Siim 2000).

The empowerment hypothesis has been criticized by feminist scholars from countries with a different gender logic for being culturally biased towards the Nordic countries. Its normative foundation is a dual-breadwinner model where both women and men are wage workers, and the thesis thus tends to undervalue welfare states based upon different family models and gender cultures. The argument is that the feminist discourse about women-friendliness is based upon the premise that women's labour market participation and economic independence is the key to gender equality. This premise tends to underestimate cross-cultural differences – ideas, meanings and values – that influence women's employment patterns (Pfau-Effinger 1998: 148). Furthermore, the focus on actors and empowerment is criticized, because it gives priority to politics and thus tends to underestimate structural patterns of gender hierarchies and segregation, especially on the labour market (Hirdman 2002).

The metaphorical strength of concept of women-friendliness is stronger than its descriptive and analytical potential. It is problematic that the criteria for evaluation of women-friendliness/unfriendliness are not clear. This makes it difficult to decide when and to what degree social policies can be characterized as women-friendly and when are they not friendly. It is also difficult to evaluate the complex developments of different gender issues, for example to compare the effect of policies that emphasize equality on the labour market with policies that focus on sexual harassment and violence against women (Lindvert 2002). Finally policies may have contradictory effects on different groups of women. This weakness becomes even more visible when it is applied to countries outside the social democratic cluster, like the liberal model (see for example the analysis of O'Connor *et al.* 1999).

A further problem with the concept is a tendency to downplay differences among the five Nordic countries. Scholars agree that it is possible to identify a Nordic gender model in terms of women's political representation and in relation to their participation in paid work. However, more detailed comparisons of the five countries reveal important differences in the form of women's mobilization, their inclusion in political parties as well as the extent of institutionalization of gender equality. A comparative Nordic study concludes that the Nordic welfare states indeed represent five different gender profiles (Borchorst *et al.* 1999). The Swedish gender profile, for example, is characterized by a high degree of institutionalization of gender equality, while the Danish gender profile is the most bottom-up oriented of all the countries with the strongest role ascribed to social movements and a limited institutionalization of gender equality as a separate and explicit goal of public policy. The Norwegian gender profile is characterized by a high degree of political integration of women into political parties, whereas Norway has been a laggard in terms of women's integration into the labour force and childcare provisions. During the 1990s there have been different political developments in relation to gender equality, and the differences in the discourses about gender, power and politics in Denmark, Sweden and Norway appear to be even more outspoken than the differences in social and political practice (Borchorst *et al.* 2002).

The Nordic countries have had an egalitarian political culture and a tradition for active citizenship based upon the participation of social movements (Skjeie and Siim 2000) and the women's movement has used this as a platform for their fight for civil, political and social rights (Siim 2000). From an analytical perspective there is, however, a crucial difference between women-friendliness and gender equality-friendliness as well as between different aspects of gender equality – on the labour market, in the family and in politics. The Scandinavian countries score high on the level of social policies towards parents, and low on poverty rates for lone parents. Political developments have also emphasized the rights of fathers, but policies to promote gender equality have not reduced gender segregation on the labour markets. On the contrary, it has been exacerbated with women employed predominantly in the public and men in the private sector (Hirdman 1990; Esping-Andersen 1999). It has also been argued that the highly developed social policies for parents paradoxically have contributed to reproduce gender segregation and inequality in the family and the labour market. This can among other things be explained by the fact that women rather than men tend to use the offer of maternity/paternity/parental leave as well as childcare leave (Åström 1992; Siim 1998).

Social equality has been taken for granted as a core value in the social democratic Nordic welfare states for many years, and gender equality has gradually become accepted as a principle in the political culture during the last 30 years. Gender inequalities in political and economic power have not disappeared and, during the 1980s and 1990s, new differentiations among women based upon generation, women's position on the labour market and ethnic origin have appeared. Feminist scholarship has increasingly become aware of the analytical distinction between gender equality and equality of ethnic minority groups as well as of the complex interrelation between gender and ethnicity. An important discursive difference between the integration of women and the inclusion of ethnic minority groups exists, because women have been defined as being 'one of us' and ethnic minorities as 'the other' (Christensen and Siim 2001). The Nordic countries currently face problems with the integration of ethnic minorities, because they have historically all been based upon a high degree of religious, cultural and ethnic homogeneity.

Hence, Hernes' term women-friendliness is biased towards the political culture, institutions and gender model of the Nordic countries. It is also an ambiguous concept that needs clarification both as a political–ideological tool that describes which social policies should be considered to be good for women, and as an analytical concept capable of differentiating between dimensions of welfare and between different aspects and interpretations of gender equality cross-nationally. Today it is contested what is considered good for women, and for which women. First, there is no longer a unified feminist movement that represents all women, and it has become a politically intricate question, who has the authority to speak for women, and who has the right to define what women want. Second, poststructuralism and postmodernism have emphasized diversity and difference and have questioned whether it is indeed possible to speak of common interests for women from different generations and across social and ethnic differences. Third, comparative research has emphasized the different and contested meanings of key concepts, like gender equality in various contexts. Finally, it is not clear how to distinguish between women-friendliness and gender equality-friendliness, and whether the interests of fathers and mothers are still contradictory.

Women's inclusion in the political elite and the growth of many types of feminisms – poststructural, postmodern and 'new' feminism – have made visible that there is no longer any political or theoretical consensus about what is good for women or how to empower women. From a theoretical perspective, the conceptualization of gender from a postmodern and anti-essentialist framework is challenging. In feminist scholarship, there is a growing consensus that analytical approaches and key concepts in gender and social policies in feminist scholarship are contested and need to be contextualized (Hobson *et al.* 2002). The methodological challenge from feminist constructivism has stimulated a debate about the relation between context, structure and agency (Bang *et al.* 2000). One key question is whether the vision of gender equality should and could be modelled on strategies, which have been widespread in the Nordic welfare states. Another crucial question is whether it is possible and desirable to link universal principles with comparative contextual research.

Comparative contextual research represents a methodological challenge to universal principles, and there is also a tension between normative principles of gender equality and poststructural and postmodern emphasis on diversity and difference. There are, however, different solutions to this challenge. Feminist research has illustrated that gender equality has a different meaning in different frames and has emphasized that the frames have an independent effect compared to structures and institutions. Equality is both relative and contextual, and there are contrasting interpretations of the norm of gender equality and different routes to equality. One response to the methodological challenge from postmodernism is to abandon normative approaches to cross-national studies of gender and modern welfare states. Bang *et al.* argue that it is logically impossible to combine a contextual approach to gender equality with a general normative (Bang *et al.* 2000). It is generally agreed that there is a tension between different positions, and they may have competing (ideal typical) logics, which offer different stories for example about Europeanization (Liebert 2003: 31). It does not follow that comparative research should abandon the debate about normative principles. The response from normative political theory has been a tendency towards a contextual and reflective approach to principles of equality and recognition (Fraser 1997). Ruth Lister's reflections about universalism are one attempt to bridge the tension between ideals of equality and universality embodied in the idea of the citizen and the postmodern emphasis on difference and diversity. She asks whether it is possible to expose the false universalism of the disembodied citizen while retaining the concept as an inspiring ideal. The solution is to combine the strengths of both universalism and difference through the notion of 'differentiated universalism' (Lister 2003: 9).

The examples illustrate that there is a dialogue between comparative cross-national gender sensitive political research inspired by poststructuralism aiming to construct research designs based upon a self-critical use of normative concepts like justice, solidarity and equality on the one hand (Hobson *et al.* 2002), and normative political theory aiming to develop a contextual theory grounded in empirical research on the other (Fraser 1997; Lister 2003). We conclude that there is a need to transcend the existing dualisms. From a comparative perspective the strategy, which we find promising, is to highlight the normative assumptions about equality and difference behind the different welfare and gender models and strengthen the comparative potential of the conceptual framework. The tensions between the different positions may become creative and productive if they form the basis for a conversation between postmodernists, comparativists and political theorists. The principle of gender equality cannot be defined beforehand with reference to one model, but should rather be the result of an ongoing conversation about equality, diversity and difference between feminist scholars from different contexts and theoretical approaches (Siim 2003).

Gender equality in mainstream welfare state research

Feminist scholarship has, since the mid-1980s, conceptualized the role of the family and care work for welfare state developments and social politics (e.g. Leira 1989; Lewis 1992; Orloff 1993).

During the 1990s, the important role of the family in restructuring the welfare state has increasingly been recognized by researchers and policy makers, and it has been accompanied by attempts to re-conceptualize the key role of the family and households in the post-industrial economy. The Italian sociologist, Saraceno (1999), has recently identified two strategies in family policy. One is de-familization or the extent to which economic and social rights are granted to individuals of all ages and family conditions or are contingent on family circumstances. The other strategy is re-familization, for example in the case of payments for care, that may also become over-familization, or forced re-familization of responsibilities and of individual rights that may in turn cause poverty and social exclusion. The Nordic countries have been the model case for de-familization, and here social policies have increasingly attempted to involve fathers in the care of children, for example by granting them specific rights to parental leave arrangements, independently of the rights of mothers.

Feminist arguments about the crucial role of the family and care work have recently been endorsed by mainstream research. In his recent book *Social Foundations of Post-industrial Economics* (1999), Gøsta Esping-Andersen has engaged in a dialogue with feminist scholars about the role of women and the family, and here he adopts some of the key feminist concepts like women-friendliness and de-familization. His main argument also seems similar to key elements in feminist theory about the household economy as the alpha and omega to the resolution of the main post-industrial dilemmas around equality and solidarity. The claim is that the social democratic welfare regime remains the only one, where social policy is explicitly designed to maximize women's economic independence through active social policies. Universalizing the double-earner household and lessening the caring burden of the family through expanding welfare services to the family is regarded as the only possible strategy for states which want to improve both the economy and the welfare of their citizens today. This is politically provocative in times of globalization, welfare state restructuring and the decline of social democracy, and it is theoretically challenging from a postmodern and contextual feminist framework.

The main point about the need for an active family policy is explored further in a recent report to the Belgian Presidency of the European Union 'A New Architecture for Europe?'. Here, the authors analyse new welfare issues in Europe and rediscover the notion of women-friendly policies and gender equality. Politics still matter in the post-industrial economy, and the optimistic argument is that a contradiction between women-friendly social policies and economic efficiency no longer exists. The report concludes that:

> a comprehensive women-friendly policy of affordable day-care and flexible leave arrangements is *sine qua non* in the pursuit of multiple goals: more gender-equality, raising female employment to offset smaller active populations and, as an added bonus, a broadening of the tax base.
>
> (Esping-Andersen *et al.* 2001: 4)

The report adds that lessons from Scandinavia indicate that this is a necessary, but not sufficient, policy, because it does not address the gender-segregated labour market.

Gender equality is today on the political agenda of the European Union and has become part of the European discourse on social policy. The new emphasis on the family, care work and gender equality is interesting, but a critical examination of this vision for the European welfare states from a feminist perspective is needed. One question is who has the economic and political power on the national and trans-national level? Other questions are: who are the actors, is this policy designed from below or from above, and who will influence its implementation? Do women's organizations, networks and the trade unions have the will and the political power to make alliances in order to work for political reforms in the European welfare states along these lines? To what extent is more gender equality by raising female employment what all women want, and parent-friendly employment policy what all men want, and what are the implications in terms of social benefits in the longer run (for instance old age pensions)? Finally, it raises the question about labour market dynamics towards globalization and flexibility. In the Nordic countries, women have mainly worked in the public sector, whereas men work predominantly in the private sector. Welfare state restructuring and the decline of social democracy makes it unlikely for all the European welfare states to adopt the Nordic labour market policy and social policy based upon the expansion of the public sector.

Finally, it is a problem that the report does not relate to the new challenges from immigration. One of the crucial questions today seems to be how to connect the vision of gender equality with social and political inclusion of ethnic minority groups in the European welfare states. In relation to the issue of diversity the Nordic 'social democratic countries' have been laggards. As Wolfe and Klausen notice: 'The Swedes have embraced the idea of diversity but rejected multiculturalism; the Danes have rejected multiculturalism and barely accepted diversity at all' (2000: 1). It is highly likely that this question will be particularly challenging in terms of family and gender structures, because the clash between Nordic cultural traditions and patriarchal family structures of a number of ethnic groups is very visible. The political parties of the centre and the left have been very defensive in addressing these problems, and thereby the extreme right has obtained an opportunity to profile itself on gender equality. This is paradoxical, since the extreme right until now has been very passive on this issue. Mainstream research as well as feminist thinking of the welfare state needs to confront these questions. It is a challenge for feminist research to develop a contextual approach to cross-national studies of gender and welfare state research based upon norms of inclusiveness of gender and marginalized social groups as well as on recognition of diversity and cultural differences (Fraser 1997).

Feminist visions of gender equality

It is a challenge to develop a contextual framework for understanding gender and other kinds of differentiation in modern welfare states that includes analytical criteria for a more critical evaluation of the gender logic of the Nordic welfare states. In the times of globalization, Europeanization and welfare state restructuring it is fruitful to have a critical debate among feminist scholars and policy experts about the normative goals for welfare state policies and different strategies to achieve them. Western welfare states are moving away from the male-breadwinner model towards an adult-worker model, but the meaning and implications of an adult-worker model in different contexts are contestable (Lewis 2001).

In her book *Justice Interruptions. Critical reflections on the 'Post socialist' Condition*, the American political philosopher Nancy Fraser (1997) argues that there is a real theoretical impasse of the equality/difference debate that cannot simply be ignored or embraced. She proposes to analyse gender equality as a complex phenomenon, and she presents an alternative to the post-industrial welfare state based upon two distinct feminist visions with different normative foundations. One based upon gender equality and the other on gender difference. Her third vision transcends the two. The three models are examined on the basis of distinct normative principles that are related to two strategies for justice *redistribution* and *recognition*. Redistribution is related to socio-economic injustice and recognition to cultural or symbolic injustice. The former tends to promote gender equality whereas the latter fosters gender differentiation.

1 The universal breadwinner model

This model is based upon the employment principle as the norm and supports women as citizen-workers. In this model women's and men's lives would be basically the same. According to Fraser, this could be seen as a utopian version of the liberal model of welfare dominant in the US and UK.

2 The caregiver-parity model

This model promotes gender equity by supporting informal care work and women as citizen-carers. The goal is to make gender difference costless. This could be interpreted as the utopian version of the conservative/familist model of welfare.

3 The universal caregiver model

This model would induce men to become more like women are now, namely balancing care work with paid work. This model is defined in the following way:

> The key to equity in post-industrial welfare state, then is to make women's current life-pattern the norm for everyone. Women, today often combine breadwinning and care giving, albeit with great difficulties and strain. A post-industrial welfare state must ensure that men do the same, while redesigning institutions so as to eliminate the difficulty and strain. We might call this vision Universal Caregiver.
>
> (Fraser 1997: 61)

The universal caregiver model is designed to deconstruct the opposition between breadwinning and care giving. Achieving gender equity in a post-industrial welfare state then means deconstructing gender. This is clearly a utopian model that would require a new view of the male role as well as a radical change in the organization of working life. The final concern could be, what will happen to policies, agency and power relations in the universal caregiver model? Fraser's answer is:

> The trick is to image a social world in which citizens' lives integrate wage earning, care giving, community activism, political participation, and involvement in the associational life of civil society – while also leaving time for some fun.
>
> (Fraser 1997: 62)

It is not accidental that this vision of women's and men's roles as democratic citizens in many ways resembles Hernes' vision of a women-friendly welfare state, because Fraser refers explicitly to the Swedish discourse of gender equality. This raises a central question of the relation between discourse and social practice of gender equality in the Nordic welfare states as well as between universal principles and their different interpretation in particular contexts. Fraser's analytical model can be interpreted as one way to transcend the dualism between normative political research, post-modernism and comparative research. Her model is based both upon universal principles of justice and on principles of deconstruction with a normative inspiration by the Swedish model of gender equality.

Globalization, welfare state restructuring and gender equality

Fraser does not discuss how the different Scandinavian and Nordic welfare states fit in her models. It is an empirical question, whether they do indeed embody a universal breadwinner model, or to what extent they link elements of the universal caregiver model with a new perception of fatherhood and a new organization of work illustrated by the development of family-friendly firms. We have argued that the Nordic countries have different gender profiles, which implies that each may combine elements and characteristics from Fraser's three models in unique ways. There has been a strong path dependency in the development of the Scandinavian welfare states, but we suggest that the evolution is not irreversible and that globalization and welfare state restructuring may contribute both to increase and decrease gender equality for different groups of women.

During the 1990s women's integration in the labour market has created a growing shortage of caring resources, conceptualized in western welfare states as a caring deficit. Family policies and care work have apparently been put high on the political agenda, but the restructuring of care has taken several forms that has both challenged and reproduced existing gender inequalities.

The Scandinavian welfare states have all, in different ways and with different timing, been under pressure for restructuring. They have still supported a universal caregiver model, albeit with some distinct differences in the character of women's mobilization and institutionalization of gender equality, as mentioned above.

Norway, which has been a laggard in terms of the integration of women into the labour force and the expansion of childcare provisions, has converged with the other two countries during the past ten years (Leira 1989; Sörensen and Bergqvist 2002). All three countries have provided relatively generous benefits for lone parents, but Norwegian policies have aimed at enabling lone mothers to care for their children themselves, whereas Danish and Swedish have sought to integrate them into the labour force. Denmark has, relatively more than the two other countries supported institutional solutions to childcare, and parental leave has for many years been shorter than in the two other countries (Borchorst 2002). Furthermore, Danish policies have granted weaker rights to fathers than Norwegian and Swedish policies, and this has become even more outspoken with the take over by a liberal–conservative government coalition in November 2001. Together with the extreme right it has extended the parental leave to one year, but simultaneously it has removed the two weeks 'daddy quota' in week 25–26, which was enacted by the previous social democratic-led government in 1997. Hereby, Denmark has chosen a different route from all other Nordic countries, which have extended the daddy quota. Furthermore, bourgeois governments in Norway and Denmark have enacted cash-for-care schemes. The question is how to establish whether these policies are friendly or inimical to women, since expanding the choice of parents, and making leave policies more flexible, may inadvertently weaken women's economic autonomy and contribute to their increased marginalization.

One of the strengths of Hernes' framework was to conceptualize the importance of women's agency and empowerment for social policy and for the future development of the welfare state. Research illustrates that the development has been contradictory on a normative level, because there is no longer any agreement about who represents women, and what are in women's best interests.

We have argued that the concept of 'women-friendliness' has a distinct bias towards social democratic welfare states that has challenged its analytical and comparative potential. One alternative is to contextualize, reformulate and deconstruct the concept to accommodate differences among women. Nancy Fraser's critical analysis of the dilemma between equality and recognition of diversity and difference is one way of doing that. One implication of this deconstruction is to distinguish between women-friendliness and policies to promote gender equality, between welfare in terms of equality and diversity, and between civil, political and social aspects of citizenship. It is neither possible nor desirable that the Scandinavian welfare states be considered as a model for gender equality for other European welfare states to follow. We have further argued that gender equality can no longer be a universal yardstick, but may indeed be used as a relative measure that is also contextual. The Nordic welfare states face new challenges of immigration, and we suggest that a relative and contextual form of gender equality is crucial to welfare policies based upon norms of both inclusion and equality as well as recognition of diversity and difference. We conclude that we should not give up the search for universal principles, but principles of equality need to be combined with principles of recognition. We need a critical re-examination of the principles of equality, diversity and welfare in terms of gender, class and ethnicity, as well as cross-national analysis between politics of recognition on the one hand and politics of re-distribution on the other hand.

Note

1 This chapter is a longer and improved version of an article that first appeared in *Nora, Nordic Journal for Women's Studies* (2002) Vol. 10 (2): 90–8. We would like to thank Stein Kuhnle and Nanna Kildal for their helpful comments.

References

Åström, G. (1992) 'Faste förbindelser. Om välfärdsreformer och kvinnors välfärd', in Y. Hirdman and G. Åström (eds) *Kontrakt i kris. Om kvinnors plats i välfärdsstaten*, Stockholm: Carlssons.

Bang, H., Jensen, P. H. and Pfau-Effinger, B. (2000) 'Gender and European welfare states. Context, structure and agency', in D. Simon and B. Pfau-Effinger (eds) *Gender, Economy and Culture in the European Union*, New York and London: Routledge.

Borchorst, A. (1994) 'The Scandinavian welfare states – patriarchal, genderneutral or woman-friendly?', *International Journal of Contemporary Sociology*, 31 (1): 45–67.

—— (2002) 'Modest changes: Danish child care policy in an era of restructuring', in S. Michel and R. Mahon (eds) *Child Care Policy at the Crossroads: Gender and Welfare State Restructuring*, New York and London: Routledge.

Borchorst, A., Christensen, A.-D. and Raaum, N. C. (1999) 'Equal democracies? Conclusions and perspectives', in C. Bergqvist, A. Borchorst, A. D. Christensen, N. Raaum and A. Styrkasdotter (eds) *Equal Democracies? Gender and Politics in the Nordic Countries*, Oslo: Scandinavian University Press.

Borchorst, A., Christensen, A.-D. and Siim, B. (2002) 'Diskurser om køn, magt og politik i Skandinavien', in A. Borchorst (ed.) *Kønsmagt under forandring*, København: Hans Reitzels Forlag.

Bussemaker, J. and Voert, R. (eds) (1998) 'Citizenship and gender. Theoretical approaches and historical legacies', *Critical Social Policy*, 18 (3).

Christensen, A.-D. and Siim, B. (2001) *Køn, demokrati og modernitet – mod nye politiske identiteter*, København: Hans Reitzels Forlag.

Esping-Andersen, G. (1990) *The Three Worlds of Welfare Capitalism*, Oxford: Polity Press.

—— (1999) *Social Foundations of Postindustrial Economies*, Oxford: Oxford University Press.

Esping-Andersen, G., Gallie, D., Hemerijck, A. and Myles, J. (2001) *A New Welfare Architecture for Europe?* Report submitted to the Belgian Presidency of the European Union.

Fraser, N. (1997) *Justice Interruptions. Critical Reflections on the 'Postsocialist' Condition*, New York and London: Routledge.

Hernes, H. M. (1987) *Welfare State and Women Power. Essays in State Feminism*, Oslo: Norwegian University Press.

Hirdman, Y. (1990) 'Genussystemet', in *Demokrati och Makt i Sverige.* Maktutredningen huvudrapport, SOU: 1990: 44, Stockholm.

—— (2002) 'Anmeldelse af Kønsmagt inder forandring', in *Nyhedsbrev for netværk for nordisk velfærdsstatshistorie*: 10–15.

Hobson, B., Lewis, J. and Siim, B. (eds) (2002) 'Contested concepts in gender and social politics', in B. Hobson, J. Lewis and B. Siim (eds) *Contested Concepts in Gender and Social Politics*, Cheltenham: Edward Elgar.

Leira, A. (1989) 'Models of motherhood. Welfare state policies and everyday practices: the Scandinavian experience', Oslo: Institutt for Samfunnsforskning.

Lewis, J. (1992) 'Gender and the development of welfare regimes', *Journal of European Social Policy*, 2 (3): 159–73.

—— (2001) 'The decline of the male-breadwinner model: implications for work and care', *Social Politics*, 8 (2): 152–70.

Lewis, J. and Ostner, I. (1994) *Gender and the Evolution of European Social Policies*, Zes-Arbeitspapier nr 4, Universität Bremen.

Liebert, U. (ed.) (2003) *Gendering Europeanisation*, Brussels: Peter Lang.

Lindvert, J. (2002) 'A world apart. Swedish and Australian gender equality policy', *NORA, Nordic Journal of Women's Studies*, 10 (2): 99–107.

Lister, R. (2003) *Citizenship. Feminist Perspectives*, (2nd edn) London: Palgrave.

O'Connor, J. S., Orloff, S. and Shaver, S. (1999) *States, Markets, Families. Gender, Liberalism and Social Policy in Australia, Canada, Great Britain and the United States*, Cambridge: Cambridge University Press.

Orloff, A. S. (1993) 'Gender and the social rights of citizenship: the comparative analysis of gender relations and welfare states', *American Sociological Review*, 58 (3): 303–28.

Pfau-Effinger, B. (1998) 'Gender cultures and the gender arrangements – a theoretical framework for cross national gender research', *Innovation*, 11 (2): 147–66.

Phillips, A. (1995) *The Politics of Presence*, Oxford: Clarendon Press.

Saraceno, C. (1999) 'Gendered politics: family obligations and social policies in Europe', paper to European Sociological Association, Amsterdam.

Siim, B. (1988) 'Towards a feminist rethinking of the welfare state', in K. B. Jones and A. G. Jónasdóttir (eds) *The Political Interests of Gender*, Oxford: Sage Publications.

—— (1998) 'Vocabularies of gender and citizenship. The Danish case', in J. Bussemaker and R. Voert (eds) *Citizenship and Gender. Theoretical Approaches and Historical Legacies, Critical Social Policy*, 18 (3): 375–96.

—— (2000) *Gender and Citizenship. Politics and Agency in France, Britain and Denmark*, Cambridge: Cambridge University Press.

—— (2003) 'Towards a contextual and gender sensitive political science?', *European Political Science*, Spring 2004, 3: 2.

Skjeie, H. (1992) *Den politiske betydningen av kjønn. En studie av norsk topp-politikk*, Oslo: Institut for samfunnsforskning.

Skjeie, H. and Siim, B. (2000) 'Scandinavian feminist debates', *International Political Science Review*, 21 (4): 346–60.

Sörensen, K. and Bergqvist, C. (2002) *Gender and the Social Democratic Welfare Regime: A Comparison of Gender Equality Friendly Policies in Sweden and Norway*, Department of Political Science UNC and Arbetslivsinstitutet.

Wolfe, A. and Klausen, J. (2000) 'Other people', *Prospect*, (December): 28–33.

7 Universalism in the age of workfare

Attitudes to basic income in Sweden and Finland

Jan Otto Andersson and Olli E. Kangas

Introduction

The Nordic countries are widely respected for their universal social policy. 'Universalism' in this context means that the right to social security is guaranteed on the basis of either citizenship or residency. Social security in Central Europe – Germany, for example – is more closely tied in with the position in the labour market, whereas in the Anglo-Saxon countries – in Australia and New Zealand in particular – benefits are conditional on the basis of need.

However, also in the Nordic countries the last resort income assistance is conditional in several respects:

1 To be entitled to a benefit, the recipient, if he/she is unable to work, must be willing to accept a suitable job or to undergo suitable training;
2 He/she must pass a means test, and is entitled to a benefit only if it can be shown that he/she has no access to a sufficient income from other sources;
3 Whether he/she can receive a benefit, and the level of the benefit, is dependent on the situation of his/her household – for example, whether he/she lives with a person who receives a sufficient income or not;
4 The conditions and level of the benefit may vary depending on where a person lives, since the administration of the benefit is entrusted to the municipalities.

The minimum income guarantee, therefore, is not ideal from a universalistic point of view. It is not a benefit – like child allowance or people's pension – to which a person is entitled independently of his/her lifestyle or life situation.

In the beginning of the 1990s Sweden and Finland were hit by an exceptionally deep economic crisis. The number of people employed fell in both countries by more than half a million between 1990 and 1994. In Finland open unemployment peaked at almost 20 per cent. In Sweden the unemployed grew sevenfold and the participants in labour market policy programmes grew eightfold. Since then unemployment has remained the most annoying economic problem. The number of unemployed in Sweden was four times higher in 2002 than in 1990. The Finnish rate of unemployment was still almost 10 per cent in 2002, more than double the average rate for the 1980s.

The dramatic change in the labour market has had an impact on the normative foundations of the welfare state. Although the main features of the welfare systems have been kept intact, a shift towards workfare has taken place. Instead of a traditional Keynesian-type expansion of the total demand and the public sector to ensure full employment, the governments pinned their hopes on supply-side measures. Especially those not being covered by income related unemployment insurance were pulled and pushed to take on employment by new incentive structures and harsher activation programmes. On the other hand – since mass unemployment has become chronic – it has become easier to remain unemployed, living on the conditional minimum guaranteed income, if one so wishes. These changes challenge the traditional Nordic universalism, since full employment was a condition for a prominent part of it. The long-term unemployed tend to fall outside 'standard security' systems, and the efforts to 'reintegrate' them – in itself a universalistic goal – has implied more stringent conditionality for the social assistance recipients. This has actually worsened their position as ordinary citizens.

The conceivably most universalistic response to a situation, where ordinary jobs have become a scarce resource, would be an unconditional *basic income* (BI), defined as 'an income paid by the government to each full member of society (1) even if she is not willing to work; (2) irrespective of her being rich or poor; (3) whoever she lives with; and (4) no matter which part of the country she lives in' (Van Parijs 1995: 35). Different names have been used for such an unconditional and universal benefit: social dividend, universal grant, citizen's income and citizen's wage (CW). The last term is the one that has been most frequently used in the Nordic countries, '*medborgarlön*' in Swedish, '*kansalaispalkka*' in Finnish. It was introduced in a Danish book called *Revolt from the Center*, which became an instant bestseller (Meyer *et al.* 1981).

There are several related schemes, which are not pure basic income schemes, since they do not satisfy all of the four conditions. If we accept a willingness-to-work test, we could go for a 'participation income' (PI) as suggested by Tony Atkinson. If the amount of the benefit is regressively linked to the incomes earned by a person (or household) the scheme corresponds to a Negative Income Tax (NIT). Different NIT-schemes were used in some local experiments in the USA in the 1970s. If we require both that a person is taking on some work and that the payment is reduced as the income of the person increases we would get a general subsidy to low paid jobs, such as the Earned Income Tax Credit (EITC) scheme in the USA. If we relax the third condition, the amount of the BI could be lowered for households with several adults. This would not imply a grave distortion of the BI-idea, nor would a dropping of the fourth condition mentioned by Van Parijs, as long as the regional disparities were motivated by, for instance, the cost of living.

A BI can be seen as an extension of the unconditional child benefits and people's pensions, which have been central components of the Nordic welfare regimes. However, only in two of the Nordic countries – Denmark and Finland – has the idea of a basic income received serious attention. The discussions in Sweden and Norway have been relatively sporadic and utopian (Andersson 2000). The fate of the citizen's wage in Denmark has been thoroughly analysed by Erik Christensen (2000). He distinguishes two phases in which the idea received a lot of attention: the grassroot movement related to the 'revolt from the centre' (*midteroprøret*) in the early 1980s and the phase when CW came on the Danish political agenda in the years 1992–1994. Among the reasons for the failure to realize the idea, Christensen mentions the difficulty to combine the visionary discourse with the discourse on how to technically rationalize the welfare state (Christensen 2000: 283, 335).

The differences between the Swedish and the Finnish attitudes to basic income can be seen both in the intellectual debates and in the activities of the political parties. In Sweden very few authors have actively proposed some version of basic income: Gunnar Adler-Karlsson at the end of the 1970s, Thomas Ehrenberg ten years later and Lars Ekstrand in the 1990s. Both Ehrenberg and Ekstrand wrote as if the idea had never been introduced in Sweden before. All three proposals were put forward in a futuristic and utopian manner. They saw a CW as a means to radically transform society, but were relatively short in the analysis of which trends and forces would actually work in favour of their visions. Adler-Karlsson's and Ekstrand's ideas did receive some attention, but they were generally dismissed (Andersson 1998, 2000).[1]

It is telling of the political climate in Sweden that Adler-Karlsson had to accept a change of the title of his book from *No to Full Employment. Yes to a Material Basic Security* to the less offensive *Thoughts on Full Employment.* In the Danish edition the original title was used. As headlines, such as 'He dreams of a citizen's wage', 'The apostle of laziness provoke' and 'A citizen's wage would feed the underworld', indicate, the reception of Ekstrand's books was not enthusiastic. His views were criticized by a leading authority on social policy, Gunnar Wetterberg, who called the idea 'the triumph of resignation'.

The Social Democrats have been the main defenders of the existing system, based on the idea of full employment and a general system of income-related social security. The Left Party has also discarded the CW-idea, but it has asked for substantial reductions in working time as an alternative strategy.

The three parties of the centre have all stressed the need for a basic security (*grundtrygghet*), but they have not accepted deviations from means testing. The conservatives favour a 'general and individual' system based on a clear correspondence between contributions and benefits plus strict means testing for those with special problems. In Sweden the only political party that has been seriously interested in a CW is the Green Party.

In Finland both the academic and public debate and the interest of the political parties have been much broader than in Sweden. During the 1980s and 1990s CW- and BI-proposals proliferated, and four parties, representing some 40 per cent of the voters – the Centre party, the Left Alliance, the Greens and the neo-liberal Young Finns – accepted the idea in their political programmes. We mention two examples to illuminate the Finnish situation.

Osmo Soininvaara (representing the Greens and Minister of Social Affairs in 2000–2002) has been an untiring champion of some form of basic income. Since the end of the 1970s he has elaborated the idea in several books and reports. *Hyvinvointivaltion eloonjäämisoppi* (*A Survival Doctrine for the Welfare State*) was awarded a prize as the best economics book of 1994. Here Soininvaara continued the discussion on basic income in a concrete and detailed way. It was based on two reports written by the author for the Ministry of Social and Health Affairs. The base of his scheme was a basic income differentiated for household composition, corresponding to the lowest levels of social assistance. The income tax rate would be 53 per cent. The author proposed two types of conditional 'extra allowances' (*lisätuki*) to supplement the basic income for special contingencies. His arguments had, however, changed if compared to his original ideas. He was now interested in creating a system that would induce everyone to contribute as much as possible to the national economy, and explicitly criticized those who wanted a CW in order to make work voluntary.

Another prominent spokesman of a basic income is the former Archbishop of Finland, John Vikström. In a speech to the unemployed in 1997 he argued for a BI in the following way:

> A basic income would send every citizen the following encouraging and motivating message: You are important. You are not a burden, but a resource. You are important by being a human being for others. Whatever work you do, in whatever situations, whether or not you are paid to do it, you still contribute to building our society.
>
> (Quoted in Andersson 1998: 372)

In her dissertation Anita Mattila compares nine different Finnish schemes. Her references – which, with few exceptions, relate to the Finnish debate – occupy no less then 18 pages (Mattila 2001).

The most explicit critics of a basic income in Finland have been the employers' organization (STK, now TT) and the national trade union organization (SAK). Both were critical towards the report made by an official working group on social security in 1986. The employers' organization interpreted the suggested income guarantee as a citizen's wage, since it was not conditional on willingness to work. It asked for a more selective social policy instead. According to blue-collar trade union central, the report had to be rewritten on a completely different premise. Social security should encourage people to work and promote full employment.

In 1994 SAK published a report on basic income. The title *Mikä ihmeen perustulo?* is perhaps best translated as 'What (a) queer basic income?' which reflects the disapproving attitude towards the idea. If a basic income scheme was introduced, the society would develop towards a low-wage-low-skill society, a 'boot-cleaner society' (Andersson 1998, 2000).

In this study we are not focusing on the intensity and character of the discussion, but on the views of the ordinary citizens. Are there large differences also in the popular opinion in Sweden and Finland? How do people in general react to ideas related to a BI? Which forms, if any, are the most popular? Who supports and who dislikes different BI-related schemes? Do the old political lines of demarcation play any role? Is it possible to explain the attitudes towards basic income by looking at different background variables and at people's views on the causes of unemployment and poverty?

The study is based on nationwide and representative opinion surveys conducted in Finland and Sweden. The Gallup of Finland collected the data in May 2002 through telephone interviews of 1,000 respondents representing the Finnish population in the age bracket of 15–80. TEMO collected the data for Sweden in June 2002 also through telephone interviews of 800 Swedes aged 16 and above (for a closer presentation of the data, see Andersson and Kangas 2002).

The questionnaire

In our surveys we tried to formulate the questions so that they would pertain to the two main models of basic income: the negative income tax model and the unconditional basic or citizen's income model. In addition to these basic income questions we asked four questions by which we tried to depict the way people would like to encourage employment. In one of these questions we wanted to know how the respondents reacted to the idea of giving the unemployed a basic income, which they could keep even though they would earn additional incomes. A positive answer to this question can be interpreted as a support for a 'participation income' of the type suggested by Atkinson (1998). We also asked the respondents to indicate a monthly level of a BI, which they thought would be appropriate. The answers to these four questions suggest how popular a basic income is.

The three other ways of encouraging employment we asked about were:

1 a public subsidy for low-paid jobs;
2 more strict conditions for unemployment compensations;
3 creating jobs – also outside the ordinary labour market – tailored to the qualifications of the unemployed.

The first of these has been used in the USA in the form of an Earned Income Tax Credit (EITC). The EITC was introduced after the NIT-experiments in the 1970s. The second and third questions show the position of the respondent towards workfare. BI has been supported as an alternative to workfare, but some BI-proposals have been linked to job creation in the informal or 'third' sector, outside the ordinary labour market.

One question lurking in all debates on the proper degree of public involvement in the distribution of resources through various welfare state measures, is how justified the individual's need is perceived to be, or how inescapable the social risks from which the need emerged are. If we see the need as unavoidable, such that the sufferer cannot remove it through his or her own actions, we generally support the rendering of help. If we perceive the difficulties to be caused by people themselves we become more stringent. They have brought their misfortunes on themselves – why should others have to help them? (Kangas 2002). Instead, they should be whipped to work. In his studies of opinions on selectivity and universality in the Netherlands, van Oorschot (1997) concluded that the first question the Dutch public is likely to ask before giving benefits is: 'why are you needy?'. Two major answers were offered. According to the first the source of need is beyond the control of the individual, and that, therefore, society should bear the main responsibility. The second emphasizes individual choices and therefore the individual is to be blamed themselves. On the basis of previous studies it seems to be reasonable to suppose that these two aspects, i.e. 'social blame' and 'individual blame' play a crucial role in people's attitudes towards welfare measures. Therefore, we also included these dimensions in our surveys in order to see if they yield any significant impacts upon opinions on basic security.

We were interested in how different background variables affected the support for basic income. Among these we have gender, age, education, income, residence, socio-economic and labour market status, and in the Swedish case unionization and family size. We were especially interested in how the party affiliation affected the attitudes towards BI.

Our questions on people's opinions on basic income and negative tax models were as follows:

1 NIT: 'What do you think about a system in which taxes and benefits are integrated so that those with very low incomes would automatically

receive an income transfer instead of paying a tax (a so-called 'negative income tax') and those with high incomes would pay taxes as normally on their income that exceed a certain limit?'

2 BI: 'What do you think about a system that would automatically guarantee a certain basic income to all permanent residents?'
3 'How large should such a basic income be?' (In *kronor* or *markka* per month)

The respondents could choose between five alternatives: very good idea; good idea; bad idea; very bad idea; no opinion/do not know. The question on amount of unconditional basic income was asked in former Finnish *markka,* since it was easier for people to reason and calculate in *markka* then in *euro.*

Another set of questions was formulated in argument form. Therefore, the response alternatives were a bit different. In the case of questions four to ten the answering options were: totally agree; agree; disagree; totally disagree; no opinion/do not know.

4 BI to support the unemployed: 'The unemployed should be encouraged to get jobs by paying them a basic income that they could retain even though they would obtain additional income'.
5 'The unemployed should be encouraged to get jobs by a subsidy to low paid jobs'.
6 'The unemployed should be encouraged to get jobs by tightening the qualifying conditions to get unemployment benefits if the unemployed refuse to take offered jobs'.
7 'The unemployed should be encouraged to get jobs by creating tailored jobs even outside the normal labour markets'.

The individual blame (8 and 10) and social blame (9) questions were constructed as follows:

8 'Unemployment is the fault of the unemployed him/herself'.
9 'Unemployment is caused by social deficiencies'.
10 'Poverty is caused by the fact that poor people are not enterprising enough'.

Previous studies (e.g. Rasinski 1989; Kangas 1997) on the impacts of wording indicate that results from opinion polls are rather sensitive to the frame in which the question is posed. In order to evaluate to what extent, if any, some of our questions are wording-sensitive, Finnish data included also an additional sample of 500 respondents where two of our ten questions were presented a bit differently. In terms of background variables (age, gender etc.) the two samples are identical. In this smaller 'framed' sample the basic income question was presented as follows: (CW-question)

Table 7.1 Opinion on negative income tax (percentages)

'What do you think about a system in which taxes and benefits are integrated so that those with very low incomes would automatically receive an income transfer instead of paying a tax (a so-called "negative income tax") and those with high incomes would pay taxes as normally on their income that exceed a certain limit?'

	Sweden	*Finland*
Good idea	43	76
Bad idea	47	14
Don't know	10	9

'What do you think about a system that would automatically guarantee a certain basic income (*citizenship wage*) to all permanent residents?'. The other framed question dealt with attitudes to harder qualifying conditions: 'The unemployed should be encouraged to get jobs by hardening the qualifying conditions to get unemployment benefits if the unemployed refuse to take offered jobs *even though those jobs would not correspond to their skills.*'

A survey of the results

We shall present our results in simple tables comparing Sweden and Finland. In the subsequent section we shall analyse the relationships in order to find some causal explanations.

Negative Income Tax (NIT)

The first question was formed to pertain to the negative income tax idea. Table 7.1 gives the wording of the question and the results.

Basic Income (BI)

Second, we tried to construct a question referring to an unconditional basic income available to every resident, see Table 7.2.

Table 7.2 Opinion about basic income (percentages)

'What do you think about a system that would automatically guarantee a certain basic income to all permanent residents?'

	Sweden	*Finland*
Good idea	46	63
Bad idea	48	32
Don't know	10	5

Table 7.3 Opinion about participation income (percentages)

'The unemployed should be encouraged to get jobs by paying them a basic income that they could retain even though they would obtain additional income'.

	Sweden	*Finland*
Agree	44	79
Disagree	50	17
Don't know	7	4

'Participation Income' (PI)

Finally, in line with Atkinson's (1998) idea, we tried to formulate a question measuring the respondent's support to a linking of a basic income to a 'participation'-test, results in Table 7.3.

Independently of how the question is framed, a majority of the Swedes are critical towards basic income, whereas in Finland a clear majority favours all three forms of a basic income. They are especially attached to a 'participation income', where a link is kept between the basic income and willingness to work. When we reframed the question on BI in the second smaller Finnish sample, using the term citizen's wage (CW), a significant decline in support took place, yet a clear majority (59 per cent) still supported the idea.

In both countries the gender difference is insignificant, while age plays some role. Young people are more enthusiastic than old. In Sweden 59 per cent of those aged 16–29 supported a BI. In Finland 78 per cent of the age bracket 15–24 support both a BI and a CW. In both countries support tends to diminish somewhat with education and more clearly with income. In Finland students (80 per cent, 78 per cent) and the unemployed (93 per cent, 91 per cent) are strong supporters of both a NIT and a BI. We do not have figures for these categories in Sweden, but both are included in the group 'others', which significantly supports both a NIT (52 per cent) and a BI (54 per cent). In both countries those living in low-income households are most in favour, and those in the highest income bracket most against a BI.

In both countries people living in the countryside tend to favour a BI. The difference between cities and sparsely populated areas is somewhat stronger in Sweden (44 versus 57 per cent) than in Finland (61 versus 68 per cent). In Sweden lone parents were significantly in favour of both a NIT (58 per cent) and especially a BI (69 per cent). We do not have the corresponding figures for Finland.

When we look at party affiliation we find some interesting results (see Table 7.4).

In both countries the conservatives tend to be more critical than those voting for other parties. In Finland the supporters of the Left and the Greens are the most pronounced adherents, which is understandable

Table 7.4 Proportion responding positively according to political affiliation

	Sweden		
Party	*NIT*	*BI*	*PI*
Conservatives (M)	29−	30−	40
Liberals (Fp)	43	51	50
Centre (C)	42	32	47
Christians (Kd)	45	42	38
Social Democrats (S)	47	52+	43
Left (V)	42	65+	47
Greens (Mp)	52	37	38
	Finland		
Party	*NIT*	*BI*	*PI*
Conservatives (kok)	63−	48−	73−
Centre (kesk)	79	61	80
Others (kd, sfp, etc.)	83	59	89
Social Democrats (sd)	82	60	74
Left (vas)	86	85+	88
Greens (vihr)	82	70	92

Note
(A significant difference is marked with + or −)

since both parties have supported the idea in their party programmes. In Sweden the relatively high support from the rank and file Social Democrats and the Left (as well as from the LO membership) is somewhat astonishing, since both parties have turned down BI-initiatives, whereas the Greens, which have promoted the idea, do not seem to have such a strong support among their voters. In these cases the official line of the party and the unofficial grassroot opinions do not fully coincide.

That the Finns are more thrilled by the idea than the Swedes becomes evident by comparing the lowest support in Finland with the highest support in Sweden. Sixty-three per cent of the Finnish conservatives like the NIT-model, whereas only 52 per cent of the Swedish Greens do so. Seventy-three per cent of the Finnish conservatives support a PI, in contrast to 50 per cent of the Swedish Liberals. As for a BI, however, the 65 per cent support of the Swedish Left beats all Finnish parties except the Left and the Greens.

Earned Income Tax Credit (EITC)

We also formulated a question, which we thought would capture the attitudes towards a US-style subsidy to low-income earners, a tax credit especially targeted for all 'working poor'. The results are shown in Table 7.5.

The difference between the Swedes and Finns is repeated when they

Table 7.5 Opinion on subsidies to low-income earners (percentages)

'The unemployed should be encouraged to get jobs by a subsidy to low paid jobs'.

	Sweden	*Finland*
Agree	49	66
Disagree	50	28
Don't know	7	6

are asked about a subsidy to low-paid work. EITC is a measure of a workfare type policy, but it could be constructed in a way that resembles a PI.

In both countries an EITC gets more support from women than from men, and more from young than from old respondents.

'More stringent conditions'

'Activation' is the magic word all social policy discourse swears on. The darker side of the activation policy is harsher qualifications and sticks instead of carrots. In our survey we tried to map this issue by presenting the following the argument showed in Table 7.6.

Both Swedes and Finns favour more stringent measures towards the unemployed if they turn down a job offer. When we reframed the question in the second Finnish sample asking how the respondent would react if the work offered did not correspond to the qualifications of the unemployed, i.e. the unemployed had higher skills than were necessary in the job offered. The acceptance of using the stick in such a situation diminishes, but still it remained surprisingly high (61 per cent).

The difference between those employed and those unemployed is large: 75 per cent and 39 per cent respectively in Finland. For Sweden this difference seems to be smaller since the group 'others' which include the unemployed differs only marginally from the average.

'Third-sector employment'

In a similar vein as activation, many analysts see the 'third sector' as a promising possibility to solve the problem of long-term unemployment.

Table 7.6 Argument on activation (percentages)

'The unemployed should be encouraged to get jobs by tightening the qualifying conditions to get unemployment benefits if the unemployed refuse to take offered jobs'.

	Sweden	*Finland*
Agree	77	74
Disagree	22	24
Don't know	2	2

Table 7.7 Opinion on jobs in the 'third sector' (percentages)

'The unemployed should be encouraged to get jobs by creating tailored jobs even outside the normal labour markets'.

	Sweden	*Finland*
Agree	49	55
Disagree	43	36
Don't know	8	9

We tried to shed some light on the popularity of this idea, and the results are shown in Table 7.7.

Swedes are somewhat more sceptical to the possibility of deviating from the normal labour market, whereas Finns once again would be willing to experiment with the idea.

'Responsible for unemployment'

As stated above, the image of the poor or unemployed may affect people's attitudes towards the proper political measures to combat destitution. If unemployment is seen as an individual problem caused by for instance bad behaviour, attitudes tend to be harsher than if the misfortune is seen to be caused by factors beyond the individual's own control. In order to measure these dimensions, we posed three questions, see Table 7.8.

Table 7.8 Opinion on responsibility for unemployment (percentages)

'Unemployment is the fault of the unemployed him/herself'.

	Sweden	*Finland*
Agree	16	14
Disagree	82	85
Don't know	2	1

'Unemployment is caused by social deficiencies'.

	Sweden	*Finland*
Agree	64	70
Disagree	32	27
Don't know	4	3

'Poverty is caused by the fact that poor people are not enterprising enough'.

	Sweden	*Finland*
Agree	22	26
Disagree	75	71
Don't know	3	3

The differences between the two countries are negligible in the three questions in Table 7.8. A large majority among both Swedes and Finns tends to blame the society rather than the individual. Despite this unanimity there are interesting and significant differences between certain groups of the population.

Women are less likely than men to blame the individual and more likely to blame society. In Sweden young people, people with only basic education and people not belonging to a trade union are prone to blame *both* the individual and the society. In Finland the youngest and the oldest, students, farmers and entrepreneurs tend to blame the individual. Those with a low education blame both the individual and society.

'Level of BI'

A crucial issue in establishing a basic income scheme is the level of benefits. We simply asked how large the basic income should be, see Table 7.9.

Table 7.9 shows the percentages of all respondents, also those who did not respond because they did not think any BI would be a good idea. Those proposing a zero BI have been left out. The Swedes are clearly more generous than the Finns, but the average in both countries is high compared to the existing lowest benefits and to the amounts (€250–500) that have been proposed in the political debates. The higher levels proposed in Sweden are certainly partly due to the higher levels in overall social security in Sweden, but it may also reflect the somewhat more utopian context of the Swedish citizen's wage debate.

In general men and older people propose a higher BI than women and youngsters. In Finland the proposed amounts rise with urbanization, but this does not seem to be the case in Sweden. In both countries those affiliated to the Left propose the highest amounts, and those with the Greens the lowest.

Explaining attitudes towards basic income

The tables presented above give a rough overview of the attitudes towards basic income. We can refine the analysis by looking at more complex

Table 7.9 Opinion on size of basic income

'How much should a basic income be?' (SEK or FIM in euro)

Euro per month	*Sweden*	*Finland*
Less than 500 (F) or 550 (S)	16%	33%
500 (550) to 670 (F), 770 (S)	6%	13%
More than 670 (F) or 770 (S)	46%	25%
Mean €/month	970	620
Not any suggestion or €0	32%	39%

relationships between different variables. Can we explain the attitudes towards basic income using the background variables and the variables expressing how the respondents tend to blame individuals or society? How are the proposed BI-levels related to the attitudes towards BI and to the background variables?

Using the answers to the NIT-, BI- and PI-questions we constructed an additive index to measure the attitude towards basic income: ATTIBAS. Since the answers to these three questions have high factor loadings in both countries we calculated ATTIBAS as a sum of the attitudes towards NIT, BI and PI. The range of ATTIBAS was coded to go from 1 (the most negative attitude) to 7 (the most positive attitude).

We also constructed another composite measure, INDIBLAM, by the use of the two questions related to individual blame. The range of this measure goes from 1 (blames the individual least) to 5 (blames the individual most). We did not include the question on social blame into this composite measure, since in both countries its factor loadings were surprisingly low.

After these transformations we analysed the data using methods of path analysis. On each 'path', using analysis of variance, we looked for explanatory models, which on the one hand gave the highest degree of explanation, and on the other only contained variables that were statistically significant. After much experimenting we could not find a structure that was adequate for both countries (one reason being that data on the labour force status were not available in exactly the same way in the two countries). We started by looking for variables to 'explain' ATTIBAS, although it is questionable if this is a continuous variable. One variable that has some significance in both countries was INDIBLAM, and we also tried out explanations for this variable (which only takes on five values). In the Finnish case both party affiliation and socio-economic status seem to explain some of the variance in INDIBLAM. We then used ATTIBAS and other variables to explain the suggested amounts of BI. This type of analysis has its drawbacks, and the degrees of explanation tend to be low. However, we find the results to be worth reporting. The relationships are not contra-intuitive, and they point to some interesting differences between Finland and Sweden.

The explanatory models we ended up choosing were the two outlined in Figure 7.1. The thickness of the arrows expresses the statistical significance of each explanatory relationship.

The degree of explanation is somewhat higher in the Finnish case. One reason may be that, in the case of Sweden, we could not separate the responses of the unemployed. In Finland the labour-force status and the individual-blame variables are good predictors of the attitudes towards BI. In Sweden income and age are the best predictors (low income or young age increases ATTIBAS). It is possible that income and age in Sweden partly correspond to the labour-force status variable in Finland. Either

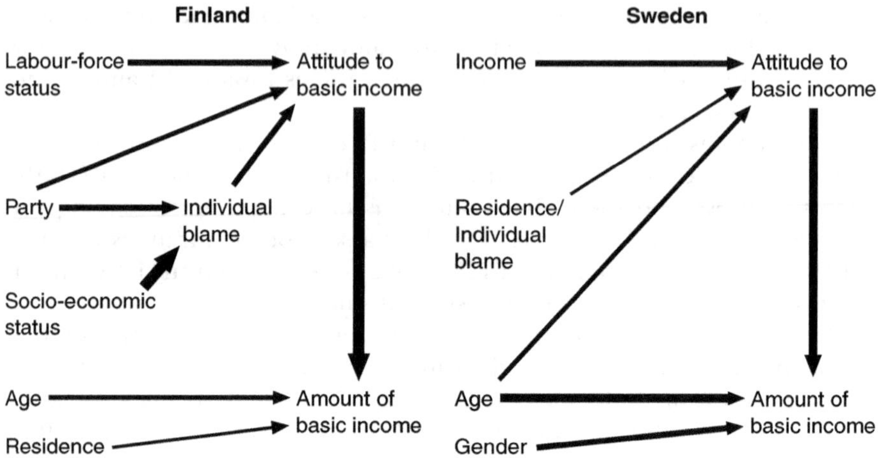

Figure 7.1 Explanatory models for basic income in Finland and Sweden.

individual blame or residence adds to the explanation in Sweden. Blaming the individual or living in cities decreases ATTIBAS. In Finland the socio-economic status affects ATTIBAS only indirectly through INDIBLAM.

In Finland party affiliation affects ATTIBAS both directly and indirectly through INDIBLAM. In Sweden we could not find a similar relationship. This may be because the debate in Finland has differed from that in Sweden. The political parties have either endorsed or rejected the idea. We also found in the Finnish case, that those who were sure of voting for a certain party also tended to agree more strongly with the party line on basic income (compared to more lukewarm supporters of the same party).

In both countries the suggested BI-amounts are strongly associated with the intensity of the attitude towards basic income in general. Age affects the proposed amount of BI in both countries. Young people are satisfied with a lower level. So are women in Sweden and people living in the countryside in Finland.

Why does a basic income thrill the Finns more than the Swedes?

The Finns are clearly more thrilled by a basic income than are the Swedes. The reasons may be sought for on the individual level, but clearly there must be some important differences in the economic, social and political situation, which could explain why BI has both been more intensely discussed and receives more public support in Finland.

There are two relatively obvious reasons why the interest for basic income has differed between Finland and Sweden. The first relates to the hegemony of the Swedish Social Democratic party and the second to the relative success of the Swedish welfare state.

Although this study shows that rank and file social democrats are not unusually critical towards a BI – in Sweden they are even relatively favourable to the idea – the social democratic parties have been averse to any basic income proposal. Both SAP in Sweden and SDP in Finland have seen basic income as a break with two fundamental principles: the 'work principle' and the 'income maintenance principle'. However, the relative influence of SAP in Sweden has always been much stronger than that of SDP in Finland. The electoral support of the Finnish SDP has normally been only about half of its Swedish counterpart SAP. It has therefore always been compelled to form coalition governments, whereas SAP has been able to govern alone for most of the time since the 1930s. In Finland the Centre Party has been as strong as the Social Democrats, and the Left Alliance (earlier the People's Democratic Alliance, which included the communists) has competed on a more equal footing. Both the Centre Party and the Left Alliance have traditionally tended to support universal benefits.

The other obvious reason for the different receptions of the basic income idea is that the Swedish welfare state is older and more sacrosanct than the Finnish, and that Sweden – until recently – has not been plagued by mass unemployment. The levels of the benefits are generally higher in Sweden. They are also more strongly related to the income maintenance principle – the 'standard social security'. The income related unemployment benefits – administered by the trade unions – has covered about 85 per cent of the earlier gross incomes. In Finland the corresponding figure is 60 per cent. The daily allowance for the uninsured has also been more generous in Sweden. It would, therefore, be relatively more costly to change the Swedish system into a pure basic income system.

Sweden was able to avoid open mass unemployment until the beginning of the 1990s. This was achieved by careful macroeconomic policies, by active labour market policies and by a rapid growth of the public service sector. In Finland mass unemployment appeared in 1976. It was gradually reduced towards the end of the 1980s but, from 1991 onwards, mass unemployment has been the principal scourge of the Finnish economy. Despite seven years of rapid economic growth the rate of unemployment is still some 10 per cent in 2004. Unemployment in Sweden has not been subdued, but it is only about half that of Finland.

Sweden is considered to be the modal example of a social democratic and universalistic welfare regime, the hallmark of which is the 'deliberate attempt to marginalize the role of needs-based assistance' (Esping-Andersen 1999: 78). It may, therefore, seem odd that most Swedes have been so reserved, and many outright hostile, towards ideas of an unconditional basic income. A paradoxical reason may, however, be that the

Swedish welfare regime has been so successful. Why support a radical change when Sweden already has managed to create the best of all existing welfare regimes? Furthermore, as Esping-Andersen remarks, 'Scandinavian welfare and employment policy has always been couched in terms of "productivism", that is maximizing the productive potential of the citizenry' (ibid.: 80). The foundational value of a basic-income regime is individual freedom, rather than a more collectivistic motivation to make everyone into an active and productive citizen. There has always been a streak of 'workfarism' in the Nordic welfare regimes, although it is far from the American urge to commodify labour. That this streak may be stronger in Sweden than in Finland, can be seen from the fact that despite the much lower rate of unemployment, on average 3.8 per cent of the Swedes were on activation programmes, compared to 2.5 per cent of the Finns, 1.7 per cent of the Finns were on unemployment pension – an inexistent welfare arrangement in Sweden. Furthermore, the Swedes leave the labour market at a much higher age; instead they eagerly make use of the generous sick-leave system (Hytti 2002).

With tongue in cheek we shall finish by offering an odd reason for why basic income is more popular in Finland compared to Sweden. According to experts on firm culture, there is a noticeable difference between the two countries. In Sweden it is necessary to be part of and receive the support from the collective. No decisions are taken without long discussions and an emerging consensus. In Finland leadership styles are more individualistic. You are allowed to be somewhat idiosyncratic and to change your opinions without engaging into long discussions. To be a village idiot – '*kylähullu*' – is honourable in Finland, but to be a '*byfåne*' is definitely not commendable in Sweden. Finns are thrilled by new technical solutions and they seem to be less afraid of sudden changes. The Swedes are well known for their pragmatism and cautiousness.

Basic income is probably most welcomed in a society which is individualistic and solidaristic at the same time. There must be a special combination of values, which allows citizens to make unconventional choices at the same time as their basic economic security is unconditionally guaranteed by the state.

Note

1 Quite recently there has been a growing academic interest in basic income in Sweden. Nanna Kildal (2001) has edited an anthology on the theme. Simon Birnbaum (2001) and Per Janson (2002) have presented interesting master essays related to basic income.

References

Andersson, J. O. (1998) 'Inkomst utan arbete? Debatten om medborgarlön i Finland och Sverig', *Historisk Tidskrift för Finland*, (2): 356–77.

—— (2000) 'The history of an idea: Why did basic income thrill the Finns but not the Swedes?', in R. van der Veen and L. Groot (eds) *Basic Income on the Agenda*, Amsterdam: Amsterdam University Press.

Andersson, J. O. and Kangas, O. (2002) 'Perustulon kannatus Suomessa' (support for a basic income in Finland), *Yhteiskuntapolitiikka*, 67 (4): 293–307.

Atkinson, A. B. (1998) *Poverty in Europe*, London: Blackwell.

Birnbaum, S. (2001) 'Inkomst utan arbete. En undersökning av argument för en ovillkorlig grundinkomst åt alla', Magistersuppsats, Stockholm: University of Stockholm, Department of Political Science.

Christensen, E. (2000) *Borgerløn. Fortællinger om en politisk idé*, Hovedland: Højbjerg.

Esping-Andersen, G. (1999) *Social Foundations of Postindustrial Economies*, Oxford: Oxford University Press.

Hytti, H. (2002) 'Miksi ruotsalaiset ovat sairaita mutta suomalaiset työttömiä?' (why are the Swedes sick but the Finns unemployed?), *Yhteiskuntapolitiikka*, 67 (4): 333–45.

Janson, P. (2002) *'Den huvudlösa idén' – medborgarlön, välfärdspolitik och en självcentrerad debatt*, Lund: University of Lund, Department of Political Science.

Kangas, O. (1997) 'Self-interest and the common good: the impact of norms, selfishness and context in social policy opinion', *Journal of Socio-Economics*, 26 (5): 475–94.

—— (2002) 'The grasshopper and the ants: opinions of just distribution in Australia and Finland', *Journal of Socio-Economics*, 31 (6).

Kildal, N. (ed.) (2001) *Den nya sociala frågan. Om arbete, inkomst och rättvisa*, Gothenburg: Daidalos.

Mattila, A. (2001) *Tarvitaanko perustuloa? Suomalaisten kansalaistulo-, kansalaispalkka- ja perustulomallien teoreettinen analyysi* (Is Basic Income Needed? Theoretical Analysis of the Civic Income, Civic Salary and Basic Income Models of the Finns), University of Kuopio.

Meyer, N. I., Petersen, H. and Sorensen, V. (1981) *Revolt from the Center*, London: Marion Boyars.

Rasinski, K. (1989) 'The effect of question wording on public support for government spending', *Public Opinion Quarterly*, 53: 388–94.

van Oorschot, W. (1997) 'Who should get what, and why? On deservingness criteria and the conditionality of solidarity among the Dutch public'. Working Papers 04/, Tilburg: Onderzoekschool Arbeid, Welzijn, Sociaal Economisch Bestuur.

Van Parijs, P. (1995) *Real Freedom for All. What (if Anything) can Justify Capitalism?*, Oxford: Clarendon Press.

8 Universalism under re-construction

From administrative coercion to professional subordination of substance misusers

Olavi Kaukonen and Kerstin Stenius

Introduction

For an analysis of the Nordic welfare state, the treatment of alcohol and drug misusers can be considered both marginal and central. From an economic point of view we are talking about a very small segment of the present welfare system. But the treatment system of alcohol and drug misusers, precisely because it operates in the margins, is a particularly sensitive indicator of normative changes in society: how much and what efforts are dedicated to this group of least resourceful citizens?

We shall discuss the postwar changes in the scope and choices in the measures against individuals regarded as substance misusers in Finland and Sweden. By comparing two countries with similar legal roots, administration and political culture in the field of alcohol and drug misuse, two countries which anyhow have taken slightly different steps at slightly different times in the development of the treatment system, we aim to gain an understanding of why and how the universalistic ambitions may now be threatened – and of what possibly protects the persistence of a comprehensive norm.

The present system of treatment of alcohol and drug misusers in Finland and Sweden have several features in common with the general social and health services: first, it is a publicly financed treatment system, available to everyone irrespective of economic position, giving the treatment a universalistic character (cf. Uusitalo 1993); and second, the responsibility to guarantee societal welfare service provision lies with the local administration, with great discretion as to how to arrange these services.

Public responsibility for welfare and equal accessibility to services are basic values of the Nordic welfare states. The municipalities have always been important for the provision of welfare services. The further decentralization of the responsibility from the state to the local level during the last two decades has been regarded as a means of securing efficiency –

placing responsibility for treatment decisions and costs at the same level – as well as increasing democratic influence.

Even if the services for alcohol or drug misusers in the postwar period have developed in parallel to other welfare services, they have characteristics that cannot easily be interpreted only with the help of the concept of social rights. One characteristic – and a very central one – is the question of coercion. The rights to treatment and the threat of coercion have been handled within the same system in Finland and Sweden.

Another aspect that characterizes substance misuse treatment is the particularly strong and persistent, even within the Nordic corporativistic system (Rothstein 1992; cf. Kuhnle and Selle 1992), involvement of the church, different voluntary organizations and private initiatives. Conflicting views, often expressed by voluntary organizations, have been integrated into the system and critical organizations have also received state support. The result has been consensual views on the problem and its solution. One consequence is the strong pressure to conformism, embodied in the persistence of compulsory treatment. The cooperation has also resulted in a particularly extensive treatment system, being one expression of universalism (Mäkelä 1988; Stenius 1999).

In both countries, the present treatment system shows features from three traditions, which can be perceived as different normative and institutional layers. The first one is a century-long historical/institutional connection with the poor relief, the alcohol question and the temperance movement. The goal has been to educate the (poor) abusers into good and sober citizens, with compulsory treatment in a lay-person dominated system. The second tradition grew out of the postwar service politics and is connected with the values of the modern, universalistic service state. The ambition within this tradition is to compensate all misusers in society, through social support and professional help, to be able to integrate and 'normalize'. Finally, the recent emphasis on expertise in the service system stresses intra-professional norms and values, giving social policy a less influential position. Professionalism has been the main strategy in increasing the reliability and quality of the services. The professionalization has been described as a 'process of displacement of social policy' (Hänninen 1998) and has certain features that can threaten the ambitions of integration and inclusion.

Today, the substance misuse services emphasize the responsibility of both the state and the municipality as problem-solvers, and the clients' own responsibility and the expert decisions of the professionals. It is a contradictory mix of norms rather than a coherent system of values.

Figure 8.1 gives a schematic description of the normative layers, stemming from three different periods.

Comprehensive descriptions of the service systems in both countries exist (e.g. Klingemann *et al.* 1992), and shall not be detailed here.[1] From an international perspective, though, it should be pointed out

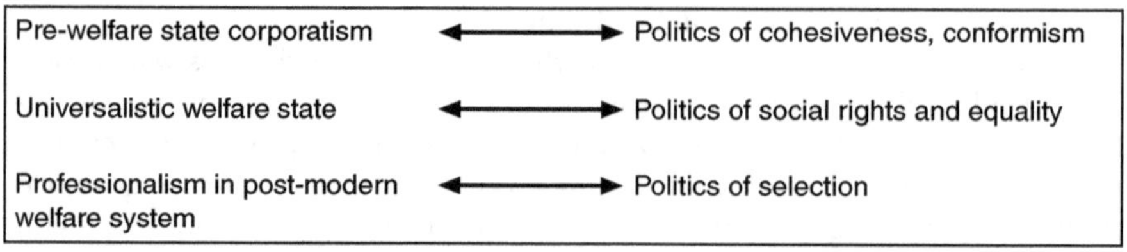

Figure 8.1 Three normative layers in substance misuse treatment in Finland and Sweden.

that the two treatment systems we are studying probably belong to the most extensive of its kind in the western world (ibid.). By treatment system we mainly refer to the specialized services for alcohol and drug misusers. In both Finland and Sweden the social service system has played a dominant role in treatment while the medical system has had a secondary role.

We shall first briefly describe the early development of the two treatment systems, followed by a focus on three features that indicate changes in the normative foundation in this area of the welfare system during recent decades. The decreasing use of coercion is one such factor. The changes in the drug treatment policies is another. Finally, we shall deal with the changes in the political steering of treatment provisions, with contracting-out of services, which challenge the normative unity in the treatment system.

From punishment to persuasion

The first Swedish Alcoholism Act was passed by the Parliament in 1913, and came into force three years later. The Act grew out of the reforms of the Poor Law and aimed at protecting society against alcoholics whose drinking impoverished their families and made them a burden to society. Compulsory detention was the core of the system. The ambition was furthermore to cure the drinker and reform him (rarely her) into a decent citizen, through temperance and religious education by lay-persons, but with the borrowed legitimacy of medicine (cf. Björkman 2001).

In Finland the same law was prepared in the late 1920s but not adopted until 1936, with a delay caused by the Prohibition (1919–1932). The first Finnish Alcoholism Act was actually a copy of the Swedish one (Rosenqvist and Takala 1987). In both countries, the municipal (elected) boards were responsible for initiating the measures against drinkers. This anchorage gave the extensive control of individual citizens a sort of collective, public and representative legitimacy. The disciplinary measures in the Nordic countries gained a special character. The municipalities, as a mediating link between the civil society and the state could:

> transfer, even on a personal level, the power relations of the civil society to the state apparatus. At the same time, they make into a governmental matter the controlling relations of civil society ... In this relation neighbourhood, the power relations of civil society and legal authority are linked together.
>
> (Mäkelä 1988: 90)

The small municipalities blurred efficiently the border between the public and the private sphere.

Central features of this first system remained almost intact in both countries until the 1980s. First, the paternalistic arguments, gradually strengthened in comparison to the utilitaristic ones, legitimizing authorities to use compulsory measures not only for the sake of society but also for the best of the drinking or drug using citizen. Second, the fact that compulsory measures, voluntary treatment and prevention were handled in the same system. Third, the strong involvement of lay-persons in treatment and treatment decisions, and the fact that the treatment system was built in a cooperative system by the state and voluntary organizations, churches, private initiatives and the municipalities became a characteristic feature.

Treatment grew very slowly in the beginning of the twentieth century, since the municipalities were reluctant to initiate expensive compulsory detention. Growth became possible with increasing economic incentives from the state, in Sweden from the 1930s, and in Finland after the Second World War.

Development was similar in the two countries, but the timing differed somewhat. The Finnish welfare state evolved later; its development seems more sudden and the solutions more pragmatic than value- or politically oriented compared with the Swedish history.

In the pre-welfare state period in both countries alcohol was seen as a social plague more than as a disease, threatening both production and social security. The drunkard was the object of severe and individualized control measures. The professions were integrated to legitimize treatment, but it was in fact performed by lay-persons or non-professional staff. The growth of the welfare state influenced the treatment of alcohol and drug misusers in the postwar period. The funding and planning became increasingly more centralized to the state authorities in both countries, somewhat earlier in Sweden than in Finland. This period saw the establishment of an internationally generously financed and extensive treatment system, where voluntary treatment and prevention gradually came to dominate and professionals became more important for the actual treatment.

Coercion questioned

After the Second World War, the Swedish treatment system was criticized for its focus on compulsory measures, for having a class bias but, above all, for being inefficient and solving neither the social nor the individuals' drinking problems. The new Temperance Act in Sweden in 1955 had a spirit of social engineering. Medicine was expected to solve the problems of alcoholics, who were now viewed as individuals in need of proper treatment, not representatives of the poor in need of reform and education. The state took an increasingly active role in the financing. The treatment system became centrally planned, regionalized and specialized, to meet the differentiated needs of misusers.

Voluntary institutional treatment was at the core of the new Temperance Act. The municipal temperance boards became obligatory and should also act on such misuse 'that can be regarded as a more private matter and where the implementation of the measure is completely dependent on the individuals own willingness to co-operate' (SOU 1961, No. 58: 20). The Swedish municipalities established both in-patient and out-patient units for voluntary treatment. Voluntary organizations were not necessarily regarded as sufficiently professional. In prevention and after-care they were, however, crucial in providing important social support and legitimacy for the system.

But compulsion and paternalism did not disappear. As Nygren (1990) states, in the case of Sweden, the use of compulsion also followed the pace of the expansion of the welfare system in the decades after the Second World War. When the welfare systems grew, the state became increasingly 'the good state', and this, paradoxically, also legitimized control of the individual. The compulsory treatment system in Sweden expanded in the 1950s (Blomqvist 1998).

In Finland, the decade after the Second World War showed growth and diversification of compulsory treatment. From the mid-1950s Finland took a partly different path from that of Sweden. Drinking problems were still mainly seen as social problems and were primarily tackled by social workers. The Finnish practice became divided – most of the problems were still handled in an administrative way by the municipalities with more coercion towards individuals and more institutionalization. On the other hand, the state supported strongly the A-clinic foundation, a non-profit organization established in 1955 to offer out-patient treatment on a voluntary basis in bigger cities.

Comparing the development in the two countries, it seems that in Finland there was a factual division of labour between the statutory authorities on the one hand, using compulsory, administrative measures, and the non-statutory agents who provided voluntary treatment on the other. This division of labour was not so clear in Sweden. In particular, the municipalities in the two countries had different roles. Finnish municipalities were not given state subsidies until the 1970s for establishing out-patient clinics, detoxification units and housing. Through the municipal involvement in voluntary treatment the role of the Swedish statutory treatment system could earlier be characterized as both 'caring and paternalistic' (Lehto 1994).

From the 1960s, the critique against the compulsory features of the treatment system was also raised in Finland. The critique was connected to a general and broad discussion on inequalities in society. Coercion as such, and especially administrative compulsion directed towards abusers, as well as the coercive procedures in the institutions, were criticized. This critique was conducive in Finland to the establishment of a treatment system as part of the welfare state. The contents and funding of the new services for alcohol and drug misusers was politically uncontroversial. Most parliamentary representatives agreed that the state should grow stronger in the area of welfare services. The planning and regulating mechanisms of the services became heavily centralized. Compulsory treatment was used significantly less often, thanks to the civil rights movement of the 1960s. In 1970, about 600 persons per year were in compulsory treatment, ten years later less than 300.

In Sweden, the first postwar critique against compulsory treatment aimed mainly at the professionalization of treatment. But with the radicalization of society in the 1970s came a social critique, which challenged the belief in social engineering. The welfare state had not solved the social problems. The state was regarded as oppressive; compulsory treatment was the most obvious example of that. The professionals could be viewed as instruments of the oppressive state (Beckman 1981). This critique re-installed the importance of lay-men influence and politicized treatment.

When the ideological wind turned right in the late 1970s, the state and its professionals came under new attack. The right argued that treatment providers related to certain social movements, such as the revivalist Pentecostal church, were not given state subsidies to the same extent as other treatment providers, and that this was a sign that the state was suffocating the civil society. From the right-wing perspective, the state-dominated system ignored the importance of traditional informal social support, within the church and the family. On the other hand, the right was much less willing than the left and the liberals to give up compulsory measures within the social service system. A new proposal to move all compulsory treatment to the mental health system was stopped by the right, with the support from the third sector organizations that were providing compulsory treatment.

For both the political left and right the state apparatus had become too strong by the end of the 1970s. There was no consensus around the content of treatment and about who should provide treatment. Whether or not to abolish all compulsory measures from the social services was a hotly debated issue.

The number of persons in compulsory treatment in Sweden was still as high as *c.*4,600 in 1960, after which it declined rapidly to less than 1,000 by the end of the 1970s (Blomqvist 1998; Palm and Stenius 2002). In Finland, the effects of the critique came around 1970. Table 8.1 shows the development of compulsory treatment in both countries.

The use of compulsory treatment in Sweden declined during the 1970s and 1980s, until the law was sharpened in 1989 (increasing the maximum detention from three to six months, somewhat extending the criteria for detention and making it compulsory for the municipality to use the law). The main motivation for the legal reform was the need to treat young drug users (Hübner 1991). No voluntary or non-profit organizations were any more involved in the provision of compulsory measures. During the 1990s the number of persons treated involuntarily declined further, roughly to the level of the late 1970s. Compulsory treatment was under pressure: from the municipalities (too expensive, in spite of state subsidies), and from research (inefficient treatment). Still, it can be argued that compulsion enjoys legitimacy in the Swedish society, as a measure to save persons from abuse. Furthermore, the Swedish state is actively supporting compulsory treatment, through subsidies, and, since 1994, by being the sole provider of this treatment (Palm and Stenius 2002).

In Finland, compulsory treatment within the social administration practically disappeared with the new Act of 1986, and was moved to the health care system, mainly based on the Mental Health Act. The discussions on civil rights were still in fresh memory and the dominance of compulsory treatment a recent experience. It was argued that the practices of treatment of alcohol and drug problems should not be more coercive than the practices applied to people with mental disorders. Compulsory care could now only be given on the basis of violent or suicidal behaviour, or if the client was causing direct, serious and immediate harm to himself/herself. There were no more earmarked state subsidies for

Table 8.1 Persons referred to involuntary treatment in institutions for substance misusers in Sweden and Finland 1960 to 2000

Year	*Sweden*	*Finland*
1960	4,647	678
1970	1,378	600
1980	973	289
1990	1,473	9**
2000	1,008*	0**

Sources: Rosenqvist and Kurube 1992: 74; Takala and Lehto 1992: 93; Lehto 1994: 16; Kaukonen 2000: 130; Blomqvist 1998; Palm and Stenius 2002; Socialstyrelsen 2001.

Notes
* Number of discharges.
** Only compulsory treatment due to violent behaviour is registered.

compulsory treatment. The number of cases dropped quickly after the introduction of the law to less than ten per year during the 1990s, consisting mainly of short term detention (five days). The absolute maximum length of involuntary treatment is 30 days in Finland.

Let us provide some figures on voluntary treatment as a background to compulsory treatment. Table 8.2 shows the number of persons in different kinds of treatment during one day at the end of 1999 in Finland (population 5.2 million) and Sweden (8.8 million).

As shown in Table 8.2, compulsory treatment in Sweden is only a small share of the whole treatment system today. But compulsory and voluntary treatments are not compensatory in Swedish treatment. The rise in compulsory treatment came in the late 1980 and coincided with the rise in voluntary in-patient treatment (Bergmark and Oscarsson 1994). As seen from Table 8.2, in proportion to the population and to the level of alcohol consumption and drug use, voluntary treatment has been at least as extensive in Sweden as in Finland.

In the question of compulsory treatment, the Finnish and Swedish systems took different routes in the 1980s. The Swedish legislation allows strong paternalism, justifying compulsory treatment for the own good of the drinker or drug abuser, while Finnish paternalism became weak, allowing compulsion only for a short time in order to empower the individual's own ability to decision-making (Häyry 1990: 78–93). In Finland you can in fact only speak of (short term) compulsory care, but not of compulsory treatment in the real sense of the word.

The use of compulsory treatment has a special political importance since the decisions about compulsory measures cannot be totally delegated from the board to the administration. These cases are in many municipalities the only ones where the elected lay-men take decisions concerning individual substance misusers. Compulsory treatment is thus still on the local political agenda in Sweden, but not in Finland.

Table 8.2 Number of persons in different kinds of substance abuse treatment or care on one day in Finland (10 October 1999) and Sweden (1 November 1999)

Treatment or care measure	*Finland*	*Sweden*
Supported housing	1,935	5,464
Out-patient treatment	2,303	10,400
In-patient treatment	859	3,172*

Sources: Nuorvala *et al.* 2000; Socialstyrelsen 2000.

Note

* Of which 257 in compulsory treatment.

The sobriety ideal questioned – changes in drug treatment

In an international perspective, both Sweden and Finland are countries with restrictive drug policies, aiming at drug-free societies. The number of drug users has been relatively lower than in other western European countries (Klingemann and Hunt 1998). In Sweden, and particularly Finland, drug use increased during the 1990s. The number of heavy drug addicts in Finland was estimated at 1,000 in the early 1990s, ten years later the figure had risen to *c.* 14,000. In Sweden, the growth was less dramatic, but the level was higher from the outset: from 19,000 in 1990 to 26,000 at the end of the decade (Olsson 2001).

In both countries there are signs of a medicalization of the treatment of alcohol and drug abusers during the 1990s. Several reforms introduced closer cooperation between social services and the health system at the local level (in Finland already from the late 1980s). In this cooperation, medicine is the stronger part. Medical doctors, contrary to social workers, have a legally regulated professional autonomy in relation to the administration and to politics and a much stronger professional role. The role of medicine in treatment has gained particular strength recently, with the growing focus on drug problems that seem to call for medical expertise. The emphasis on the need to develop evidence-based treatment in social work, where medicine has become the model for development and professionalization of social services (see for instance Månsson 2000), is another sign of medicalization of the alcohol and drug treatment field.

In drug treatment the traditional abstinence-orientation of the treatment systems has been challenged. Of greatest interest, and much debated, has been the question of substitution and maintenance treatment for heroin or other opioid dependent addicts. Substitution treatment has been controversial in the Nordic countries, since it de facto accepts the possibility of a chronic need of a legally administered drug. Needle or syringe exchange has been another much debated question, and has been regarded by its critics as a sign of social acceptance of drug use which does not provide society with very substantial possibilities to interfere with rehabilitative measures. On these two questions the two countries opted for different paths in the 1990s.

Sweden was one of the first countries in Europe to introduce methadone treatment of chronic opiate misusers in the mid-1980s. This was done in a strictly regulated system, with the long term aim of a drug-free life. The number of persons treated is still low, maximum 800 in the whole country. In Finland, where heroin use was rarer in the 1980s, this treatment was not actualized until the 1990s, when there was an epidemic of HIV among drug users in Finland, and the drug question became a serious problem of public health.

In 1997, the Finnish Ministry of Social Affairs and Health opened up for regulated substitution and maintenance treatment, at first in the bigger cities, later throughout the country (Hakkarainen and Tigerstedt 2002). A recent estimate gives the figure 3,000 opioid addicts in Finland, of which around 400 receive substitution treatment (Partanen, personal communication 2003). Even though the opioid addicts make up only 20 per cent of the heavy addicts, the professional discussion focuses heavily on this group, since there seems to be a promise of cure or alleviation through the medically administered substitution treatment.

The needle and syringe exchange and substitution programmes in Finland were permitted from 1997 and developed quickly. The syringe exchange programmes reached a notable proportion of hard drug users. In 2001, it was estimated that around 8,000 drug users have taken advantage of needle exchange programmes in Finland (Partanen, personal communication 2003).

Sweden has had a less dramatic and more restrictive harm-reduction policy during the 1990s. In addition to the methadone patients, a roughly equal number of persons (600–800) in 2002 get substitution treatment with buprenorphine (Kakko, personal communication 2003). This latter subscription is, interestingly enough, lacking national regulation. The total number in Swedish substitution treatment is thus today 1,200–1,600.

The estimated proportion of opioid drug addicts in substitution treatment is between 13–20 per cent of opioid addicts in the two countries by the year 2000. The number of needle and syringe exchange programmes is remarkably higher in Finland, where they exist in most bigger towns, than in Sweden, with two programmes in two cities in the south of Sweden (EMCDDA, Annual report 2002). But in March 2003, the Swedish 'drug tsar', Björn Fries, declared that he was willing to suggest an increase in the number of these programmes, but that they should be combined with offers of rehabilitative measures.

The development in the drug treatment in the 1990s shows that the intention to rehabilitate into sobriety has become more relative in the two countries, sooner and more in Finland, and that this process in the case of substitution and maintenance treatment has been accompanied by a referral of the responsibility for treatment decisions to medicine and its logic, where the alleviation of suffering and saving of lives has priority over conformism and the cohesiveness of society.

Contracting out services – and decision-making

Both countries entered the 1980s with a larger and more expansionist treatment sector for alcohol and drug abusers than ever before, with ambitions to reach new groups of misusers and to attack new and less severe problems in a service-oriented spirit (Rosenqvist and Stenius 1986). This happened in a period with no immediate economic threats to the welfare system. In both countries there was a growing concern over the costs of the treatment system (ibid.). Growing ambitions combined with increased economic consciousness led to attempts to emphasize the cheaper out-patient instead of in-patient treatment.

A decentralization of the responsibility for the steering, financing and supervision from the state to the municipalities was expected to lead to higher efficiency. The 1980s saw a number of reforms in Finland and Sweden implying a withdrawal of the state from the planning and provision of social services and a growing freedom to design substance treatment systems at the local, municipal level. The financial regulation of the treatment system was decentralized to the municipalities in 1984 in Finland and two years later in Sweden. The reforms meant an end to the state budget funding of treatment institutions. State subsidies were instead given to the municipalities for unspecified treatment of alcohol and drug misusers and the municipality bought services on the bases of performance. As service providers, public and non-public organizations were put on the same line.

Decentralization was also expected to increase the democratic influence over treatment planning. In fact, though, the professionalization of individual treatment decisions led to increasing restrictions for political priority-setting. The definition of needs started to move from political fora to the professional system (Lehto 1991). The new social service acts of the 1980s in both countries were also explicitly intended to move the decisions concerning individual citizens from the politically elected boards to the social workers and other professionals, and confirmed the diminishing role of lay-men in daily contact with the misusers.

Decentralization, deregulation, the availability of resources and the lack of professional constraints led anyhow to a growth of in-patient treatment instead of out-patient services, which was the political aim. Another largely unexpected process in the in-patient treatment field in Sweden was that in less than a decade the public dominance was substituted by a non-public one in the provision of institutional treatment. Treatment institutions in the form of corporations became a large group. New entrepreneurs were successful on the new local treatment markets. This trend continued during the 1990s (Figure 8.2).

The privatization trend in Sweden strengthened in the 1990s, and notably the for-profit institutions grew steadily in importance in Swedish in-patient treatment. With a share of 40 per cent the for-profit provision is much higher in this sector than in most parts of the welfare system (Trydegård 2001). Even if Swedish out-patient treatment is mostly provided by municipalities and covers many more individuals yearly than the in-patient treatment (Holmberg 2001), the privatization of institutional care is remarkable in terms of allocation of financial resources and as a mark of the impact of a new logic in the welfare thinking.

In Finland the volume of the in-patient treatment provision also grew towards the end of the 1980s. Following a new regulation by the government in 1987, increasing subsidies were given to non-profit (but not to for-profit) service organizations through the Finnish Slot Machine Associ-

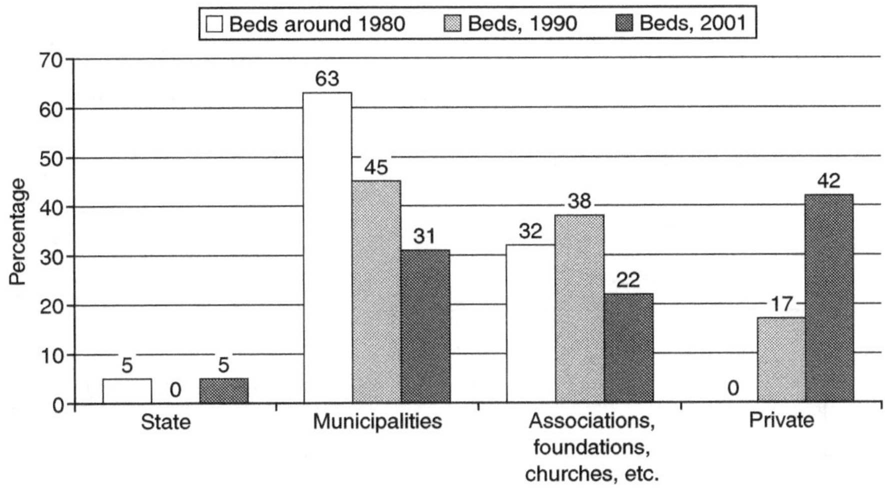

Figure 8.2 Provision of institutional treatment for alcohol and drug misusers in Sweden, number and percentage of beds according to type of provider in 1980, 1990 and 2001 (Source: Stenius 1999 Socialstyrelsen 2001a).

ation (SMA).[2] The SMA subsidies to non-profit organizations in substance misuse treatment grew quickly from the year 1988 and during the 1990s. One might say that the Finnish state became more active in promoting non-public treatment provisions. SMA became the invisible hand of the state in the Finnish treatment market. The services expanded unexpectedly towards more institutional care and treatment.

The Finnish state stopped producing any specialized services for alcohol and drug misusers in 1994. The municipalities produced around 65 per cent of the services in the beginning of the 1990s, but less than half by the end. Services for the drug users were by then produced to a greater extent on a non-profit basis (60 per cent) as a result of the subsidies to this sector. The development in Finland meant less a privatization in terms of a growing share of third sector or for-profit providers of services but rather a 'privatization', in the sense of professionalization and de-politicization of the decision-making. There was a change of emphasis in the service delivery on the one hand from the specialized social services for substance misusers to the more general health and welfare services: an expansion of care and treatment especially in psychiatric hospital wards (Figure 8.3).

The 1980s was the decade of expansionism and diversification of the system in both countries. In voluntary treatment, the decade saw an all-time peak in special treatment available for alcohol and drug misusers. The clientele of at least the Swedish alcohol and drug treatment, which had been very stable (poor alcoholics), was probably somewhat broadened, to include more persons with social anchorage – jobs and intact families – than before (Rosenqvist and Stenius 1986; Blomqvist 1998). The comprehensiveness had

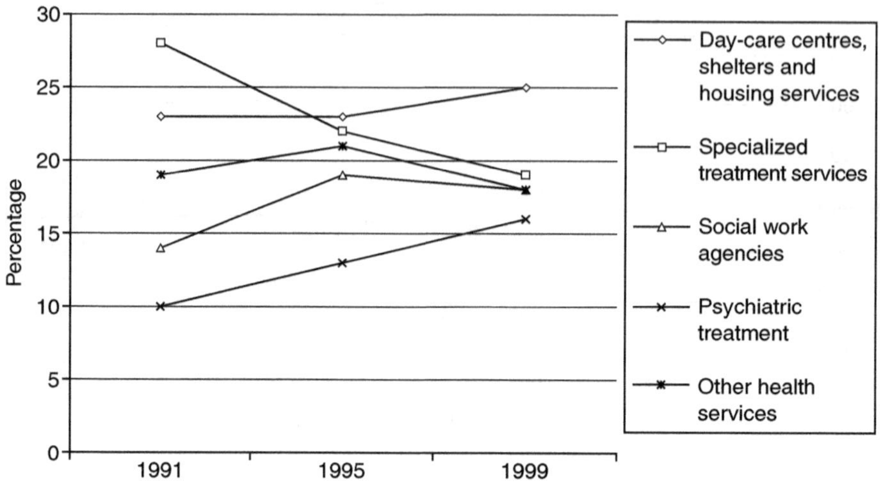

Figure 8.3 Distribution of visits (percentage) of alcohol and drug abusers in different social and health care services during one day in 1991, 1995 and 1999 in Finland (Source: Stakes 2000).

reached its peak. In Finland, though, the proportion of non-working class people has never been higher than 5 per cent in specialized treatment (Kaukonen 2000).

The 1990s started dramatically in both countries. The most important decentralization reforms – the new Municipal Acts in Sweden and Finland, which increased the freedom to organize the municipal decision-making, and marked the end of all ear-marked state subsidies (in 1993) – came just after the economic crises had reached the public economies (Bergmark 2001). Bergmark (1995: 149) shows that treatment of alcohol and drug misusers belonged to the parts of the municipal welfare system that was least prioritized in the public programmes by the Swedish administrators in the 1990s. Also in Finland the treatment for misusers had a very posterior status according to citizens, social workers, administrators and politicians (Niemelä *et al.* 1995). But 'the invisible hand of the Finnish state' (the Slot Machine Association, SMA) compensated the non-public providers not only for the withdrawn state subsidies, but also for the overall effect of the very deep economic depression in the beginning of the 1990s. There are obviously differences between municipalities but, as a whole, the services for substance users in Finland did not suffer from the depression as much as some other services. Also in Sweden it is difficult to detect any real shrinking of the total volume of the specialized treatment for alcohol and drug misusers during the 1990s. The costs for substance abuse treatment in the municipalities were basically unchanged during the decade (Oscarsson 2000).

The access to in-patient treatment was anyhow somewhat restricted in Finland in the years of economic depression in the 1990s. But it seems that it was actually the increased professionalization, not the economic hardship, which was the main reason restricting the clients' access to services. The amount of clients receiving specialized out-patient treatment did not grow in spite of the restrictions on institutional care and a relatively dramatic increase of both alcohol consumption and drug use towards the end of the 1990s (*Yearbook of Alcohol and Drug Statistics* 2002; Nuorvala *et al.* 2000). On the other hand, there was a growth of shelters and daycare wards for homeless misusers. There was a sharpening selection within the specialized treatment services that led to a de facto lower quality of the services to the poorest. Also in Sweden, there are signs that both chronic and socially more integrated alcohol misusers receive less institutional treatment, and more caring measures without curing ambitions were given to the chronic alcohol users from the 1990s, while drug misusers were treated to the same extent as before (Oscarsson 2000).

Neither country cut the total funding of the service systems, but the new market-oriented political and ideological choices led to a more professionally directed systems, with smaller possibilities even for local authorities for political steering. By the year 1994, shortly after the new municipal law of 1992, a quarter of all Swedish municipalities, mainly the bigger ones, had introduced some kind of purchaser-provider models in their administration of alcohol and drug abuse treatment (Bergmark and Oscarsson 1994a). These administrative reforms, which aim at separating production from politics, tend to shrink the role of the politicians – it becomes reactive rather than active (Montin *et al.* 1993; Premfors 1998). The market-inspired models may have led not only into a destabilization of the treatment system – with short contracts and increasing economic insecurity (Stenius 1999) but also to a growing separation of different branches of the municipal administration, and thus a weakened overall view of the policy and planning. In these administrative models, the role of voluntary organizations, foundations and churches in treatment also changed in both countries. They got less subsidies as pressure groups. The organizations got a new, economized and emphatically service producing relation to the state and the municipalities (Lundström and Wijkström 1995). They were forced into a role of actors on a treatment market, rather than defenders of the clients.

Without going into a discussion about problems with consumer steering in the field of addiction treatment, we should note such problems as the weak consumer's influence when he or she does not pay for the service him/herself; the fact that an informed choice is illusionary when there are serious difficulties to compare the quality between different services, if there de facto is only one option to be chosen; or if a client is coerced into treatment (see Gilbert 1984: 69).

The popularity of market-oriented administrative models seem to be based less on ideological arguments about democracy and the freedom of the consumer, and more on their promises of cost-efficiency (Rose 1995: 33–7; Bergmark and Oscarsson 1994a), although there seems to be little evidence of the economic promises having become true.

Conclusion: de-politicization as a threat to universalism

The 1980s can be characterized as the decade of pluralism and decentralization, with growing integrative ambitions and a vivid pluralistic ideological impact on the system, through the many new third sector or private institutions. The 1990s, on the other hand, could be viewed as a period when the two inclusive traditions were weakened: both the first 'protect and punish' tradition of the system, which aimed at educating, even with compulsion, the abusers into good and sober citizens and the later, postwar persuasive tradition, which set out to help the misusers through social support and professional treatment to integrate and become good and sober citizens. They were supplemented by an expert-driven treatment-tradition, with more restricted ambitions to treat the alcohol and drug related problems, so that the negative effects of drinking and drug use are minimized for the users themselves and society. Further professionalization, selection, documentation and scientification, contracting out for efficiency and a weakened emphasis on the social political side of the drinking and drug use problems worked in this direction.

The fact that the total volume of the Swedish and Finnish specialized treatment systems for alcohol and drug abuser was not more affected by the economic crises of the 1990s can be interpreted as a sign of the persistence of the institutionalized welfare state and its universalistic and inclusive ambitions. On the other hand it is possible, or even probable, that the treatment needs increased in both countries during the last decade, due to other social factors, such as growing alcohol and drug consumption, increased unemployment, lack of housing and segregation, and that the real needs of treatment were thus growing.

As shown above, the 1990s may have brought about a split of the service system. There is, at least in Finland, an increased alcohol and drug related use of the general health and social service systems, and, on the other hand, a growing amount of care with low rehabilitative ambitions. The therapeutically oriented specialized treatment has neither been effective enough nor interested in clients with poor capacity for therapeutic interaction (Kaukonen 2000). Some signs of the same development can be registered in Sweden (Oscarsson 2000).

The decentralization of treatment decisions in the 1980s was intended to increase the political influence of citizens/lay-persons, with the necessary involvement of the many more local politicians in policy decision. The simultaneous professionalization worked in the other direction. The New Public Management models strengthened the de-politicization.

The state has withdrawn from the steering of the services system. The municipalities have been de-politicized. The voluntary organizations have less and less possibilities to put new needs on the agenda, due to the hardened competition and the dominance of economics in the treatment market. From the client's point of view, service policies are even more decentralized than before, consisting of individual needs testing by professional gate-keepers and with economic arguments ever more present. The service politics have been replaced by the policies of services – by the treatment prescription of experts and by market-oriented administrative models promising cost savings.

In both countries, what was in the institutionalized welfare state a coherent social policy of the alcohol and drug misuse services has been replaced by the (social service) administration of a complex system and by professional expertise. While the funding is still public, the treatment provision is increasingly privatized, the decision-making within the services is less and less a public political decision, and the needs of the client are often invisible for the decision makers, interpreted only by the clinicians in a more and more medicalized language. The value based discussion has been replaced by economic and scientific-professional rationality.

The division of labour is a necessary precondition and consequence of modernization. Professionalization is not only a feature of the care and cure of intoxicant users, but has been the main strategy in the service policies and in the regulation of the admission to services in general (Lehto *et al.* 1999: 131–2). The dominance of professions in today's service decision-making has radically changed the balance of power between the political and administrative systems. The main strategy and quality guarantee of the welfare state – steering by information, education and professions – may have come to a critical point, where 'the second modernity' starts (Beck *et al.* 1994): a reflexive development, where modernization and its dynamics develop by its own force outside the political sphere and starts to undermine its own objectives. In this case study, it is difficult to blame the usual suspect (i.e. globalization) for the processes of de-politicization. The main reasons are of domestic origin: professionalization, externalization and the change of values in the political thinking.

The professionals cannot be blamed for this development. The political decision makers have consciously given away the social politics to the social service administration. The cultural cohesion, the conformistic norms, and thus also compulsion, have been on the retreat. More problematic is that the values of equality and universalism through this process have been transformed into governing with the 'best' selection. Universalism is threatened more from inside the welfare state than from outside.

The transformation in both welfare states seems to have changed the basic ideas of universalism in practice. The public financing has not been cut, but it has been more short-sighted and less welfare and equality oriented. Universalism is constrained by continuous economic negotiations, and so is the availability of different kinds of services. The professional steering, gatekeeping and selection of clients have been strengthened in both countries.

So far, citizens or clients themselves have always had very little influence on services. The clients of the substance misuse treatment system have often very small personal, social and economic resources and depend on the service system. They are, however, often capable of choosing. To give them more influence could be one way of defending the crumbling comprehensiveness of the social and health care services in the margins. Another way to empower the clients could be the traditional – and most comprehensive – means of the Nordic welfare states, social insurance, the most advanced way of producing social security (Ewald 1995: 74).

Notes

1 For the historical data we have drawn upon earlier research: Takala and Lehto (1992) and Kaukonen (2000) have analysed the Finnish development, Rosenqvist and Kurube (1992), Abrahamson (1989), Bergmark and Oscarsson (1994), Blomqvist (1998) and Stenius (1999) have described the Swedish system.

2 The Association has monopoly on gambling in Finland, and the profits are used for the public good.

References

Abrahamson, M. (1989) 'Synen på missbruk – 80 år av diagnostisk rundgång', *Nordisk Sosialt Arbeid*, 9 (2): 38–49.

Beck, U., Giddens, A. and Lash, S. (1994) *Reflexive Modernization. Politics, Tradition and Aesthetics in the Modern Social Order*, Cambridge: Cambridge University Press.

Beckman, S. (1981) *Kärlek på tjänstetid – om amatörer och professionella inom vården*, Stockholm: Arbetslivscentrum.

Bergmark, Å. (1995) *Prioriteringar i socialtjänsten. Rättvisa och ekonomi.* Rapport i socialt arbete nr 73, Stockholms universitet, Institutionen för socialt arbete, Edsbruk: Akademitryck AB.

—— (2001) 'Den lokala välfärdsstaten?', in Marta Szebehely (ed.) SOU 2001: 92 *Välfärdstjänster i omvandling*, Stockholm: Socialdepartementet.

Bergmark, A. and Oscarsson, L. (1994) 'Från producenternas paradis till marknadens retorik. Den socialtjänstbaserade missbrukarvården under 1980- och 1990-talen', in U. Pettersson (ed.) *Socialtjänstens klientarbete. från vision till marknad?*, Stockholm: Studentlitteratur.

—— (1994a) 'Swedish alcohol treatment in transition? Facts and fiction', *Nordisk Alkoholtidskrift* (English supplement), 11: 43–54.

Björkman, J. (2001) *Vård för samhällets bästa. Debatten om tvångsvård i svensk lagstiftning 1850–1970*, Stockholm: Carlssons bokförlag.

Blomqvist, J. (1998) *Beyond Treatment: Widening the Approach to Alcohol Problems and Solutions*, Stockholm University: Stockholm Studies in Social Work.

EMCDDA (2002) *Annual Report on the State of the Drug Problems in the European Union and Norway*, European Monitoring Centre for Drugs and Drug Addiction, Lisboa.

Ewald, F. (1995) 'Vakuutusyhteiskunta', [Insurance Society], in R. Eräsaari and K. Rahkonen (eds) *Hyvinvointivaltion tragedia. Keskustelua eurooppalaisesta hyvinvointivaltiosta* [The tragedy of the welfare state. Discussions about the welfare state in Europe], Gaudeamus, Tampere.

Gilbert, N. (1984) 'Welfare for profit: moral, empirical and theoretical perspectives', *Journal of Social Policy*, 13 (1): 63–74.

Hänninen, S. (1998) 'Is Finland going beyond the age of entitlement?' in S. Hänninen (ed.) *Displacement of Social Policies*, Jyväskyla, Finland: Sophi.

Hakkarainen, P. and Tigerstedt, C. (2002) 'Ristiriitojen huumepolitiikka – huumeongelman normalisaatio Suomessa', in M. Heikkilä and M. Kautto (eds) *Suomalaisten hyvinvointi 2002*, Stakes. Jyväskylä: Gummerus.

Häyry, H. (1990) *Freedom, Autonomy and the Limits of Medical Paternalism*, Helsinki: University of Helsinki, Department of Philosophy.

Holmberg, R. (2001) 'En kartläggning av det svenska behandlingsystemet: IKB 1999', *Nordisk alkohol- & narkotikatdiskrift*, 18 (2): 190–7.

Hübner, L. (1991) *Missbruk och tvångsvård: de nordiska ländernas lagstiftning om vård av missbrukare utan eget samtycke*, Stockholm: Nordiska kontaktmannaorganet för narkotikafrågor.

Kaukonen, O. (2000) *Päihdepalvelut jakautuneessa hyvinvointivaltiossa* [Substance abuse services in a divided welfare state], Helsinki: National Research and Development Centre for Welfare and Health (Stakes), Research report 107.

Klingemann, H. and Hunt, G. (eds) (1998) *Drug Treatment Systems in an International Perspective. Drugs, Demons and Delinquents*, Thousand Oaks, London and New Delhi: Sage Publications.

Klingemann, H., Takala, J.-P. and Hunt, G. (eds) (1992) *Cure, Care, or Control. Alcoholism Treatment in Sixteen Countries*, Albany: State University of New York Press.

Kuhnle, S. and Selle, P. (eds) (1992) *Government and Voluntary Organizations*, Aldershot: Avebury.

Lehto, J. (1991) *Juoppojen professionaalinen auttaminen* [Professional help for drunkards], Helsinki: National Board for Social and Health Care.

—— (1994) 'Involuntary treatment of people with substance related problems in the Nordic countries', in M. Järvinen and A. Skretting (eds) *Missbruk och tvångsvård*, NAD-publikation nr 27, Helsinki: Hakapaino.

Lehto, J., Moss, N. and Rostgaard, T. (1999) 'Universal public care and health services', in M. Kautto, M. Heikkilä, B. Hvinden, S. Marklund and N. Ploug (eds) *Nordic Social Policy. Changing Welfare States*, London and New York: Routledge.

Lundström, T. and Wijkström, F. (1995) 'Från röst till service? Den svenska ideella sektorn i förändring', Stockholm: Sköndalsinstitutets skriftserie No. 4.

Mäkelä, K. (1988) 'Suomi ja sen hyvinvointivaltio, valtio ja sen Suomi' [Finland and its welfare state, the state and its Finland], *Tiede ja edistys* XIII (2): 88–96.

Månsson, S.-A. (2000) 'Kunnskapsutveckling inom sosialtjänsten och den akademiska forskningen' [The development of the knowledge base within social work and academic research], *Socionomen*, (8): 4–9.

Montin, S., Fridolf, M. and Sköldberg, T. (1993) 'Radikala organizationsförändringar i kommuner och landsting', SOU 1993: 73. *Rapport till Lokaldemokratikommittén 1993*, Stockholm.

Niemelä, P., Knuutinen, M., Hyvärinen, S., Kainulainen, S., Myllykangas, M. and Ryynänen, O.-P. (1995) *Sosiaali- ja terveydenhuollon priorisointi. Tutkimus priorisointiprosessista ja – näkemyksistä kunnissa*, [Priorities in social and health care services in Finland], Helsinki: National Research and Development Centre for Welfare and Health (Stakes), Reports 174.

Nuorvala, Y., Metso, L., Kaukonen, O. and Haavisto, K. (2000) 'Päihde-ehtoinen asiointi sosiaali- ja terveydenhuollossa 1995 ja 1999' [Intoxicant related services in social and health care 1995 and 1999], *Yhteiskuntapolitiikka* 66 (3): 265–76.

Nygren, R. (1990) 'Tvångsvård och rättsröta eller historien om riksdagens anstaltsombudsman', in P. H. Lindblom (ed.) *Process och exekution. Vänbok till Robert Broman*, Uppsala: Iustis förlag.

Olsson, B. (2001) 'Tungt narkotikamissbruk i Norden 1995–2000', in P. Kouvonen, P. Rosenqvist and A. Skretting (eds) *Bruk, missbruk, marknad och reaktioner. Narkotika i Norden 1995–2000*, NAD-publikation Nr 41, Helsingfors: Hakapaino.

Oscarsson, L. (2000) 'Den socialtjänstbaserade missbrukarvården under 1990-talet – förutsättningar, utveckling och behov', in SOU 2000: 38. *Välfärd, vård, omsorg.*

Palm, J. and Stenius, K. (2002) 'Sweden: integrated compulsory treatment', *European Addiction Research*, 8 (2): 69–77.

Premfors, R. (1998) 'Reshaping the democratic state: Swedish experiences in a comparative perspective', *Public Administration*, 76 (Spring Issue): 141–59.

Rose, N. (1995) 'Eriarvoisuus ja valta hyvinvointivaltion jälkeen' [Inequality and power after welfare state], in R. Eräsaari and K. Rahkonen (eds) *Hyvinvointivaltion tragedia. Keskustelua eurooppalaisesta hyvinvointivaltiosta*, Tampere: Gaudeamus.

Rosenqvist, P. and Kurube, N. (1992) 'Dissolving the Swedish alcoholism treatment system', in H. Klingemann, J.-P. Takala and G. Hunt (eds) *Cure, Care, or Control. Alcoholism Treatment in Sixteen Countries*, Albany: State University of New York Press.

Rosenqvist, P. and Stenius, K. (1986) 'Nya målgrupper för alkoholistvården', *Alkoholpolitik -Tidskrift för nordisk alkoholforskning*, 3 (4): 215–19.

Rosenqvist, P. and Takala, J.-P. (1987) 'Two experiences with lay boards: the emergence of compulsory treatment of alcoholics in Sweden and in Finland', *Contemporary Drug Problems*, 14 (1): 15–38.

Rothstein, B. (1992) *Den korporativa staten: intresseorgansiationer och statsförvaötning i svensk politik*, Stockholm: Norstedts juridik.

Socialstyrelsen (2000) *Vårdinsatser för vuxna missbrukare och övriga vuxna 1999*, Stockholm: Socialstyrelsen, www.sos.se/plus/statistsik.asp?mAmne=missbruk.

—— (2001) *Vårdinsatser för vuxna missbrukare enligt LVM*, Stockholm: Socialstyrelsen.

—— (2001a) *Förteckning över hem for vård eller boende & familjevårdsenheter 2001*, Stockholm: Socialstyrrelsen.

SOU 1961: 58 *Översyn av nykterhetsvården. Betänkande av nykterhetsvårdsutredningen*, Stockholm: Socialdepartementet.

Stakes (2000) National surveys of intoxicant-related cases in health and social services in Finland (years 1991, 1995 and 1999), unpubl. database, Helsinki: Stakes.

Stenius, K. (1999) *Privat och offentligt i svensk missbrukarvård. Arbetsfördelning, samverkan och styrning under 1900-talet*, Lund: Arkiv Förlag.

Takala, J.-P. and Lehto, J. (1992) 'Finland: the non-medical model reconsidered', in H. Klingemann, J.-P. Takala and G. Hunt (eds) *Cure, Care, or Control. Alcoholism Treatment in Sixteen Countries*, Albany: State University of New York Press.

Trydegård, G.-B. (2001) 'Välfärdstjenster till Salu: privatisering och alternation driftsformer under 1900-talet", in SOU 2001: 52. *Välfärdstjenster i omvandling.* Antologi från Kommiféen för Välfärdsbokslut. Stockholm.

Uusitalo, H. (1993) Pohjoismaisen hyvinvointivaltion arvot ja käytännöt [The values and practices of the Nordic welfare states], in J. O. Andersson, A. Hautamäki, R. Jallinoja, I. Niiniluoto and H. Uusitalo (eds) *Hyvinvointivaltio ristiaallokossa*, Helsinki: WSOY.

Yearbook of Alcohol and Drug Statistics 2002, Helsinki: Stakes.

9 After equality? Normative innovations from Lindbeck to Svegfors – towards a dynamic conservatism?[1]

Sven E. O. Hort

> At some rare moments a nation pauses to reflect on its future. Such moments usually occur in periods of decline and crisis. The ability of a nation to reconsider past decisions and rejuvenate itself is then put to the test. Today Sweden is experiencing its most serious crisis since the 1930s. How Sweden works to overcome the crisis will mark the country for decades to come. The form the solution will take is still an open question.
>
> (Lindbeck *et al.* 1994: 1)

Introduction: equality and the limits of the welfare state

In the pioneering work of the first generation of comparative welfare state research, the normative basis of the welfare state is highlighted already in the title of its prime example: *The Welfare State and Equality* (Wilensky 1975). This work reached above, but also summarized, very much the emergence of a research tradition that started with studies of individual nation states characterized by ambitious social programmes and institutions such as Germany and Britain. For instance, the German experience up to the Nazi regime had been thoroughly analysed by Karl Polanyi in *The Great Transformation* (1944). In the UK in particular, Marshall and Titmuss had scrutinized the normative foundations of the paths towards the modern welfare state. In historical and macro-sociological perspective the egalitarian welfare state stood out against the poverty and poor relief of earlier stages in the development of modern democracy and industrial capitalism. Equality is not the obvious, only or unquestionable answer to an investigation of the normative basis of the welfare state, but it definitely has its advocates (cf. Rothstein 1998). Wilensky was never alone, and long before the advent of the welfare state, from the American and French revolutions onwards, equality has been one of the hallmarks of modernity. Of course, there have been alternatives as well as complements such as democracy, efficiency, freedom/liberty, (social) justice, security and solidarity (or fraternity) associated with authors from de Toqueville to Okun (Bobbio 1996).

The egalitarian emphasis in comparative welfare state research of the 1970s resonated very well with the public mood of the time in advanced capitalist democracies. Equality became the ethos of the time – *zeitgeist* – and closely affiliated with welfare state developments in western Europe. In the new, recently emerged model welfare state of the time – without modesty Sweden – this approach had found its most outspoken proponent in a report presented to the Social Democratic Party Congress in 1969 – the *Equality Report* (1969) – by one of the original signatories behind the major programme of the 1930s for modernization and against poverty, Alva Myrdal. Together with her husband Gunnar, she was the author of *Kris i befolkningsfrågan* (1934) where they argued for a 'prophylatic' and 'productivist' social policy, and laid out a programme for large-scale welfare and anti-poverty reform. Thirty-four years later, the party had been in power almost uninterruptedly since the early 1930s and the national party campaigned vigorously and fairly successfully for (full) employment, (social) security and (cultural, social and economic) development without being outspoken on equality as such. Nevertheless, the party successfully reaches back to an older egalitarian theme in Scandinavian society and together with its main partner, the trade union movement, managed during the three decades of political rule to reach a consensus with other major social actors in Swedish society, in particular the farmers, the teetotallers and the employers. This programme came to a temporary halt in the 1960s when leading Social Democrats declared that the party basically had achieved its fundamental welfare objectives. However, this laid-back attitude was challenged by a younger generation in the party as well as by important sections of the trade union movement.

In the mid-1960s, the Social Democratic government appointed a State Commission – the Low Income Commission under the chairmanship of LO-economist Rudolf Meidner – to evaluate to what extent the goals had been reached, which also stimulated Scandinavian and Nordic welfare research and in particular the level of living approach. Simultaneously and parallel to this work by mainly economists, sociologists and statisticians, the Social Democratic party set up the Equality Commission headed by Alva Myrdal. Thereby the party in terms of normative catchwords went from (social) security (*trygghet*) – still the slogan of the 1968 election campaign together with (full) employment and (socio-technical) development – to what most people considered the more radical equality (Östberg 2002). Furthermore, the emphasis on equality and egalitarian living conditions was invested in the new 1974 Swedish Constitution, and this is further expanded upon in the 1980 social service legislation, actually introduced during one of the brief spells of a centre-right coalition government.

Thus, the institutions that were built during most part of the twentieth century were impregnated by the values of the working class movement and adjacent popular social mass movements including the farmers. Of course, also representatives of the 'Other'; the power elite or the economic and, much weaker, political bourgeoisie, had a say in this process that has often been called the Swedish model of compromise and consensus, of peaceful reform and social engineering (Therborn 1989). In particular the powerful representatives of 'big business' should be mentioned in this regard, and the Wallenbergs became the new 'royal family' or 'financier of the welfare state' as the title of the obituary was in the *Financial Times* in 1982 when Marcus Wallenberg jnr. passed away; like Lorenzo the great grandson of the founder of the dynasty (Olsson 2001).

In the first years of the new millennium Sweden is living during the reign of Marcus Wallenberg III, the Social Democratic Party is still in power and has so been for more than 60 out of 85 years of full democracy, or 19 out of the last 23. However, during the last two decades, in particular during the 1990s, Sweden and its welfare state – like other comparable welfare states – has gone through rough waters and it is a matter of dispute whether it is still alive and in good health (cf. Hort 2000, 2002, 2003). Is the pause over or is the nation still reflecting on its future? Obviously global power constellations have changed dramatically since the heyday of the Swedish model. Most researchers have come to the conclusion that the welfare state is still there though, in a comparative perspective pruned and downsized to a certain extent (Kuhnle 2000). How much and how far this process has gone is a bone of contention (Korpi and Palme 2003; Nordlund 2002; Björnsson 2001). And it is definitely a matter of dispute whether equality still is the normative basis of the welfare state (Åmark 2004). Is Sweden back to a glacial vision of the productivist social policy approach or is it still also a prophylactic and civilized version of workfare, the Lutheran work ethic of agrarian society before this was blended with the new (still Protestant according to Max Weber) work ethics of the social movements of industrial–capitalist society?

The Lindbeck Commission: economic efficiency and growth

Soon after the extraordinary monetary crisis in late 1992 that forced the new non-socialist government to opt for an accord – a consensus agreement with far-reaching consequences for future policy options – with the traditional political rulers of Sweden, the Social Democrats since September 1991 in opposition for a consecutive three years period, the Bildt (1991) government appointed a State Commission to search for a new welfare model, to define the scope of government welfare provision and to find new ways of financing public welfare. The Commission was headed by the chairperson of the selection committee of the Bank of Sweden Laureate in memory of Alfred Nobel, the economist Assar Lindbeck. Lindbeck was not only an academically established professor and a World Bank expert but also a former Social Democrat, for a long time closely affiliated with Olof Palme, who had left the party in protest against the so-called wage earner fund proposal(s) (cf. Sassoon 1996). The Commission also included one Norwegian and one Danish economist as well as a well-known Swedish political scientist, Olof Petersson. The secretary was drawn from the inner circles of the Ministry of Finance, Per Molander, an intellectual of the *kanslihushögern* (the Swedish equivalent of a Whitehall Right; cf. Molander 1994), for a while at the most respected think tank of Big Business (SNS) as well as a former secretary-general of the Ministry's own think tank, the Expert Group for Studies in Public Economics, which had produced a flow of controversial studies of Swedish welfare policies and practices during the 1980s and well into the 1990s. The Lindbeck or Economics Commission produced a final report to the Government as well as some 40 expert reports published in two appendices volumes (Ekonomikommissionen 1993). Less than one year after its domestic release, the final report appeared in English as *Turning Sweden Around* (Lindbeck *et al.* 1994).

The outcome of the work of the Commission was an analysis that pointed out a number of macro-economic policy mistakes and institutional 'failures' during the last quarter of the twentieth century. Sweden had fallen from a top position among the advanced capitalist countries and since the mid-1970s 'lagged behind' in terms of economic growth and prosperity. Added to this was the unemployment crisis of the early 1990s. The focus was on economic efficiency and the Commission was mainly preoccupied with the negative and unintended consequences of a huge public sector for efficiency and growth. The Swedish welfare state was in great need of rejuvenation, renovation and transformation. It was no longer a solution to the problem, but a source of the problem as defined by the analytical framework of the Commission. For the Commission nothing in the old model was sacred – except economic growth – and pointed out 113 wide-ranging proposals to adapt and adjust existing policies and institutions to new socio-economic circumstances. The proposals spanned between major macro-economic policy recommendations and larger institutional changes to more immediate but mundane directives to various government bodies such as the National Board of Education. I happened to be at the Ministry of Finance with some 30–40 officials in front of the TV monitor at the Department of Macroeconomics when the main report from the Commission was delivered and made public, and even the most loyal civil servant smiled for a second when the Commission came to one of its final proposals: more homework for pupils in elementary and secondary schools. Also the proposal to raise the educational level of journalists made people raise their eyebrows.

However, at the heart of the work of the Commission was various ways to improve macro-economic efficiency. Furthermore, Lindbeck had for long been preoccupied with the marginal tax rate and tax wedges, which continued to influence the analysis of the Commission. The Commission recognized that there were fundamental, systematic problems in Swedish society, which had been building up over a long period of time, and that comprehensive reform was necessary. Gone was the old rhetoric on equal distribution of material resources and full employment. Instead, the proposals from the Commission can be seen as a continuation and prolongation of a number of changes in government policies at the turn of the last decade of the last century: such as the change of government top priority from full employment to low inflation as outlined by the Social Democratic government in the autumn of 1990 when the Swedish application for membership in the EU was announced by Prime Minister Ingvar Carlsson (2003), the general tax reform of the early 1990s, and simultaneously the Bank of Sweden became more independent from the government in running monetary policy. The Lindbeck Commission continued along these lines when it proposed major institutional changes such as a cap on government expenditure, a limitation in the power of parliament to impose budgetary expansion, and abandonment of any attempt at fine-tuning (a major blow to the earlier reigning Rehn-Meidner model of macro-economic steering). Furthermore, it proposed a continuation of the temporary freezing of local government expenditure. Income must meet outlays and no concessions should be made to public borrowing, was the main message from the Commission which devoted many pages to a discussion of the need for a balanced budget and which made many suggestions as to how to achieve such a balance. Hence, government income – high taxes or huge deficits – should not be allowed to hamper economic growth.

The question was whether this approach signified a return to the prophylatic and productivist policies of the 1930s and 1950s? The report of the Lindbeck Commission was in many left-leaning quarters regarded as a blueprint for a neo-liberal welfare regime change – an adjustment to global macro-economic trends and a reversal of an earlier Swedish socio-economic model. This is probably too rapidly drawing conclusions, which ignore the fact that the members of the Commission were closer to equilibrium thinking than doctrinaire positioning without subscribing to artful, but sterile compromise. Although the Commission was driven by a clear vision close to the free market approach of academic economics – 'capitalism cannot function without capitalists – despite apparent hopes to that effect among some Swedish social reformers' (Lindbeck *et al.* 1994: 96) – it underlined that both the public and the private sector in Sweden were marked by significant inefficiencies. It proposed a number of measures to improve competition in the private sector, but in focus was the public sector, in particular social insurance, which should be based on actuarial principles. Apart from the above-mentioned proposals, the Commission also advocated more use of the price mechanism in the public sector and recommended incentives to reward efficient (but still publicly financed) welfare producers as well as wider opportunities for consumer choice in childcare, education, health and old age care. Labour market reform was also on the agenda with the aim of letting work pay off. To end, the Commission argued for a smaller welfare state, a slimmed down version close to the original productivist – perhaps less so prophylatic – model of the 1930 to the 1950s, i.e. 'before equality'.

The Social State project: civil society and human dignity

At the end of the 1980s and early 1990s, the think tanks of big business in Sweden initiated a major academic project on the welfare state supported by a few major private foundations in Sweden after the Bank of Sweden Tercentenary Fund had denied it funding. In conjunction with the set-up of a private university in downtown Stockholm, these circles, through the City University, launched a project to provide a trenchant analysis and radical re-thinking of the aims, methods and effects of existing welfare programmes in Sweden. This project provided a much-needed boost to the idea of a private university in an otherwise public system of higher education. Privatization was possible, despite that this was done on the most rocky soil of neo-liberalism. The project was headed by one of the most internationally known Swedish sociologists and opinion researchers, Hans L. Zetterberg – for a short while also editor-in-chief of *Svenska Dagbladet* – but also included political scientists as well as historians, economists and social psychologists. Moreover, a number of intellectuals and political activists – mainly young neo-liberal student politicians – were also attached to the project. The main part of the Social State project, as the official name was, was produced and published during the latter part of the period of non-socialist government in the first half of the 1990s, *in toto* 14 books or booklets, and some minor reports, but its final report was published after the return to the helm of social democracy in late 1994 and more or less deliberately avoided by the intellectuals of the national party-cum-movement. At the concluding open seminar of this project, with the exception of the biographer of Per Albin Hansson, the cultural editor of the national weekly of the trade union movement and one or two low-ranking officials at the Ministry of Finance, the absence of people – academics as well as other professionals – from the centre-left of Swedish society was most visible.

The outcome of this project differed from the neo-liberal State Commission. If Lindbeck was close to the norms of the liberal market approach, it was another set of normative values that Zetterberg adhered to. To him, it was not the Anglo-Saxon free market ideals that governed his scrutiny of the social state, but the status-securing conservative, continental welfare model. Thus, the Esping-Andersen triad (see below) became a useful tool in polemics against the institutional, universal or social democratic welfare regime type. De-commodification and stratification, two key notions in the latter's analysis, were pitched against each other by

Zetterberg. De-commodification was the source of the problem as it contributed to the financial problems of the welfare state and undermined the Protestant work ethic necessary to support a big welfare state. Hence, Zetterberg leaned towards Max Weber's conceptions and in particular when he discussed stratification and status groups. However, the answer to this problem was not market liberalism and increased economic efficiency. Social bonding had to be rejuvenated, and to Zetterberg, *human dignity*, which is not provided by the market to most people, was essential to any modern society. Human dignity, and help to self help in groups of one's own discretion became the norm of the day. Instead of all-embracing universal state welfare schemes, Zetterberg advocated something similar to the continental model with its emphasis on selectivity and in-group solidarity relying on a mix of the subsidiarity principle and communitarian theory.

Hence, Zetterberg introduced the notions of civil society, welfare populations and social patronage. Civil society became an alternative to state and market provided welfare. According to Zetterberg in modern society there are four universal welfare populations – the young, the sick or disabled, the elderly and the destitute – as well as a number of special welfare populations, such as the unemployed. By calling support for a welfare population social patronage, he implied that social support should come from parts of society other than the state, for instance the market or civil society. Moreover, he emphasized that welfare populations from the start have a strong normative position in civil society. In any civil society and even the most advanced welfare state, it is an obvious and expected human action to help those that for various reasons deserve social support. In contrast, welfare populations have a weak position on the market as they are short of money, have few assets and social insurance has become a welfare state institution for strengthening the position of the welfare populations on the market. Thus, also in the explicitly critical perspective of Zetterberg, a country where the state has a large social patronage is defined as a social state, which is the more appropriate notion as state patronage is most often larger than pure 'welfare', while its normative foundation has also made its social scientists home-blind.

> Research in Sweden on the Swedish welfare state usually blissfully and tacitly takes its point of departure in those values of popular rhetoric which have come to dominate within the department and the institutions of public welfare and in the unions whose members run the welfare state. Swedish welfare researchers usually hold that any measures aiming at equality by means of state guaranteed rights are good. In our research the underlying principle has been that anything adding to human dignity is to be considered valuable, even if it does not always imply total equality.
>
> (Zetterberg 1997: 289)

Human dignity is, thus, the normative basis of this alternative approach to a more or less pure or maximalist system of state welfare. Human dignity has its natural foundation in civil society where people care for their next of kin or their neighbours. This is also the natural source of social solidarity and the popular social mass movements so typical of modern Scandinavian society. However, these pro-state movements have been so successful that they have made themselves more or less unnecessary as the state has taken over their role as welfare providers. The retreat of the state during the 1990s provided an excellent opportunity to rethink the optimal balance between the state, market and civil society. Explicitly referring to the continental welfare model, Zetterberg admitted that this is not less expensive than the Nordic welfare model but allows for a greater role for civil society and the market and welfare populations will have a more dignified existence in return for reasonable investments on the whole of society when an optimal division of labour has been achieved between civil society, the market and the state. The Zetterberg report can, parallel to the report from the Lindbeck Commission, be regarded as a blueprint for a conservative welfare model – an accommodation to trends towards European integration and an adjustment to continental welfare policy – and human dignity is explicitly contrasted with equality as a value underpinning this model.

The LO Social Justice Commission: power/knowledge

In the aftermath of the Swedish unemployment crisis of the early 1990s and the earthquake election of 1991, the worst electoral result for the Social Democrats since 1928 and which ousted the party from power if only, as it turned out, for three consecutive years, the powerful blue collar Swedish Trade Union Confederation (LO) initiated another welfare reform project, or perhaps more accurate a no-to-welfare cutbacks project, the Committee of Inquiry of Justice as the formal name was. At the LO headquarters Ingemar Lindberg, a former under-secretary of state at the Ministry of Social Affairs, was in charge of the project, in everyday parlance the Social Justice Commission, and he reported directly to the chairman of the LO. Lindberg had during the late 1980s spent a sojourn at the comparative welfare state research project at the Stockholm Institute for Social Research under the direction of Walter Korpi and his associates, most notably, of course, Esping-Andersen. At LO, Lindberg gathered a broad group of researchers, intellectuals and activists who wrote against the current, and in the social policy reform tradition of the (old) labour movement. For instance, Lindberg managed to recruit the controversial secretary of the State Low Income Commission of the 1960s, the former LO economist Per Holmberg, who was fired as Commission secretary by the Social Democrat government in the early 1970s. Also the former head of the Economic Analysis Department of the LO, Clas Erik Odhner was involved in the work of the Social Justice Commission. But Lindberg also managed to involve such intellectuals as the novelist Maj-Gull Axelsson, who wrote on living and working conditions at home and abroad for this commission. Thus, Lindberg succeeded in developing a global perspective on what hitherto had been looked upon, at least among the traditional left, as aspects of the national welfare state (Lindberg 1998; cf. Svallfors 2000). This occurred during the years of membership negotiations between Sweden and the European Union, an entity considered a threat to the Swedish welfare state by many left-leaning Swedish social democrats, and during the referendum campaign in the autumn of 1994 several well-known intellectuals close to the Social Justice project actively supported a 'No-to-Europe' vote when growth was pitched against welfare and the elite stood against the people.

More important, Lindberg and his associates managed to mobilize the trade union movement and during the years 1992–1995 involved almost 30,000 local activists in some 2,500 groups, in meeting and study circles. The Social Justice Commission was a very different undertaking from the rest of the band (four commissions/projects discussed in this article). Not only did it take issue with welfare issues such as an unfair distribution of resources and growing social cleavages, it also raised the issue of power in society and within its own organization/movement, the trade unions and the Social Democrat Party. The outcome of this inquiry was not a blueprint for a new welfare project on the part of the labour movement and other, 'new' social movements. Instead, it was a rebuttal of the neo-liberal approach by the proponents of the (outgoing?) model.

Nevertheless, the LO inquiry managed to move the normative focus of the traditional welfare project: from national equality of the 1960s and 1970s to global and local – or glocal – social justice. Isiah Berlin's negative and positive freedoms – fair play on the markets as well as in jurisdiction and politics, and freedom from oppression (emancipation and self-determination) – were merged with the fair distribution approach of the traditional left into a triangular concept of social justice. Furthermore, this approach included a strong adherence to gender equality. Actually, the Commission rejected the traditional emphasis on class:

> The conflicts between social classes and between the sexes should instead be seen as two sources of oppression, equal in significance. This involves far-reaching change in basic attitudes and conduct. This change must in turn lead to an open discussion about changes in the trade union movement's methods of work and ways of operating.
>
> (LO 1996: 5–6)

Added to this: 'Oppression has many faces. Disparagement and oppression of immigrants is a social conflict which the Swedish trade union movement must also see and react to' (ibid: 6). Class, gender and ethnicity on equal terms were new to Sweden in the mid-1990s (Jensen and Mahon 1992; cf. Earles 2004).

Instead of social surveys and *enquêtes* LO opted for meetings with specific themes – focus group meetings – and thereby managed to give voice to a fair number of people who perceived themselves as disadvantaged and never listened to by their own leaders who were looked upon as part of the elite. Despite the fact that this Commission did not produce what most academics would regard as new knowledge, together with the appearance of the new urban middle class women's movement, *stödstrumporna*, this blue-collar mobilization definitely contributed to the downfall of the non-socialist government in the election of 1994 (Stark 1997; Earles 2004). Together, this class-genus mobilization from below gave the Social Democrats a great advantage in the election campaign despite the fact that the party in advance of election day advocated harsh measures – such as cutbacks in welfare benefits – to come to terms with the unemployment and state financial crisis.

This mobilization is perhaps the most obvious sign of the paradox of the 'normative turn' from equality and egalitarian policies towards top priority for budgetary consolidation and welfare cutbacks. The immediate impact of this mobilization on welfare policy is hard to see – the new Social Democratic government of 1994 pursued retrenchment policies – but this mobilization continued also during the first years of the SD government, in particular within the movement and at the party Congress in March 1996. The main report of the work of the Justice Commission, however, was presented at the LO (TUC) Congress in September 1996. The Social Justice report became a focal point at this Congress. The cooperation between the trade unions and the party was rejuvenated through this mobilization and after the next election in 1998 – when the SD government managed to remain in power despite a defeat almost as great as in 1991 (but its junior partners, the Greens and the Left Party, gained) – the government set up a new State Commission to investigate welfare developments over the full decade.

The report from the trade union Social Justice Commission can in contrast to the Lindbeck and Zetterberg reports be looked upon as a defence of the uniqueness of the Swedish welfare model in the context of a new global order and a counterattack on those who one way or another just wanted to adjust to the current wave of globalization and regional European integration. Glocal social justice was put forward as an alternative to the liberal emphasis on economic efficiency/growth as well as to the conservative human dignity. While the LO project comes close to the spirit of the radicalism of the third way of the 1980s and the normative foundation of the social democratic regime type, the slow but gradual departure from this 'normative regime' is visible in the next State Commission to be scrutinized.

The Palme Welfare Balance Sheet Commission: towards a fourth road?

In February 1999, half a year after the party's severe national election defeat – in the postwar period comparable only to the 1991 earthquake result – a rejuvenated Social Democratic government appointed a State Commission consisting of seven respected social science researchers – three women, four men, among the former the coming Minister of Environment Lena Sommestad (1998), a Ph.D. in Economic History and then the Director of the Institute for Future Studies – under the chairmanship of Joakim Palme, a younger, but close colleague of Korpi and Esping-Anderson, and the eldest son of the late Olof Palme (PM until his untimely death in 1986). The government called a non-parliamentary group of researchers, not the traditional broad-based parliamentary commission. Thus, this Commission can be compared with another State Commission from the early 1990s, the above-mentioned Lindbeck Commission, set up in order to discuss the normative basis of the contemporary welfare state. Moreover, this Commission was given the mandate and resources to scrutinize welfare trends and to evaluate welfare developments in the 1990s. Over a period of two and a half years, the Commission published – with the support of the social indicator research community as well as the major producers of social statistics in Sweden – 13 reports on various aspects of welfare and welfare policy plus a final report delivered in October 2001 (Palme *et al.* 2002; Hort 2002). Apart from housing conditions and housing policy – which virtually disappeared in Sweden in the early 1990s – the Commission succeeded in covering all the relevant social policy areas.

Thus, the explicit motivation for the appointment of the Commission was, apart from the mobilization within the labour movement, the concern raised in state and society about the magnitude of the effects of the crisis of the 1990s on the welfare of individuals and families living and working in Sweden. Since the economic crisis also triggered change in virtually all areas of social policy, the question how this affected the nature of the Swedish welfare model was also on the agenda. Implicitly, thus, the normative foundation of the Swedish welfare state came to the fore.

The outcome of this State Commission was a massive balance sheet comparing the situation of welfare resources in Sweden at the beginning and the end of the 1990s. The Commission explicitly and closely followed the Scandinavian tradition of welfare research with its emphasis on availability of and access to material resources. Although without taking into account the enormous cyclical variations over the years, the Commission managed to paint a picture of shortcomings and achievements of the Swedish welfare state focusing on the distribution of resources in the early and late part of the decade respectively along lines of class, gender, generation and ethnicity. There was also a special focus on disadvantaged groups such as lone mothers, drug addicts and homeless people (the only avenue into housing conditions). In conclusion, the Commission argued that the empirical analysis pointed at both negative and positive signs:

> Increased problems could be observed with regard to; employment, working-life stress and ill-health. On the negative side, the disfavourable development for disadvantaged groups; youth, single mothers and immigrants, should definitely be added ... In other aspects of welfare, improvements could be registered; real wages, levels of education, and mortality are good examples.
>
> (Palme *et al.* 2002: 15)

Furthermore, the Commission evaluated the impact of the balance sheet on the Swedish model:

> Full employment, one of the cornerstones of the model, was not restored from mass-unemployment during the course of the decade. Also, the active labour market policy, which is often associated with the full-employment strategy, could not accommodate the rapid increase in unemployment. When it comes to social policy, the large number of changes that made provisions less generous is perhaps the most characterizing feature of the 1990s. Yet it would be misleading to conclude that the model has been abandoned. Universal social services and benefits, as well as earnings-related social insurances are still dominating the system. However, a number of decisions, as well as non-decisions, might trigger more systematic change in the longer run by changing the interest formation around social policy institutions. It might be that non-decisions are most important in a model-perspective. As ceilings in most systems are not changed, and real wages increase, this means that an increasing number of citizens have earnings above the ceilings. This in turn might in the long run transform the earnings-related system into a flat-rate one, presumably shifting the responsibility of insurance to private schemes ... the sustainability of the particularities of the Swedish model of welfare remains an open question.
>
> (Palme *et al.* 2002: 15–16)

Although the starting point of the Commission was the traditional Scandinavian approach to welfare and its emphasis on equal distribution, the introduction of the conceptual tool 'balance sheet' points towards influence from business economics and a market driven approach. Thus, it is probably fair to say, that despite its explicit adherence to the notion of equality as the normative basis of the welfare state, the investigation of welfare developments over the 1990s implicitly came to regard (social) security and fighting poverty as the over-arching objectives of welfare policy. Target groups such as the homeless return to the centre of stage. Thus, there is both a tendency towards emphasizing the possibility of basic security – flat-rate schemes – combined with private insurers – voluntary welfare – and a focus on disadvantaged – target – groups close to the focus of the residual welfare model.

The report by Palme *et al.* is no blueprint for reform, neither a deviation from the essence of traditional social democratic welfare policies (Lindberg 2002). However, it makes or takes a subtle detour away from the upheld regime type of 'the three worlds of welfare capitalism' towards a more diffuse variety of alternatives as proposed by Korpi and Palme in their 1998 article in the *American Sociological Review* on the paradoxes of distribution into or back to the welfare mix of the 1980s. The Swedish welfare state is in flux somewhere between the basic security, corporatist and encompassing models. Thus, this envisages the normative turn of the most recent Swedish State Commission dealing with the (re-) organization of social welfare. If the Social Justice Commission tried to stick to the third way, the Welfare Balance Sheet Commission tried to find a fourth way away from and beyond the obstacles of the 1990s – or back to the future?

The Svegfors Responsibility Commission: towards dynamic social conservatism or a fifth normative model?

After the most recent general election of 2002, a better showing by the national party which cemented the social democratic grip on power, again with the help of its junior partners in the centre and to the left, the government in 2003 appointed another State Commission to exclusively deal with the various levels of responsibility in the organization of welfare by state and society. This time, the government did not appoint a die-hard Social Democrat, but one of its recently appointed County Governors – historically a most respected position within the Swedish civil service – namely Mats Svegfors. Svegfors, once a close ally of former Prime Minister Carl Bildt and an intimate collaborator of Gösta Bohman, the successful leader of the Swedish Moderate Party of the 1970s and early 1980s and former Minister of Economics in the first postwar non-social democratic government. In the early 1980s, Svegfors became the CEO of the main think tank of the Swedish employers, and later editor-in-chief of its main daily *Svenska Dagbladet* where he became a most visible commentator on Swedish politics and public issues, and also frequently on air in various TV channels. Thus, he never fully subscribed to neo-liberalism, but explicitly advocated a conservative interpretation of the communicative action-dialogue of Jürgen Habermas (cf. Svegfors 2000) and from the Responsibility Commission there are obvious links back to the intellectual powerhouses of the 1980s and early 1990s.

This State Commission – the Responsibility Commission as it official name is – is closely linked to another State Commission on constitutional affairs under the leadership of Per Nuder, Minister of Coordination in the Government and, in reality, second-in-command after Göran Persson (1998), Swedish PM since 1996, with whom Nuder has worked closely for almost a decade. Svegfors reports on and off to Nuder. Thus, there is an explicit link between the preparation for the future formal order and the social engineering or creation of a future social order. Of course, it is still an open question if such a joint venture will take off, but the links between government and opposition, the right and the left, are obvious and rather close. However, already during the existence and operation of the two commissions, the Prime Minister in an interview with the main Swedish daily during the spring of 2004 hinted at the possibility of a third state commission solely devoted to the financing of the welfare state (*Dagens Nyheter* April 10, 2004). Of course, tax policy and the construction, and implementation, of innovative levies are at the heart of the big welfare state, but in late June 2004 Svegfors' mandate was finally extended 'to follow in the tracks of Axel Oxenstierna', the seventeenth century founder of the Swedish public administration (Nuder 2004; cf. Wetterberg 2002). The timing of this extension is noteworthy: just two weeks after an extremely serious defeat for the pro-EU forces and, in particular, the social democratic leadership in the European Parliament election.

In late 2003 the Svegfors Commission produced a first, preliminary report on governance or the responsibility of various authorities and main actors in Swedish state and civil society: 'Developmental power for sustainable welfare' (SOU 2003). But the emphasis on the notion of innovation capacity for sustainable welfare – and, furthermore, social responsibility – is a striking sign of a gradual policy turn of the Swedish welfare state away from full state responsibility towards a mix of individual, group and organizational responsibility for sustainable welfare at various levels of society. Moreover, this is an indication of a normative turn away from the ethos of the left towards the centre and right of intellectual reasoning. To use the language of innovation research, this is the dynamic conservatism of twenty-first century Swedish social democracy. The notion of scarcity is fundamental to an understanding of this approach. New ways of dealing with the problem of distributing scarce resources are, thus, at the heart of the work of the Commission. It is in this context that notions of innovative capacity, productivity growth and solidaristic responsibility have to be evaluated.

In particular focus are the welfare producers, i.e. local government, and the division of responsibility between central and local government in the production of welfare. The concrete ambition of the Commission is to develop dynamic strategies to ensure an equivalent level of public services and equal treatment of citizens throughout the country. Moreover, it will try to enhance cooperation between various government-financed agencies including mainly project financing through the EU, and welfare service producers at the local level. In a second round, it will consider the possibility to abolish the county councils and find a new division of responsibility at the level of local authority and in particular regarding health care and overall regional development. Hence, innovative design and productivity growth are key issues in this context. Likewise, the Commission has also made explicit deliberations on social obligations and individual responsibility, capacity-building and involvement of citizens in welfare service production. Furthermore, the Commission stresses the necessity to consider a change in public sector commitments as demand for public welfare provision will continue to grow in particular due to demography. It is within these parameters that the citizen is not just a welfare beneficiary or client but also a responsible elector and taxpayer, i.e. a subscriber to the Lutheran work ethic on Sundays as well as workdays.

Thus, this third State Commission under scrutiny in this chapter points to the influence of not only the most recent investigation into the distribution of welfare but also the alternatives and rethinking of the early 1990s – from Lindbeck and Zetterberg to the right to Lindberg and Palme to the left. Instead of the early visions of neo-liberal and neo-conservative strands, and the defence of the left as expressed by the Social Justice and the Welfare Balance Sheet Commissions, the Svegfors Commission tries to transcend the different ethos of left and right into a realist-provisional utopia of *Lagom.* Thus, scarcity and responsibility are linked with solidarity, i.e. social responsibility at a time of scarce public resources. Whether this vision of the future will be a fifth 'normative welfare model', or no more than a preparation for conflictual compromise and a middle ground between the main political parties is to early to tell.

Concluding remarks: a normative turn or social innovations – towards a new conflictual consensus?

Efficiency, growth, human dignity, social justice, (social) security (*trygghet*), (social) responsibility or welfare in itself – none of these catchwords have so far managed to fully replace equality as the normative foundation of the welfare state. Nevertheless, over a 15-year period, gradually a normative turn has occurred in Sweden as well as in other advanced welfare states. In Sweden, is this a sign that the nation state has successfully reconsidered past decisions and been able to rejuvenate itself? Furthermore, can this mix of alternative notions be seen in the perspective of a culmination of welfare state developments and model-building that occurred in the late 1980s in which the Swedish welfare state was still presented as the epitome of the gospel of equality, de-commodification and social rights?

In 1990, the second generation of comparative welfare state research made its imprint through the publication of the celebrated work by Gösta Esping-Andersen: *The Three Worlds of Welfare Capitalism* in which Sweden was singled out as the archetype of the social democratic welfare state model. That year also saw the first signs of a major breakdown of the strength of the Swedish working class movement with the walkout of the Minister of Finance K. O. Feldt (1991) and the demise of the first Ingvar Carlsson (2003) cabinet (cf. Andersson 1993; Petersson 1999). One year later, the Social Democrats suffered their worst election result since 1928. Back in power from September 1994, social democracy has continued at the helm and managed to overcome election results as bad as 1991. As mentioned, the European Parliament election of June 2004 was another major blow to the Social Democratic leadership.

According to Esping-Andersen, no longer was there one arch-typical welfare state, but several alternatives, three to be exact: the conservative, the liberal and the social-democratic regime type. Instead of Titmuss' three models of social policy – the institutional, the achievement–performance and the residual model – Esping-Andersen distinguished between three welfare regimes. Instead of historical stages in the development of citizenship rights and the modern welfare state, the typologies developed by Marshall and Titmuss were used as starting-points to look for differences and similarities between contemporary welfare states. While the major work of the first generation of comparative welfare state research took 64 countries as its empirical observations, although 22 advanced welfare states were singled out for more intensive scrutiny (see above Wilensky 1975; cf. Wilensky 2002 – which covers 18 advanced welfare states), Esping-Andersen confined himself to 18 of the latter type – though not exactly the same as the late Wilensky sample – and left out the rest of the world which during the last decade, much more than in the first generation of this type of research, has come to the forefront in comparative welfare state and global social policy research (Gough and Wood 2004; Kuhnle and Hort 2004).

In the work of Esping-Andersen, the social democratic regime type was contrasted with the conservative and liberal ones which roughly corresponds to Titmuss' three models of social policy – the residual, the industrial achievement–performance and the institutional – and fundamentally there is also a correspondence to Marshall's three types of citizenship rights (civil, political and social). While the equality of the first social democratic regime type is unquestioned by Esping-Andersen and elaborated through the concept of de-commodification, by Korpi and Palme through the concept of social rights, the Conservative model cultivates hierarchy and status – highlighted through the central concept of stratification – and the liberal economic efficiency and individual dualisms. Despite considerable admiration for the clarity and simplicity of the *Three Worlds of Welfare Capitalism*, there was widespread discontent with the ambiguities involved in this kind of complexity reduction, not least among feminist researchers in this field (cf. Arts and Gelissen 2002). In the aftermath of the three worlds, several researchers from various parts of the world suggested a minor enlargement of the number of ideal-types, in general from three to four or five.

I have already alluded to the proposal by Korpi and Palme in their two articles in the *American Sociological Review* and *American Political Science Review*, respectively (1998, 2003), in which they at a slightly different level of analysis present five ideal-typical models of social insurance institutions. Looking back on the initial work of Korpi on social policy in advanced welfare states in which he subscribed to a dichotomy based on the residual versus the institutional model (1980), this is a substantial enlargement of the number of models. Apart from the residual or liberal type and the corporatist or conservative type, Korpi and Palme recently also put forward another minimalist type called 'voluntary state subsidized' as well as two types close to the universal or social democratic model namely the 'basic security' and the 'encompassing' models respectively, the latter one, of course, the one that comes closest to the old egalitarian model. With only 18 cases at their disposal, the enlargement of models from three to five simultaneously both sharpen and dilute the modelling. The encompassing model still has its normative counterpart at the level of ideal-types, at another level of analysis the slow, but gradual, development of the Swedish case points in other directions: towards the withering away of equality as the normative guide to the advanced welfare state.

Moreover, while the work of Esping-Andersen is founded on the empirical and theoretical research by, in particular, Walter Korpi, also the surrounding research environment with projects such as the one headed by Peter Flora (1986–1987) on 12 western European welfare states or the state-centred approach advocated by American researchers in this field (cf. Skocpol and Amenta 1986) paved the way for diversity and innovation on the normative side. In particular Flora tried to evade the Titmuss spatial temptation, half a page is devoted to the modelling business in the Introduction to *Growth to Limits* (1986–1987: XXI), and instead rested on the temporal aspects of the nation-building and state-formation approach developed by Stein Rokkan (cf. Flora *et al.* 1999). Critical to the welfare backlash perspective – 'primarily a protest against taxation and bureaucracy, and much less against social benefits and public services' (Flora 1986–1987: XXIV), nevertheless the theme of limits to welfare state expansion – and the possibility of institutional adaptation and reform – was early on exposed by Flora. The accelerated growth of the welfare state during the 1960s and early 1970s had already, in the late 1970s, been succeeded by a much slower pace of development. The challenges posed to the welfare state were rather similar throughout western Europe, and despite the diversity, Flora emphasized the common origins of the European welfare state. To him, (social) security, and solidarity, much more than equality, stand out as the common landmark of welfare state development.

Thus, the role of equality as the normative foundation of the welfare state in policy-making as well as in comparative social research probably reflects a specific period, the golden age and its aftermath, and also shows the strength of (some of) the dynamic social forces behind the welfare state. In Sweden, this theme reached a peak in the late 1960s and early 1970s and managed to make its imprint also on the international level. The egalitarian impulse is still there but pronounced in other words, and deeds. Sweden has not (yet) turned around in normative terms, in that sense 'the nation' is still conservative, but the struggle over the leifmotif of the welfare state over a 15 years period illustrated above through the innovative epigraphs of five major 'welfare reform' projects points towards a new era 'after equality'.

Note

1 I would like to thank all of those who over the years have provoked me in writings, public discussions or through oral and written communications. A complete listing would be impossible. However, apart from the editors of this book (cf. Chapters 1 and 2 of this volume) and the participants in the Bergen seminar in May 2002, this time it is fair to mention Erik Allardt (1989), Rita Liljeström and Hans L. Zetterberg. Furthermore, outside Scandinavia Sang-Hoon Ahn (2003), Jolanta Aidukatite (2003), Daniel Cohn, Rebecca van Voorhis and Neil Gilbert inspired continuous (re-)writing of a comparative perspective on welfare policy in Sweden.

References

Ahn, S.-H. and Hort, S. E. O. (2003) 'The welfare state in Sweden', in C. Aspalter (ed.) *Welfare Capitalism around the World*, Hong Kong: Casa Verde.

Aidukaite, J. (2003) 'From universal system of social policy to particularistic? The case of the Baltic states', *Journal of Communist and Post-Communist Studies*, 36: 405–26.

Allardt, E. (1989) 'Recent developments in Scandinavian sociology', *Annual Review of Sociology*, 15: 31–45.

Åmark, K. (2004) 'Makt, normer och aktörer i aktuell nordisk välfärdsstatshistorisk forskning', *Arkiv för studier i arbetarrörelsens historia*, (92) (in press).

Andersson, S. (1993) *I de lugnaste vatten...*, Stockholm: Tiden.

Arts, W. and Gelissen, J. (2002) 'Three worlds of welfare capitalism or more?', *Journal of European Social Policy*, 12 (2) (May): 137–58.

Bildt, C. (1991) *Hallänning, svensk, Europe*, Stockholm: Bonniers.

Björnsson, A. (2001) 'Systemskiften – en explorative essä', Report No. 35, Göteborg: Förvaltningshögskolan.

Bobbio, N. (1996) *Right and Left*, Cambridge: Polity Press.

Carlsson, I. (2003) *Så tänkte jag – politik och dramatik*, Stockholm: Hjalmarson & Högberg.

Earles, K. (2004) 'The gendered effects of the reregulation of the Swedish welfare state', *Socialism and Democracy*, 18 (1): 107–34.

Ekonomikommissionen (1993) *Nya villkor för ekonomi och politik. Ekonomikommissionens förslag*, Stockholm: Finansdepartementet (SOU 1993:16 med Bilaga 1–2).

Esping-Andersen, G. (1990) *The Three Worlds of Welfare Capitalism*, Cambridge: Polity Press.

Feldt, K.-O. (1991) *Alla dessa dagar*, Stockholm: Norstedts.

Flora, P. (ed.) (1986–1987) *Growth to Limits – The Development of the West European Welfare State Since World War II.* Vols I, II and IV, Berlin: Walther de Gruyter.

Flora, P., Kuhnle, S. and Urwin, D. (1999) *State Formation, Nation-Building and Mass Politics in Europe: The Theory of Stein Rokkan*, Oxford: Oxford University Press.

Gough, I. and Wood, G. (eds) (2004) *Insecurity and Welfare Regimes in Asia, Africa and Latin America*, Cambridge: Cambridge University Press.

Hort, S. E. O. (2000) 'Sweden – from a generous to a stingy welfare state?', in N. Gilbert (ed.) *Targeting Social Benefits*, New Brunswick: Transaction.

—— (2002) 'Bokslut över Välfärdsbokslut', *Tidsskrift for velferdsforskning*, 5 (3): 168–73.

—— (2003) 'Back on track – to the future? The making and remaking of the Swedish welfare state in the 1990s', in N. Gilbert and R. Van Voorhis (eds) *Changing Patterns of Social Protection*, New Brunswick: Transaction.

Jensen, J. and Mahon, R. (1992) 'Representing solidarity: class, gender and the crisis in Social Democratic Sweden', *New Left Review*, (201): 76–100.

Korpi, W. (1980) 'Social policy and distributional conflicts in the capitalist democracies', *West European Politics*, 3 (3).

Korpi, W. and Palme, J. (1998) 'The paradox of redistribution and strategies of equality: welfare state institutions, inequality and poverty in the western countries', *American Sociological Review*, Vol. 63 (5): 661–87.

—— (2003) 'New politics and class politics in the context of austerity and globalization: welfare state regress in 18 countries 1975–95', *American Political Science Review*, 97 (3): 425–46.

Kuhnle, S. (ed.) (2000) *Survival of the European Welfare State*, London and New York: Routledge.

Kuhnle, S. and Hort, S. E. O. (2004) 'The developmental welfare state in Scandinavia: lessons to the developing world', in H. J. Kwon (ed.) *Social Policy in a Developmental Context*, Geneva: UNRISD.

Lindbeck, A., Molander, P., Persson, T., Petersson, O., Sandmo, A., Swedenborg, B. and Thygesen, N. (1994) *Turning Sweden Around*, Cambridge: MIT Press.

Lindberg, I. (1998) *Välfärdens idéer*, Stockholm: Atlas.

—— (2002) *Ett bokslut över välfärden*, Stockholm: Arena.

LO (1996) *Kongressrapport: Rättvisa och arbete*, Stockholm: Landsorganisationen.

Molander, P. (1994) *Akvedukten vid Zaghouan*, Stockholm: Atlantis.

Myrdal, A. (1969) *Jämlikhet*, Stockholm: Prisma.

Myrdal, A. and Myrdal, G. (1934) *Kris i befolkningsfrågan*, Stockholm: Bonniers.

Nordlund, A. (2002) 'Resilient welfare states – Nordic welfare state development in the late 20th century', Umeå: Department of Sociology (Dissertation Series no. 27).

Nuder, P. (2004) 'Pröva om landstingen behövs', *Dagens Nyheter*, 28 June 2004.

Olsson, U. (2001) *Furthering a Fortune: Marcus Wallenberg – Swedish Banker and Industrialist 1899–1982*, Stockholm: Ekerlind.

Östberg, K. (2002) *1968 – När allt var i rörelse*, Stockholm: Prisma.

Palme, J., Bergmark, Å., Bäckman, O., Estrada, F., Fritzell, J., Lundberg, O., Sjöberg, O. and Szebehely, M. (2002) 'Welfare trends in Sweden: balancing the books for the 1990s', *Journal of European Social Policy*, 12 (4): 329–46.

Petersson, T. G. (1999) *Resan till mars*, Stockholm: Bonniers.

Polanyi, K. (1944) *The Great Transformation*, New York: Basic Books.

Rothstein, B. (1998) *Just Institutions Matters: The Moral and Political Logic of the Universal Welfare State*, Cambridge: Cambridge University Press.

Sassoon, D. (1996) *Hundred Years of Socialism: The West European Lefty in the Twentieth Century*, London: I. B. Tauris.

Skocpol, T. and Amenta, E. (1986) 'States and social policies', *Annual Review of Sociology*, 12: 131–57.

Sommestad, L. (1998) 'Privat eller offentlig välfärd? Ett genusperspektiv på välfärdsstatens historiska formering', *Historisk tidskrift*, (4): 48–64.

—— (2003) *Utvecklingskraft för hållbar välfärd*, Stockholm: Ministry of Finance (SOU 2003: 132).

Stark, A. (1997) 'Swedish women', in J. Mitchell and A. Oakley (eds) *Women and Social Policy*, London: Routledge.

Svallfors, S. (2000) *Sidospår*, Umeå: Borea.

Svegfors, M. (2000) 'Sju teser om demokratin och politiken år 2049', in A. Björnsson and P. Luthersson (eds) *Efter partistaten*, Stockholm: Hjalmarsson & Högberg.

Therborn, G. (1989) *Borgarklass och byråkrati*, Lund: Arkiv.

Wetterberg, G. (2002) *Kanslern – Axel Oxenstierna i sin tid*, 1 and 2, Stockholm: Atlantis.

Wilensky, H. (1975) *The Welfare State and Equality*, Berkeley: University of California Press.

—— (2002) *Rich Democracies: Political Economy, Public Policy and Performance*, Berkeley: University of California Press.

Zetterberg, H. L. and Ljungberg C.-J. (1997) *Vårt land, den svenska socialstaten*, Stockholm: City University Press.

Part III

Towards a paradigm shift?

10 Changing normative bases of the Nordic welfare state? The case of pension provision in Norway

Rune Ervik

Introduction

This chapter focuses on the pension system and the National Insurance (*Folketrygden*) as a normative institution of central importance to the Norwegian welfare state. The National Insurance system of Norway is taken to be representative of the Nordic elements of universalism and social insurance redistributive schemes of income security in old age. The National Insurance is seen as founded on different normative principles, on different understandings of fairness as concerns distributive justice that together encompass a robust whole. A focus on pension provision in normative terms means addressing the question of how to share burdens and goods in a fair way by constructing institutions that provide legitimacy to outcomes and procedures of these institutions.

The chapter addresses changes in the pension discourse and analyses those in terms of an altered balance between different normative principles historically.

First, what is called the original normative bases of the pension system in Norway is presented by focusing on an analysis of the parliamentary debate on the enactment of the National Insurance in 1966. These lines of argumentation on the normative underpinnings are briefly related to three major traditions of philosophical/normative thought on distributive justice. In this section Norway is also placed within the Nordic pension system at the time to expose the internal divisions and commonalities within the Nordic model.

Second, discursive changes of pension provision are presented signifying a change of the normative content of the National Insurance as well as opening up for more prominence to other tiers of pension provision. A brief description of reforms in other Nordic countries follows.

Finally, the chapter concludes by drawing implications for the question of changing normative bases of the Norwegian pension system and welfare state and the relevance of this in a Nordic context of welfare states.

The original bases of the National Insurance

When the National Insurance *(Folketrygden)* was enacted in 1966 it was seen as being the 'jewel in the crown' of the welfare state (Bjørnson 2001). Formerly separate insurance programmes covering old age, disability, sickness, unemployment and compensation for families with children were incorporated into one institution. Since then the Norwegian public pension system is universal: every resident of Norway (minimum three years of residence) has the right to a basic pension (*Grunnpensjon*) independent of labour market participation, and those with income from employment, above a certain minimum, receive an additional earnings-related pension (*Tilleggspensjon*). Through the PAYG system of financing, based on general and progressive taxes, the system implies vertical redistribution.

Norway shares with the other Nordic countries, save for Denmark, the basic combination of a universal basic pension and a system of public earnings-related pensions, financing through PAYG and defined benefit arrangements. Sweden introduced universal basic pensions in 1948 and an earnings-related system in 1959. Finland did the same in 1957 and 1961, respectively. Norway introduced universal basic pensions in 1957 and earnings-related pensions in 1966. Denmark removed means-testing and introduced universal benefits in 1957.[1] In 1964 public supplementary pensions (*Arbeidsmarkedets Tillægspension*) were introduced. This system differed from the earnings-related public pensions of the other Nordic countries by being a flat rate system, based on years of labour market participation. The right to a full pension required 40 years of earning. In contrast to the Danish system, the Finnish system was much more geared towards earnings-relatedness of public pensions in that no upper ceiling on earning pension benefits was introduced. The Swedish and Norwegian systems shared an upper ceiling above which additional earnings did not give additional pension benefits. The Norwegian ceiling was lower than that of the Swedish system. Thus in terms of pension benefits these were more widely dispersed in the Swedish case.

I shall go back to the political discussions and enthusiasm expressed at the time of the enactment of the 1996 law to see how political actors conceptualized the normative foundations of the new institution. The parliamentary debate in 1966 reveals some of the normative underpinnings. To get an impression of how different political actors conceptualized the values and normative foundations of the new legislation representatives from all political parties are looked at.[2] Let me first go to the spokesman for the issue (*saksordfører*) Halvdan Hegtun from the Liberal Party (Venstre).[3]

> The debate on which we now are to embark is uncommon in more than one way. First, it is unusually comprehensive, as it establishes a

> compulsory scheme for the entire population. One may also say that it is epochal, as we set the ambitious goal that each Norwegian citizen not only should have the necessary minimum of economic security, but should be able also to maintain a reasonable and good standard of living in old age, if one is bereaved of work capacity or has lost one's breadwinner ... the most remarkable of all this is perhaps that this great reform with such a broad scope and this courageous effort that will cost so much today gains almost complete agreement between all the political parties. This is a joyful expression of how far we have reached in this country as regards social consciousness and will to practical social solidarity. All our people will now have the people's insurance (*Folketrygden*) and we are willing to take on the burdens that is needed and distribute them in a reasonable and fair way.
>
> (*St.forh.* 1966: 223, *author's translation*)

The above quote contains several important normative principles that not only make up the foundations of this institution in question, but also reflect the broader foundation of the Norwegian and Nordic welfare state as such. First of all, there is the extensiveness of the system including all residents; each and every citizen (resident) has the right to a defined minimum of economic security. This constitutes the core element of universalism, although that specific word did not appear in the debate. The second element is that of standard security in old age, becoming old shall not mean a drastic reduction in the standard of living obtained through the period of active working life. This can be designated as an achievement-oriented normative element in that differences in pension benefits to some extent reflect previous differences in labour market success (in monetary terms). This view is formulated well in the last part of the following quote from the Conservative parliamentary member, Jo Benkow's, statement:

> the societal view underpinning the National Insurance is developed through a long process of maturation. Although the National Insurance encompasses a comprehensive legislative piece, its basic thought is simple enough: To create reciprocal security on ever more areas and to cover a need far beyond the direct monetary benefits, a need also to feel safe. The result has been an increased security for all, entailing that what each one of us have to pay is a very reasonable price. At the turn of this year we are binding ourselves to a lifelong, but very favourable paying off contract for others and our own best. In the whole system of the National Insurance the benefits are calculated such that they encourage active participation and not passivity. The National Insurance first and foremost encompasses a new distribution of those means that society disposes for consumption, but it shall be a

> new distribution which liberates creativeness, the joy of work and the will to achieve – a distribution which can imply a new dimension in the relations between human fellow beings ... Today a modern achievement stimulating view on pensions has definitively made its way. We must create an arrangement that ensures that the living standard of the pensioner is not to be substantially depreciated when entering into the pension age. This we cannot realize by a uniform basic pension that is equal for all.
>
> (*St.forh.* 1966: 242–3, *author's translation*)

On this last point there was also broad agreement, but the (small) Socialist People's Party was critical to the balance between the earnings-related and the basic pension elements. It was a principled critique of the institutional structure of the *Folketrygden*, which in their view to a too large extent mimicked the logic of private insurance, according to Finn Gustavsen:

> The National Insurance is proposed to be organized mainly in the same way as private and other insurance schemes and I think that one has been restricted and bounded by pure insurance technical principles, and we see no reason for this in connection with a social security scheme (*trygd*) for all people ... We are against building up a pension institution locking in the present income distribution, and we advocate a scheme with enhanced equalization ... All in all this system will mean that we reduce the share of the income related supplementary pensions of the total pension system and at the same time raise the basic pensions up to a higher level than the majority of the Parliament wants.
>
> (*St.forh.* 1966: 252, *author's translation*)

The quote suggests that occupational and private pension schemes played a role in formulating the goals of the national insurance. The public state employee scheme *Statens Pensjonskasse* functioned as the norm both as goal of standard security in terms of replacement rate, that was to be two-thirds of average gross work income and in setting the upper income ceiling for pension earning (*Innst. S.* nr 247 1964–1965).[4] The actuarial fairness of private pensions was also set up as a reference. That is, deviations from an actuarially neutral scheme in terms of premiums paid, expressed part of the redistribution of the system. Thus an income of NOK 9,500 would in the National Insurance pay 91 per cent of what would be an actuarially fair premium, whereas an income at the upper income ceiling would pay 120 per cent of an actuarially fair premium. This was called the 'solidarity premium' (Sosialdepartemenetet 1963–1964; *St.forh.* 1965: 130; *Innst. S.* nr. 247 1964–1965). In the words of the representative from the Christian People's Party, Lars Korvald, redistribution is strongly connected to the universal right to equal treatment:

> There is no doubt that the result of this law will be that large sections of the community will be saved from worries about their future . . . From an economical point of view the National Insurance means that also 'the little man' – he who for different reasons does not manage so well in the struggle of life and for the goods of well being may look to the future with more hope. The National Insurance is a distribution of our common goods on a national scale. It recognizes that every member of society has a right to the goods of society and that the weak must be helped to obtain the same right as those who enjoy being fully capable of work . . . It is in line with the basic idea of the National Insurance that no group of the people is to be treated unequally. The feeling of safety, which so far has been enjoyed only by greater or smaller groups of the people through public or private insurance schemes, is now, on the basis of the National Insurance idea, to cover all people. For me, this extension of coverage is the decisive point.
>
> (*St.forh.* 1966: 293, 295, *author's translation*)

In this account the principle of redistribution is implicit in the universal character of the system: in order to grant everyone the right to a pension the burdens have to be distributed in a fair way, i.e. according to ability. How did the Labour Party see the normative basis of this institution? Also, the insistence on equality is central. The Parliamentary Social Committee Chairman, Oskar Skogly, puts it this way:

> What started as a demand for reducing suffering from want, has become a demand for security – for all . . . Those employed by the state or municipalities have long had pension schemes. The same goes for salaried employees within the private sector. Now previous inequality in this area is to be abolished. With the National Insurance we legislate that security of a pension is to be a right and a duty for all, so that everyone through this is secured a justifiable and reasonable pension benefit, that only the most successful and better off groups of society today enjoys . . . Now other major groups in society follow, and have through the National Insurance, covered the same human need for security . . . Therefore I consider it right to say that the accomplishment of the National Insurance is the greatest social effort in this country's history.
>
> (*St.forh.* 1966: 234, *author's translation*)

Here the rooting of the institution in the terms of a human need for security is central. Because all humans are considered equal in this respect he questions and finds the hitherto unequal treatment illegitimate. The quotation points to the value of equality as equal treatment and equal access to security, but not in the meaning of equality of results in monetary terms, that legitimizes the comparison between different occupational groups and their pension coverage. Finally, the speaker from the Centre Party, Johannes Gilleberg, points to the historical changing development of institutions with responsibility for the security of our human fellow beings:

> The single individual searches consciously or unconsciously for security, and for most of us security is the basis for the realization of abilities. Previous generations always sought solutions for this problem. The man of the Middle Ages found security in the family, later generations tried to secure their future in private organizations. In the previous century, another tendency was increasingly dominant: The state undertook more and more of responsibility for social policy, because the family and private organizations did not manage on their own the task of solving the individual's need for security in a world of ever higher speed of transformation. The current legislative draft represents in this perspective a highlight in the development, which sees the state as taking on main responsibility for the security of the individual ... The National Insurance is to be an obligatory common scheme for all people. No single individual is to be excluded and left to fall behind. This is a reality that justifies the notion of 'a new epoch', a reality that all parties support.
>
> (*St.forh.* 1966: 246)

Also for Gilleberg the principle of equality was the foundation of fairness. No individual was to be excluded as the search for security was of equal importance for any person and a basic condition for individual autonomy.

Taken together, there are descriptive and normative arguments that appear to be shared by all the parliamentary actors referred to above. First, the value of equality and universality is a shared normative foundation. Every individual is to be treated equally and have equal access to the social security provided by the scheme. There is a strong focus on the universal social rights of the individual, i.e. that this institution is established to fulfil the individual need for and right to security, and that this need because of its universal status applies equally to all members of society. Second, there is an insistence on security as a social concern that belongs to the public sphere and ought to be addressed as a collective responsibility. This view encompasses not only basic security, but also standard security. The stress on the institution as a result of collective effort and expressing a form of social solidarity visible in formulations such as 'the Norwegian people' and 'all people' indicates this sense of public state responsibility as well as the inclusiveness of the security scheme. The name of the institution, *Folketrygden*, that is closer to 'people's security/safety' in content than National Insurance, also implies this collective and universal character of the scheme. Redistributive intervention by the public hand was also justified by pointing to the social or cooperative character of the output from production, visibly in terms such as 'our common goods' and 'those means society disposes for consumption' opening up for a democratic control of distribution outside the market. Third, a close connection between the social right and the compulsory element can be seen, i.e. that everyone is obliged to be member of the system and hence these two sides constitute a reciprocal element and open up for seeing the institution as a social contract (confer the quote from Benkow above). For the standard security element this reciprocity seems evident, in that contributions and benefits are linked together through the benefit formula. As regards the universal minimum the reciprocity cannot be constituted in narrow monetary terms. But if reciprocity allows for taking into account differences in ability to pay or contribute this opens up for also seeing 'non-contributors' as fulfilling their duty on equal terms as to those of 'contributors'. This points to the essential ambiguity and contested nature of concepts such as 'reciprocity' and 'contribution' (Kildal 1999; Ervik 2001).

A final point must be made concerning the concept of freedom. The libertarian insistence that redistribution by state institutions is unjust and restricts individual liberty (O'Neill 2000) was not part of the debate on the National Insurance. What we do find is a notion of freedom as positive freedom in the passage from Benkow above and the state as a liberating institution: 'a mighty and decisive factor in creating freedom from suffering of want and freedom from the fear of suffering of want' (Nikolai Molvik, Christian People's Party, *St.forh.* 1966: 249). Thus the Nordic historical and cultural legacy of seeing the state more as conducive to individual freedom than as an oppressive institution (cf. Stråth and Sørensen 1997; Trägårdh 1997) seem to have also been valid for the politicians behind the National Insurance institution.

Not only was the National Insurance an institution representing social justice and providing individual freedom it was also seen as a rational way of providing security, by reducing administrative costs as compared to a situation with fragmented occupational and private schemes (Sosialdepartemenetet 1963–1964: 16; see also Benkow pp. 173–4).

Summing up, the National Insurance institution was pragmatic in trying to unify to some extent opposing normative principles of fair distribution. It did not follow the individual/private insurance logic with its insistence on actuarial fair premiums to its extreme. On the other hand, a purely redistributive scheme insisting on equality of outcomes was also avoided. The most widely held principle was that of universalism in terms of coverage and the equal right to a basic income in old age irrespective of previous labour market participation. If we think in terms of substance, there is of course a pragmatic consideration or balance involved in how to define what constitutes the sufficient minimum of basic security. Thus, the substance of universalism was balanced or compromised against the fairness ideal of the contribution-based element and both principles had to be adapted to the overall national economy. Given this account it is justifiable to see the National Insurance as encompassing a social right foundation of income security in old age and as incorporating plural principles of distributive fairness therein, and by this making it into a robust social institution.

Traditions of distributive justice and existing pension institutions

Practical distributive principles can be related to different theoretical traditions of distributive justice. A simplified taxonomy of fairness principles suggests three basically different concepts of fairness. Fairness arguments can be based on appeals to equality, to deviations from equality or to personal choice (Linneroth-Bayer 2001: 50). Young (1994) presents a similar threefold division: parity, proportionality and priority. Parity means that the claimants are treated equally, because they are equal or because there is no clear way to distinguish between them. Proportionality acknowledges differences between claimants and divides the good in proportion to these differences. For instance the Aristotelian equity principle simply states that goods should be divided in proportion to each claimant's contribution (Young 1994). In cases where the meaning of contribution is specified and accepted among the parties this is a way to proceed, but very often, if the contribution of each is difficult to specify, or is heavily contested, the equity principle is invalidated and leads to nothing specific in terms of how to proceed to share burdens and goods. Another weakness is that the principle only works when goods are divisible, not when goods are public and/or cannot be divided. Priority asserts that the person with the greatest claim to the good gets it. These fairness principles could be connected to more overarching theories and philosophical ideas of distributive justice. Three broad positions may be identified: the communitarian position, the consequentialist reasoning based on a utilitarian account of value and the contractual approach.

The communitarian position argues that normative principles and conceptions of fairness are dependent on local contexts (O'Neill 2000: 119–21). This perspective opens up for different conceptions of distributive justice within different societies and is therefore indeterminate as to choosing between them. Rather than being a philosophical tradition it is more of a sociological theory concerned with the conditions for evolving moral communities. Thus, in this account, it does not have much to say about principles for distributive justice within a pension system apart from insisting on these principles' connectedness with different conceptions of the good life.

Within the consequentialist tradition, the justice of an action is to be judged by its consequences for its contribution to human happiness and well-being. This is the classical utilitarianism known in the philosophy of Bentham: the greatest good for the greatest number. There are several shortcomings of the utilitarian approach, the most serious in ethical terms is that it sets no limit to the intrusion into people's lives. Unbearable sacrifice put on one individual may be justified if it contributes to increasing total human welfare. Within the utilitarian approach there are, however, radically different accounts as regards the consequences in terms of what ought to be done. This is illustrated clearly within the debate on trans-national global justice. In contrast to Peter Singer (1972) advocating a massive redistribution from the rich world to the poor, Garret Hardin (1974) sees such a transfer of resources as encouraging unsustainable practices of poor people in poor countries having children they cannot support. Thus, consequentialist reasoning may lead to very different conclusions as regards distributive questions:

> Consequentialists have not replaced quarrel with calculation in discussions of transnational (*or national*) justice: the evidence is the diversity of their own proposal for virtually all policies that might affect economic entitlements.
>
> (O'Neill 2000: 124, *italics*; my addition)

Also within the contractual or rights-based justice conception contradictory voices exist. The libertarian justice position insists that all rights are either universal liberty rights, i.e. negative rights, or special rights based on voluntary agreements and contracts. In terms of pension institutions, the only legitimized form of distribution is the private insurance contract where the individual enters voluntarily into the contract and where the principle of actuarial fairness is adhered to. Proclamation of other universal rights is denied because they would violate the universal liberty rights. Within this universe there is no place for redistribution either at the national or the trans-national level (Nozick 1974). This laissez faire version of the contractual perspective resembles the Malthusian inspired version of utilitarianism in terms of policy recommendations on economic justice.

Against this position those arguing for the existence of positive rights as universal rights to cover basic material needs find redistributive efforts fully legitimate. They also question the alleged opposition between negative rights of freedom and positive rights of welfare, instead they assert the importance of material rights in order to achieve or accomplish the rights to freedom. John Rawls' theory of justice is relevant in this respect as it concerns the basis for fair distribution of what he denotes social primary goods: liberty and opportunity, income and wealth, and the basis of self-respect. Here his first principle of equal and maximal liberties for all is qualified by his second principle requiring that inequalities are to be permitted:

1 only, and only if they are to the advantage of the worst off person (Difference principle);
2 only if attached to offices and positions open to all under conditions of fair equality of opportunity (Rawls 1971: 302–3; Malnes and Midgaard 1992: 311).

How can these different theories of distributive justice be connected to the empirical facts of distributive rules inherent in different pension systems? Figure 10.1 tries to signify the different distributive logics in a simplified and purified form. A triangle is made up where three different normative distributive justice accounts are placed in each of the three corners together with some historical/empirical examples of pension institutions operating fairly close to these principles. The Nordic countries are also placed within the space of the triangle. Needless to say Figure 10.1 does not pretend to give full justice to all concerns and dimensions of different fairness theories or empirical institutions for income security.

The Nordic countries make up a family of nations clustering fairly close to the social right corner where the distributive principle of universal equality reigns. I have placed Rawls' theory of justice here as one possible philosophical underpinning of the social right to an equal universal minimum. Here the most relevant part of his perspective on fairness in income terms concerns the maximum principle of which it follows that for each of the parties in the original position, i.e. behind the veil of ignorance, the contract would contain agreement on a minimum income as high as possible. Clearly 'as high as possible' will be a contested point in which ongoing discourses on positive and negative incentive effects will influence the account of how much inequality of income is to be tolerated and (how generous the minimum income may be) and would be consistent/compatible with the maximum principle.[5] Because of this his theory in principle opens up for having smaller or greater tax and income transfer payments as well as greater or smaller use of the market mechanism (Føllesdal 1993) and thus his theory could also be placed somewhere in the middle of the distributive fairness space.

As noted above real life distributive institutions are usually mixes of different distributive principles. Here the Nordic cases in the heyday of the welfare states differed and so Finland is placed closer to the proportionality principle because of its system's stronger earnings relatedness. Sweden and Norway also contain this element, but to a lesser degree. And finally Denmark is placed closest to the strict egalitarian corner of universal basic security.

Altered ways of framing the pension problem

Space does not allow a detailed presentation of institutional changes since 1966. A very brief summary based on previous research gives the following

Aristotelian concept of justice. Proportionality.
Deviations from equality: merit, need.
Work oriented. Standard security.

Example: Bismarckian compulsory social/worker's insurance.

Standard security

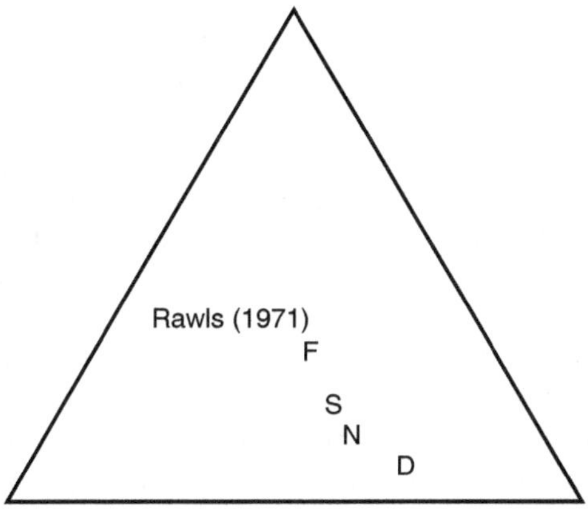

Individual savings and insurances

Libertarian contractual theories. Negative universal liberty rights and special rights emanating from freely entered contracts. Fairness conception: actuarial fairness. Redistribution only as voluntary gifts.

Examples: The private voluntary pension insurance contract and individual savings.

Universal basic security

Social rights. Contractual theory: Liberal conception of justice. Positive universal liberty rights. Rawls (1971).
Universality requires redistribution to secure every member the equal right to dispose primary social goods such as income.

Examples: Danish people's pension and basic flat-rate pensions in the other Nordic countries. Universal basic income as an even more clear-cut case.

Figure 10.1 Philosophical approaches to distributive fairness and their presence in pension institutions.

picture (cf. Ervik 2001; Ervik forthcoming): the composition of basic and standard security within the National Insurance has been altered. When compared to the original design the basic security element has been strengthened. The earnings-related element of the system has correspondingly been weakened, especially in terms of gross income replacement levels. This has created more space for occupational and individual pension schemes as well as other forms of savings and sources of income in old age. Reforms within these other tiers of pension provision in terms of pension scheme design has opened up for less socially redistributive elements within the occupational schemes and increased the pure market logic and risk exposure within the private pension schemes. Accompanying these institutional transformations there has been a visible change of discourse in the pension field. Here the account will be limited to the debate on the newly legislated reforms of occupational pension schemes.

From a social right perspective towards an individual savings perspective in the pension discourse?

In Norway occupational pension schemes in both the private and public sector have been based on defined benefit arrangements, in which pension benefits were calculated as a certain percentage of previous earnings (two-thirds of previous earnings, final annual salary, within public occupational schemes). The recent legislation on occupational pensions (NOU 1999: 32) opens up for introducing defined contribution-based pension schemes with tax incentives as well as opening up for contribution-based elements within traditional and existing occupational schemes. There will also be more individual choice in terms of investment composition and risk exposure. The new laws will make it easier in economic and administrative terms for firms within the private sector to provide occupational pension schemes for their employees, thus a result may be an extension of coverage within the private sector to groups that have not previously been covered. The focus on these novel forms of pension provision marks a turn away from the political arena towards the labour market and the insurance industry concerning the goal of standard security. The view from one of the central political actors is clear:

> There is more disagreement on allowing defined contribution arrangements. The employee organizations have in this case, unbelievably so, been strong opponents of such designs and this has also been transmitted to the largest political party, the Labour Party, that until only a few years ago resisted such a set up of occupational pensions. This must be seen in relation to the fact that defined benefits are pleasant for those employees having such arrangements because then they are guaranteed the benefit and the risk wholly rest with the employer. In defined contribution schemes the contribution of the employer is given for each year, whereas benefits depend on return on investments, thus with more risk bearing on employees. The reality is that a defined contribution scheme is the only possible one in securing those who are now without an occupational pension to get one, even though it is risk prone. This view has gradually come to be more accepted also within the labour movement.
>
> (Political actor, PEN-REF Interview No. 2, June 2000)

This quote illustrates well the change away from the National Insurance as an institution serving both basic and standard security. Strengthening the earnings-related part of the National Insurance is not considered to be an option at all, occupational pension provision through the market sector is seen as the only feasible one. It is of interest to contrast this view put forward at a time when Norway has a formidable strong public economy and is part of a globalized and internationalized economy exposed to international competitive pressures on firms with the situation back in 1966, with a less strong public economy, but already then strongly integrated in an international trade economy:

> For economic reasons, a large part of our business life has unfortunately so far, not been able to get their own pension arrangements. Many leaders of firms therefore view the National Insurance as a good support to accomplish social security for their workers. Especially smaller and labour intensive firms now get an economical manageable chance to compete with more profitable units also in the social area. Therefore I believe the National Insurance in the long run will represent, despite a substantial burdensome restructuring, a way of securing the most exposed workplaces. If the less profitable workplaces are to be able to compete for qualified workforce, then it is not enough with the so-called direct wage, the social element must also be part of this.
>
> (Jo Benkow, Conservative Party, *St.forh.* 1966: 245–6, *author's translation*)

Here the question of cost competitiveness was used as an argument for sharing social costs at the societal level to put firms on an equal competitive footing.[6] Today the cost argument is an argument for reconstructing the institutions of occupational pensions in a way that reduces costs and responsibility of the firms and correspondingly put more trust in the individual and in the pension insurance industry. Thus, besides the possible effect of the new law in increasing fairness through the broadening of coverage the law also initiates a break with the past concerning the way of thinking about what pensions are. From considering pension within a perspective of rights, defined contribution arrangements represent pension as a pure savings arrangement. This change is aptly captured in the following respondent's statement that:

> We have spent over a hundred years building a so-called rights perspective on pensions even within the occupational system. This way of thinking is now about to be changed toward a savings perspective.
>
> (Insurance industry actor, PEN-REF interview No 14, June 2000)

The altered thinking about pensions in the direction stated above also has strong implications for how notions of fairness are structured. Within the social rights perspective the question of security and solidarity marks out discourses on fairness and is strongly connected to the public discourse and public policy as we saw in the first section of this chapter.

Framing the pension issue as an issue of individual insurance and savings arrangements give prominence to fairness as a question of equal individual treatment in accordance with actuarial criteria. Whereas within the social rights perspective cross-subsidies and redistribution are considered to be fair and legitimate, within the individual saving approach such elements are considered to be unfair and alien to the system. Attention is on concepts such as individual investment choice and fund returns. In terms of distributive fairness the symmetry between contributions and benefits at the individual level is legitimized. That is a framework biased towards the terminology of the market and individual opportunity and also away from the political agenda and the collective responsibility of elected representatives:

> This results from a development where one distances oneself from a form of paternalist pension policy towards a pension policy where pension ought to be a concern for individual influence. There is a stronger degree of individualization, where the ideological objections against the private market are reduced. Even the trade union organization LO thinks the insurance industry has something to contribute.
> (Insurance Industry actor, PEN-REF Interview No. 3, June 2000)

Whether this change of the occupational pension system should be designated as a 'pension revolution' as respondents from the pension industry formulate it, (it may be a reflection of some wishful thinking on their behalf), is too early to judge. It will depend on the success of the system in terms of increased coverage within the private sector. It will also depend on the extent to which this way of thinking will exert influence also within public sector occupational pensions and the earnings-related part of the National Insurance system. And it remains to be seen whether recent international stock crashes will have an impact on the discourse and reform efforts.

The pension scheme coverage issue was and is important in the tariff negotiation between the parties of the labour market within the private sector in 2002. The result has been local solutions and voluntary schemes dependent on the economy of the firms. Regarding the public sector schemes, some municipalities have left the *Kommunal Landspensjonskasse* (KLP; municipal sector scheme), covering most of the municipal employees of the country, and entered into agreements with private insurance companies. Their motivation has been to reduce costs for instance by taking advantage of demographic advantages. This represents a break with the solidarity principle of the KLP system where such differences and their costs are shared between all the municipalities.[7]

Also for the National Insurance the achievement oriented norm as basis for evaluating distributive justice within that institution has increasingly come to the fore in public debate. Given institutional changes which have pushed the public pension scheme more towards an equalization of benefits, there may be a problem of alienating those groups who value and see as just the principle of symmetry between contributions and benefits. When established, the difference between the lowest and highest National Insurance pension was 1:4, in 2000 this was diminished to 1:2 (Finans-og tolldepartmentet 2000–2001: 315). The increasing importance of individual achievement oriented values and savings based view on pensions is also evident in the public debate on funding the earnings-related part of the National Insurance. Back in 1966 when a National Insurance fund was set up as a buffer to smooth economic fluctuation, it was seen by all parties as representing 'all people's savings money' (*St.forh.* 1966), i.e. as a collective savings effort under public democratic control. In the contemporary debate that consensus is broken. Both the Conservatives and the Progress Party have announced their support for a model of defined contribution with individual investment choice and privately managed funds.

In sum, the discursive changes points to a pension edifice increasingly cast in terms of the private insurance contract and where the conception of fairness is structured around the notion of actuarial correctness or fairness. The scope of the social contract is diminished to cover universal basic security founded on the equal status and rights of individuals and provided through the traditional redistributive social insurance logic. Increasingly the standard security element is divested from the original National Insurance consensus and placed within the labour market and the individual insurance contract market.

Nordic pension system reforms and some implications for distributive justice

Whereas Norway has not yet seen any major reform of its public pension system, reform processes in the other three Nordic countries have altered somewhat the distributive principles of their system. Let me present a brief account of these changes which also serve to set the Norwegian case in perspective.[8]

In 1999, Sweden introduced a reformed pension system consisting of three parts: income pension (*inkomstpension*), premium pension (*premiepension*) and guarantee pension (*garantipension*). The system is life-course and contribution based, but with an income contribution ceiling. The standard security element is accomplished through the income and premium pension. The total pension premium is 18.5 per cent. Of this premium, 2.5 percentage points (i.e. *c.*13.5 per cent of the total premium) are placed in individual pension accounts in which the individual may freely choose between different investment objects. For this part of the pension, benefits are wholly dependent on market performance of the invested amount. The income pension is calculated on the basis of the 16 per cent contribution and the accumulated pension assets (these are so-called notional and not real assets) this results in. However, these pension assets are divided by a factor that takes into account changes in expected longevity at the time of pensioning. In addition, an expected growth factor is accounted for (1.6 per cent annual growth). If expected growth is higher this will result in higher pension benefits and if growth is lower this will imply lower pension benefits. The pension is flexible as a pension (fully or partly) may be taken up as from 61 years of age. The basic security element is achieved through a guaranteed minimum pension for those who have not earned sufficient pension rights. This pension is tested against the earned income-related pension above the level of the guarantee pension.

The Finnish pension reform from 1996 has also introduced selectivity in the basic security pension. The system consists of two parts; the public people's pension system and the work pension system. The people's pension guarantees a minimum pension to those without a work pension. If the work pension reaches above a legislated ceiling the people's pension is not to be paid and hence a selective means test is introduced. Also in Finland the earnings-related pensions have been changed towards stronger life course basis. Whereas before 1996 the two years in between of the last four years was the basis for pension income, since 1996 the last ten years will count. Each year of work earns 1.5 per cent of income in pension benefits. To keep people working an incentive is given for those above 60 years of age, earning 2.5 per cent each year. A flexible pension option is offered as from 60 years with pension reductions when retiring before 65 and pension increases when continuing to work.

The Danish case reveals similar changes as those of the others with respect to the basic security element as stricter income testing was introduced as of 1993 (Petersen and Åmark 2002). Starting out as a broad agreement between labour market organizations in the period 1989–1991 most employees within the public and private sector were covered by labour market pensions. In this respect Denmark has become more similar in their public/quasi-public pension system to the other Nordic countries i.e. by combining standard security and income security.

The reforms of the three countries all point in similar directions in terms of conceptions of distributive justice/fairness. The first significant change concerns the principle of universality in terms of benefits. The change from unconditional (apart from age and residence) basic pensions towards economic means-tested guarantee pensions denotes a step away from universality in terms of benefits towards selectivity. The second trait is the shift towards a single metric of measuring contributions based on life-course income. Here it is the proportionality principle of distributive fairness that is heeded. This is explicitly stressed in the principles of fairness laid down in the Swedish reform:

> in order to avoid distributive conflicts it is important that there is connection between what is paid in from the individual person and what is paid out as a pension benefit. There is a simple and easily understandable justice in a close relationship between contributory payment and benefits.
>
> (Hatland 1999, based on a summary of SOU 1994: 20, *author's translation*)

However, even though accepting the term contribution we may argue that this term is empty, i.e. it may be filled with wholly different conceptions of how this is to be measured. The Norwegian development until now deviates from that of the other Nordic countries. But there is reason to believe that Norway will be back on the Nordic track. The preliminary report of the Pension commission (Pensjonskomiteen 2002) sorts out two possible choices for a public pension system design for the future: an equal basic state pension to every pensioner or a modernized National Insurance system. In the first case the state will cease its responsibility for standard security and leave this to the labour market and private market schemes. If this alternative is chosen tax reductions will accompany this reform. The commission has not decided whether these arrangements should be organized as compulsory or voluntary schemes and this is of course a key question with importance especially for those without labour market pensions today. This decision will directly impact the social division of welfare in pensions.[9] The other alternative is what is called a modernized National Insurance where:

> the connection between work income and pension is strengthened. The pension ought to be proportional to the amount of work income the individual person obtains throughout his or her working career up to a specific ceiling.
>
> (Pensjonskomiteen 2002, *author's translation*)

The first solution will be close to the previous Danish situation, whereas the second is close to the recent pension reform in Sweden; this is also the model mostly referred to in the report. Whatever solution is chosen, the distributive fairness implications are close to those of the other Nordic countries by sticking closer to the Aristotelian principle of proportionality where life-course work income increasingly is seen as the correct and fair metric of contribution and effort. In addition the possibility of investing part of the contribution in funds represent a novelty closer to the principle of individual choice and the bias of actuarial fairness. The reform options also contain a possibility of introducing a guarantee pension as in the other Nordic countries and thus introducing an element of selectivity, and hence in my account, a possible weakening of universalism as a principle of justice and distributive fairness.

Conclusion: universalism challenged and less equality in old age?

Transformations within the National Insurance give reasons to speak of a changing normative basis in terms of distributive justice. These changes point towards a future situation of equalized public pension benefits. This development seems to be at odds with the discursive changes pointing to an increasing prominence of individual achievement oriented values. Thus, we may speak of a legitimacy gap in normative terms created by the increasing distance between institutional outcomes in terms of pension benefits and discursive changes. To the extent that responsibility for standard security is increasingly removed from the public sphere and replaced by income from other tiers of pension provision one outcome is very likely to be increasing inequality in old age and a retreat from what has been called 'the taming of inequality in retirement' (Pedersen 1999). If so, it is an open question whether such a development will have repercussions on the formal and substantial content of the universal basic pension.

In 1987 Gösta Esping-Andersen and Walter Korpi expressed the view that the *Folketrygd program* (National Insurance programme) could 'stand as the hallmark for all the four [Nordic] countries' social policy ideal' (Esping-Andersen and Korpi 1987: 51). Today such a statement is less correct as a description of common social policy norms within pensions. Both in a broader European, as well as in a Nordic comparative perspective, Norway stands out as exceptional by strengthening the basic security elements of National Insurance, whereas other countries have tried to strengthen the link between contributions and benefits through their pension reforms (Hatland 1999; Hinrichs 2000). Thus, we may speak of a Norwegian *Sonderweg* in public pension provision. However, the preliminary report of the pension commission and the present public debate on pensions, which stresses the need to credit contributions and the general 'benefits to work line' *(arbeidslinja)* in social policy, point to a future of public pension reforms in Norway that will put Norway back on the new Nordic track of pension provision.

Notes

1 However, there was an income test for parts of the pension benefit. This was partly removed in 1964. Thus, still a part of the pension benefit is subject to an income test (Vesterø Jensen 1985: 116–17). Also for the other Nordic countries there are elements of income testing for components of the minimum pension, i.e. the basic pension and/or the pension addition (Øverbye 1991: 11–14).

2 Rather extensive quotes are in most cases chosen to indicate and capture several normative and descriptive arguments and statements that are linked together into a more or less coherent whole in terms of general normative bases.

3 All translations from Norwegian into English are mine. Some of the elegance of the original formulations may be lost in the translation.

4 However, there was a difference because the occupational scheme guaranteed two-thirds of the *final* salary, whereas the National Insurance aimed at securing two-thirds of *average* gross work income of a typical industrial worker.

5 It is important that this position, i.e. the universal social right to a minimum income (equal basic security), is not to be confused with egalitarianism in the strict sense. A purely egalitarian position would not accept the maximum principle. That is, they would prefer a situation of absolute equality even to a situation where those in the worst position would be better off, but maintaining a situation of greater overall inequality.

6 As concerns the present globalization debate it is interesting to note that to be competitive social costs were included, i.e. the social element was a prerequisite for being competitive both at the national and the international level. However, underlying the debate in the parliament was also a strong consciousness of the fact that Norway was a small open economy dependent on trade and world market prices. Social costs had to be compatible with this international competitive situation. Reforms and expansion of social security was dependent on economic growth.

7 The trade union organization *Landsorganisasjonen* (LO), took these municipalities to the Court of Labour (*Arbeidsretten*) as they saw the opting out from the KLP as a violation of the central tariff treaty. In October 2002 the court ruled in favour of the LO (*Sunnmørsposten*, 9 October 2002). Still, the outcome of this struggle at the political level is yet to be decided.

8 The presentation of Nordic reforms mainly rely on Hatland (1999) and Pensjonskomiteen (2002).

9 But the withdrawal of the state in respect of standard security is only seemingly. Whatever the choice will be, the visible and the invisible hand of the state will reveal itself through regulatory policy and tax policy measures. Thus, for the last point, there still may be substantial revenue costs in pursuing a policy of basic security only, as the experience from especially the English-speaking family of nations illustrates (Ervik 2000).

References

Bjørnson, Ø. (2001) 'The Social Democrats and the Norwegian welfare state: some perspectives', *Scandinavian Journal of History*, 26 (3): 197–223.

Ervik, R. (2000) 'The hidden welfare state in comparative perspective: tax expenditures and social policy in eight countries', Doctoral Dissertation, Department of Comparative Politics, University of Bergen.

—— (2001) *Pension Reform in Norway*, LOS rapport R0107, Bergen: LOS-Senteret.

—— (forthcoming) in S. Ney (ed.) *The Politics of Pension Reform: Solidarity, Equity or Efficiency?*, Edward Elgar.

Esping-Andersen, G. and Korpi, W. (1987) 'From poor relief to institutional welfare states: the development of Scandinavian social policy', in R. Erikson, E. J. Hansen, S. Ringen and H. Uusitalo (eds) *The Scandinavian Model*, Armonk, NY: M. E. Sharpe.

Finansdepartementet (2000–2001) *St. meld.* nr. 30. Langtidsprogrammet 2002–2005.

Føllesdal, A. (1993) 'John Rawls', in T. Berg Eriksen (ed.) *Vestens Tenkere*, III, Oslo: Aschehoug.

Hardin, G. (1974) 'Life-boat ethics: the case against helping the poor', *Psychology Today*, 8: 38–43.

Hatland, A. (1999) 'Sosial Trygghet. Nordisk alderspensjon under ombygging', Det 21. Århundredes velferdssamfunn. Rapport Nr. 32, Oslo: FAFO.

Hinrichs, K. (2000) 'Elephants on the move. Patterns of public pension reforms in OECD countries', *European Review*, 8 (3): 353–78.

Innst. S. nr 247 (1964–1965) Instilling fra sosialkomitéen om folkepensjon.

Kildal, N. (1999) 'Justification of workfare: the Norwegian case', *Critical Social Policy*, 19 (3, August): 353–70.

Linneroth-Bayer, J. (2001) 'Pension reform in Austria', PEN-REF Project, IIASA, Vienna.

Malnes, R. and Midgaard, K. (1992) *Politisk tenkning fra antikken til vår egen tid*, Oslo: Universitetsforlaget.

NOU (1999: 32) Utkast til lov om innskuddspensjon i arbeidsforhold.

Nozick, R. (1974) *Anarchy, State and Utopia*, New York: Basic Books.

O'Neill, O. (2000) *Bounds of Justice*, Cambridge: Cambridge University Press.

Øverbye, E. (1991) 'Offentlige og private pensjoner i Norden. En analyse av deres framvekst og samfunnsøkonomiske konsekvenser', INAS-rapport, 91: 10, Oslo.

Pedersen, A. W. (1999) 'The taming of inequality in retirement. A comparative study of pension policy outcomes', FAFO-report No. 317, Oslo: FAFO.

PEN-REF Interviews (2000) Interview No 2, 3, 14, June 2000.

Pensjonskomiteen (2002) 'Mål, prinsipper og veivalg for pensjonssystemet: Foreløpig rapport fra Pensjonskommisjonen 4 September 2002', Oslo.

Petersen, K. and Åmark, K. (2002) 'Old age and supplementary pensions in the Nordic countries, 1880–1920', Paper at workshop on 'The Nordic model of welfare – a historical re-appraisal', Helsingør 31 May–2 June.

Rawls, J. [1971] (1997) *A Theory of Justice*, Cambridge: The Belknap Press of Harvard University Press.

Singer, P. (1972) 'Famine, affluence, and morality', *Philosophy and Public Affairs*, 1 (3, Spring): 229–43.

Sørensen, Ø. and Stråth, B. (1997) 'Introduction: the cultural construction of Norden', in Ø. Sørensen and B. Stråth (eds) *The Cultural Construction of Norden*, Oslo: Scandinavian University Press.

Sosialdepartemenetet (1963–1964) *St. meld.* nr. 75: Om folkepensjon.

—— (1948) *St. meld.* nr 58: Om Folketrygden.

St.forh. (Stortingsforhandlinger) (1964–1965) Innstilling fra sosialkomiteen om folkepensjon, 21 June 1965.

—— (1965–1966) 1) Lov om folketrygd 2) Tilleggsinstilling om lov om folketrygd, 9 June 1966.

Sunnmørsposten 9 October 2002.

Trägårdh, L. (1997) 'Statist individualism: on the culturality of the Nordic welfare state', in Ø. Sørensen and B. Stråth (eds) *The Cultural Construction of Norden*, Oslo: Scandinavian University Press.

Vesterø Jensen, C. (1985) 'Det tvedelte pensionssystem', Forskningsrapport, Institut for samfundsøkonomi og planlægning, Roskilde Universitetscenter.

Young, P. (1994) *Equity in Theory and Practice*, Princeton: Princeton University Press.

11 Paradigm drift in the Swedish welfare state?[1]

Marcus Carson

Introduction: a crisis in the Swedish welfare state?

The American writer Mark Twain was reported to have remarked upon seeing his prematurely printed obituary in the newspaper: 'reports of my death are greatly exaggerated'. Some parallel between Twain's situation and that of Sweden's welfare state is easily apparent. Intermittent battering from economic slowdown and some three decades of periodic discussions of welfare state crisis has prompted more than an occasional pronouncement that the Swedish model[2] is dead. Newspaper headlines in late 1999 in the Swedish capital, such as 'Nearly All Stockholm Is For Sale'[3] (*Metro Tidningen* 15 November 1999) and 'System Shift Continues' (*Expressen* 16 November 1999), appeared to herald a transformation of what are considered to be some of the core locally managed institutions of Sweden's welfare model. A wide range of public facilities and services – rental housing, a major hospital, primary care services, even crisis services for women – were being sold outright or considered for contracting out to private management by the Moderate-led governing coalition. The process continued in fits and starts for the next three years until by a razor-thin margin, the 2002 elections shifted political power in Stockholm back to Social Democratic (SAP) leadership.[4]

These concrete developments were accompanied by changes in policy discourse. Surveying the content of the discourse providing the backdrop for Stockholm's political struggles, *Dagens Nyheter*[5] editorial writer Barbro Hedvall pondered:

> Is a business the highest, the ideal form of human activity? Those who read and listen to debate in the end of the 1990s easily get that impression ... one can hear any of a number of Social Democratic local government councils throwing around terms such as opening up for competition, purchasing, and above all, striving after 'putting one's municipality "on the map", in competition with other municipalities ... Today the folkhem has become an Ikea-concept – democratic

> furnishing for high or low with a workload that all can manage. Now it is business that counts, and Sweden, Inc. that makes the wheels turn.
>
> (*DN* 31 August 1999)[6]

Hedvall's observations, in a newspaper seldom criticized for harbouring social democratic sympathies, suggest that neo-liberal ideals may have set deeper roots in Sweden than might generally be conceded. They also point to a significant development: while public support for welfare institutions remains high, confidence in the effectiveness of those institutions has eroded and the willingness to experiment with market approaches has greatly increased. The long-term consequences such developments have for Swedish welfare institutions are heavily influenced by how they are reflected in policy discourse, in particular kinds of institutional reforms, and where boundaries are drawn.

It seems almost certainly premature to declare the Swedish model dead. Many observers remain confident of its continued vitality, characterizing the struggles and changes taking place largely as the necessary routine adjustments to changing external conditions. Within this framework, Sweden's welfare institutions are considered still too robust and their normative foundations too deeply embedded to be vulnerable to significant erosion or fundamental change. Esping-Andersen (1996: 14) captured the underlying confidence of this perspective in observing:

> there is a drift towards decentralization and privatization of service delivery, particularly in Sweden. It would, however, be a mistake to see this as a neo-liberal strategy of marketization. All providers remain subject to centrally defined, stringent norms and the move appears much more motivated in terms of efficiency criteria and in terms of allowing services to vary more in accordance with differentiated client demands . . . nevertheless, the drift of these reforms is marginal adjustment, not a paradigmatic shift away from the basic principles of the welfare state.

The underlying premise of Esping-Andersen's analysis was that institutional changes taking place were largely superficial, and that the core norms, values and principles of the welfare state – the cognitive/normative foundations upon which the welfare state institutions were built – remain stable. Esping-Andersen's conclusions predate the most recent developments in Stockholm, but important points remain valid. Core principles such as equality and universality, rather than the public provision of services per se, continue to be seen as the defining characteristics of Sweden's welfare state. At least for a time, public provision of services was more of an effective means to that end than an end in itself. Nevertheless, in the context of the policy discourses and developments at the end of the 1990s, the above analyses seem problematic.

It remains an open question, however, whether the kind of privatization of which Stockholm is an example constitutes the demise of the Swedish welfare model. Sweden's Social Democrats have themselves participated in introducing market-based incentives in hopes of improving economic efficiency and growth. Yet, the Social Democratic-led national government found the developments in Stockholm sufficiently problematic to legislate a stop to the Moderate government's selling off of Stockholm's hospitals. When the Social Democratic-led coalition regained control of Stockholm's city and county governments, many of the privatization plans were killed in their tracks. Does this mean that the uniquely Swedish characteristics of Stockholm's local welfare institutions were preserved, or has some critical threshold already been crossed? Either way, how does one determine where to draw the line?

This chapter offers an analysis that runs counter to arguments that Sweden's welfare state remains stable and solid. The central arguments of this chapter are that:

1 there is an identifiable paradigmatic drift taking place in the form of new policy discourses, explanations and strategies, and these legitimize different institutional approaches for organizing welfare than prior to the 1990s;
2 the core principles, goals and norms guiding policy reforms reflect different rank ordering of priorities than those upon which the welfare state was built;
3 the contradictions and inconsistencies this reordering of principles fosters create tensions in the guiding policy paradigm, or belief system, and that the 'drift' of reforms therefore reaches deeper than 'marginal adjustment'.

The thrust of the case made here is that such paradigmatic drift sets the stage for institutional reforms that contribute to changing the characteristic nature of Sweden's welfare institutions. Paradigmatic change is both cognitive and normative. It is cognitive in that the conceptual model Swedish citizens and political elites use to interpret Sweden's welfare state contains growing unexplained problems – anomalies. It is normative in that there is an increasing gap between the values associated with Sweden's welfare model and the ways in which new incentives are influencing people to act. Such changes begin with marginal adjustment in response to specific problems, but as they are further legitimized by policy reforms, they affect the core principles and goals underlying the Swedish welfare model. While these developments do not entail the inevitable demise of the Swedish model, they contain the seeds of fundamental institutional change and therefore pose a formidable challenge.

Such an analysis implies a pair of distinct political battlegrounds. The first is cognitive and normative – over the values that define what welfare means and cognitive models that describe how these values can be best realized. This conceptual contest is fought through political and policy discourse; the aim is to offer persuasive, credible accounts for why and how things work – or ought to work – and to contribute meaning to people's lived experience. The other struggle is institutional and systemic, and focuses on the nature of reforms of formal rule systems and organizational structures. For the supporters of Sweden's welfare state institutions, protecting gains already made through selective reforms is a crucial goal. For actors who subscribe to a more market-oriented paradigm, the goal is to use incremental reforms to demonstrate the validity and legitimacy of the challenger paradigm – and eventually to implement it. Developments in Stockholm provide an empirical example, and even if the developments in Stockholm are not completely generalizable to Sweden as a whole, many do tend to span both local and national levels.

On a theoretical level, this chapter examines in particular the ways in which specific public policy discourses frame and articulate reality (Kemeny 1999a; Olsson 1990; Spector and Kitsuse 1987) and, in doing so, relate critically or in support of particular institutional arrangements. These discourses are generally interrelated in complex ways that can be captured in the concept of public policy paradigm. Briefly sketched here, the concept has been developed elsewhere in detail (Burns and Carson 2002; Carson 2004; Hall 1993). The institutional approach employed here emphasizes the importance of the relationships between paradigmatic ideas that guide social welfare policy and the institutional arrangements intended to realize those goals and ideals.

The relationship between equality and efficiency as guiding principles and policy goals is particularly important. Both Tilton (1990) and Esping-Andersen (1990) have noted that the reconciliation of the two principles, often seen as contradictory or incommensurable, has been one important factor in the development of Sweden's welfare model. Until the 1990s, the reconciliation of these principles was accomplished not by simply taking account of both, but by consciously placing efficiency in the service of equality. Equality was presented rhetorically as improving efficiency. Significant policy developments of the late 1990s suggest that this ordering of guiding principles has been reversed.

Policy paradigms and the normative bases of welfare

The public policy paradigm is an important cognitive–normative concept that facilitates the analysis of changes in public policy that emerge over time. It is based on the contention that policy-making processes are structured not only by existing institutional arrangements, but also by organized sets of ideas. Hall (1993), Burns and Carson (2002) and Carson (2001, 2004), outline a concept of policy paradigm change generated by policy failures and anomalies leading to broader, partisan policy debate and eventual institutional reforms.

A public policy paradigm serves to structure, represent, describe and analyse, as well as to guide action and regulation. It contains a generally coherent complex of assumptions, ideas, beliefs and values. It is expressed and communicated through policy discourses that define social problems and related solution complexes and suggest the assignment of authority and responsibility in a given policy area (Burns and Carson 2002; Carson 2001). Supportive discourses or paradigms are embedded in all institutional arrangements (Dryzek 1996: 104). A policy paradigm therefore represents a cognitive framework through which the world is viewed, and which necessarily focuses attention on certain phenomena while overlooking or obscuring others. In this respect, it shares commonalities with concepts such as 'master frame' (Snow and Benford 1992), within which individual issues or policy questions can be contextualized and 'framed'. The 'policy paradigm' should not be confused with Kuhn's (1970) classic scientific paradigm. Although they share important commonalities, they are distinguished by the logical rigour, methods and standards of evidence they employ (Carson 2004: 38).

Each paradigm is grounded in a particular set of fundamental assumptions and beliefs that a group of actors shares about reality, and it serves as the foundation for organizing their perceptions, communication and action. They assign value to certain actions and conditions, while discouraging or even prohibiting others. Since they are collectively produced and collective identities and interests are often closely associated with them, they are usually changed reluctantly.

Policy paradigms, institutions and structure

Two analytical distinctions are of particular interest in connection with change processes:

1 the one between paradigm and institution;
2 the general core–secondary pattern, or hierarchy of principles.

The first refers to an important analytical distinction between the paradigm as a shared cognitive–normative model and its realization in institutionalized form. While the paradigm serves as a sort of blueprint, institutions are constructed imperfectly, over long periods of time, and in response to a variety of imperatives. Gaps and inconsistencies between the two provide a basis for critique and challenge.

Hall (1993) and others identify a distinction between core policy goals and principles (core) and the policy instruments employed to achieve them (secondary). The various core elements of the policy paradigm also differ in importance, and where core principles come into conflict (such as between equality and efficiency), rules are applied that tend to systematically favour one principle over the other. It is the 'incommensurability' (see Kuhn 1970; Carson 2004) of the complex of core elements that distinguishes one paradigm from another. The practices, procedures and forms of accounting or measurement they define form the secondary characteristics that distinguish variations on a single given paradigm – and as Kuhn observed, may even be shared with a competing paradigm. Table 11.1 illustrates the core–secondary conceptualization of paradigmatic structure.

Paradigmatic and institutional change

Within any paradigm, certain developments (what Kuhn referred to as anomalies) inevitably emerge that can be neither adequately explained nor dealt with within the cognitive framework connected with the institutionalized paradigm. Such developments may be explained away or simply ignored. However, if their effects are sufficiently powerful (as with a crisis), or if they attract a sufficiently influential constituency of actors, these anomalies may lead to either adaptation of the existing paradigm (secondary, or marginal adjustment) – or to its eventual replacement by a competing paradigm. Paradigmatic shift tends to be led and followed by changes in actors' behaviour and choices, and may be realized over time in institutional–structural changes. A paradigm whose central principles are not sufficiently institutionalized will be weak and/or short-lived. Correspondingly, a public policy paradigm whose core principles, values and norms are deeply embedded in institutional structure will be accordingly durable and resilient.

Incongruencies and incompatibilities between a public policy paradigm and corresponding institutional structure may produce tensions and conflicts. Such inconsistencies can be conceptualized as a form of cultural–

Table 11.1 Core/secondary elements of public policy paradigm

Level of significance	*Elements of policy paradigm*
Core	• Underlying assumptions (often hidden and taken-for-granted) including conceptions of justice and fairness, rights • Identities, relationships with power and authority • Ideal and material interests • Us/them definitions
Peripheral (secondary)	• Strategies • Trusted sources of expertise • Giving of accounts • Situational adjustments

Source: Carson 2004.

institutional dissonance, a sociological version of Festinger's 'cognitive dissonance'. However, the status of any particular phenomenon as a social problem is not solely the result of its inherent qualities or inconsistencies with the paradigm. It arises from the process of social groups defining the phenomenon as a problem in terms that are relevant to society, and demanding a remedy (Spector and Kitsuse 1987). *These tensions and change processes should therefore be seen as actor-driven rather than functional.* Since a policy paradigm is essentially a cognitive model of how a particular area of public policy should work (including the normative component containing assumptions regarding what is good and appropriate, right and wrong), the policy itself represents an ongoing experiment in actualizing that model. The data, which emerge as people's lived experience, may seem to confirm the theory, falsify it or produce indeterminate results.

Equality, cooperation and collective responsibility

Equality, cooperation and consensus, and collective responsibility with democratic engagement form an essential part of the core principles and policy goals of the Swedish welfare state (Tilton 1990; Esping-Andersen 1988). The conceptual basis for this complex of core principles is artfully articulated in Per-Albin Hansen's *Folkhem* speech and by subsequent social democratic intellectuals (Tilton 1990). And although the principle of equality is perhaps most often referred to, each of these principles supports and reinforces the others. One of the notable characteristics of the Swedish model is the extent to which public policy has been constructed in ways consistent with these principles.

A second notable characteristic of the Swedish model, and one that has arguably contributed to its effectiveness and resilience is that each of these principles has been explicitly 'reconciled' with principles often considered incompatible or incommensurable. Equality is paired with efficiency, cooperation and consensus with competition, and collective responsibility with individual engagement. At one level, this reconciliation is cognitive – persuading people there is no tradeoff between the pairs and thereby reducing potential conflict. If consensus is reached, the potential for political conflict is reduced. But the reconciliation was also quite practical, with institutional arrangements constructed in order to minimize undesirable effects by consciously structuring tradeoffs. In each case, this is managed by making the latter an adjunct to the former – a pragmatic means to facilitate the attainment of the primary goal. They were embraced based on a pragmatic understanding of competing needs, and of social change processes and the difficulty of getting where one wants to go from where one currently sits. The importance of these pairings and developments that have tended to shift their prioritization relative to one another in the development of policy reforms, are outlined below. These two complexes can be described in simplified form in terms of ends and means, with equality-related principles the ends, and efficiency-related principles a part of the means to those ends.

Equality and efficiency

The importance of SAP's efforts to reconcile equality and efficiency is well established. Esping-Andersen (1988: 38) points out that 'the success of Swedish Social Democracy owes much to its intellectual capacity to harmonize these seemingly conflicting goals'. Tilton (1990) adds to this insight, pointing to the active effort by Social Democratic leaders to not only reconcile efficiency with equality, but also to argue that greater equality would contribute to greater efficiency. This clearly amounts to more than an intellectual or political exercise; investing energy and close attention in fostering economic efficiency served as a means of achieving progress towards the social democratic goal of greater equality. What is clear in both characterizations is that efficiency is an adjunct to equality; efficiency was seen as secondary to a higher goal, while socio-economic equality was seen as an important goal in itself. Increased efficiency not harnessed to overall long-term improvements in equality would in fact have been quite contrary to social democratic values, as the benefits would have accrued primarily to the owners of capital.

Two aspects of this reconciliation are particularly important, one in practical policy terms, the other in terms of aligning potentially competing societal interests. Gustav Möller, among others, recognized that redistributing the small amount of available concentrated wealth might improve equality, but not to a level that eliminated poverty. Möller concluded that the only solution was to promote sufficient economic growth to increase the size of the pie to be distributed (Tilton 1990). In this respect, the 'intellectual capacity' to which Esping-Andersen refers lay in a pragmatic recognition of certain realities – one that more ideologically dogmatic intellectuals might have missed.

The other element represents wise political strategy. Equality was presented to commercial interests as a means to their goals of increased efficiency and productivity. For this to be effective and persuasive, of course, both an internally consistent set of arguments and credible supporting evidence had to be presented. That task was ably taken up by the Myrdals, Gösta Rehn, Rudolf Meidner and others.

Cooperation versus competition

Sweden's penchant for building cooperation through consensus and compromise – and effectively externalizing competition (both politically and economically) provides a second important element. Neo-corporatism – defined as the active incorporation of all relevant interests in policy-making to maximize coherence and buy-in within defined parameters –

has been an important element of the Swedish policy-making model. Its legacy continues to exert an influence, and Swedish politics can still be considered less combative than the pluralist systems of the US or the UK. Within Sweden's market economy, negotiative and consensual approaches have had a sufficiently important role as to be considered unusual, and characterized as a negotiated economy, even though neo-corporatism was formally repudiated by the Swedish Employers Federation (SAF) in the 1980s (Pestoff 1999). Sweden's tendency towards large, export-based industries has also had the effect of externalizing competition. Particularly in the 1990s, however, competition has gained an increasingly prominent role within Sweden – at the expense of cooperation and consensus – as a means for achieving political and economic goals. This change is expressed not only in the denunciation of neo-corporatism and intensification of ideological debates, but also in many of the policies implemented to improve the performance of social welfare institutions such as public rental housing and health care. At the same time the Swedish Employer Federation (SAF) officially denounced corporatism, it announced its new efforts aimed at influencing public opinion.

Collective responsibility and individual engagement

Active engagement in political and economic life has been another core principle of the Swedish welfare state. Individual engagement in the context of collective responsibility implies democratic engagement in which individuals play roles that are relatively pre-defined, or are redefined by consensus, and power to influence is based on citizenship. In contrast, individual engagement where individual responsibility and competition are the norm (such as in the neo-liberal market paradigm) is more open to self-definition and entrepreneurial activity, and more likely to produce clear winners and losers, leading to greater inequality. This element is important in the context of balancing the equality/efficiency principles and goals, and balancing the cooperation/competition means for achieving them.

Social problem/goal focus

The social democratic paradigm and its *Folkhem* metaphor identified inequalities leading to poverty and hardship as Sweden's most urgent social problem; reducing or eliminating these problems was the most important purpose of the Social Democratic government. Equality has been a core goal, with cooperation and collective responsibility part of the larger complex of core policy goals and a means of striving for greater social equality. The existence of poverty and hardship were thus seen as resulting from a fundamental failure of the way in which unregulated markets distributed societal resources. A second and related problem was that economic growth was needed in order for redistribution to have practical meaning. The appropriate solution, therefore, was for the state to intervene in arenas that had been largely the domain of markets, both in order to achieve a more equitable distribution of resources, and to manage the necessary economic growth. Such intervention, following these principles, extended into a variety of areas of welfare, including housing and health care.

Policy discourses and reforms in housing and health

In housing, the principle of equality has been expressed through policies aimed at creating widespread availability of good quality, affordable and secure housing. This goal has been pursued in part through channelling public resources into apartment construction through reduced interest rates and outright subsidies. Negotiation between interested parties has played a central role in setting rent levels, with citizen participation channelled through organizations such as the Tenants Union (*Hyresgäst-förening*), as well as the municipal housing companies (*Allmänyttan*). As described below, market mechanisms have had a role, but a circumscribed one, operating within politically-defined parameters.

Access to health care has been pursued along comparable lines. The organization of health services is based first on the principle of equality – that health services should be provided independently from a person's particular social or economic status – and on the principle of need – that resources should be channelled to the individual(s) or particular sector where health needs are greatest. Cost-effectiveness is also explicit as a principle, such that 'a reasonable relation between costs and effects should be obtained, measured as improved health and higher quality of life'. However, 'the principle of cost effectiveness is subordinated to the other two' (Hjortsberg and Ghatnekar 2001: 36). Collective responsibility has been reflected in the almost entirely publicly-financed health services, and in the decentralized, county-based management of most health services in the context of a national regulatory framework. Moving into the 1980s, health services were almost entirely publicly financed and managed, with private entrepreneurship and market competition largely squeezed out of the system and considered incompatible with health care goals.

During the 1980s, a new set of problems began to emerge in both housing and health. Waiting lines for apartments (Stockholm area, among others) and health services began to appear, but a strained economy appeared not able to sustain the higher tax rates that would be necessary to resolve these access problems via increased spending. With financial constraints driving a need to make do with comparable or reduced expenditures, attention turned towards boosting efficiency. As decentralization and other efforts to make public management more effective failed to resolve availability problems, attention began to shift to competition as a remedy. The perceived inefficiency and ineffectiveness of public management began to dominate public discussions, while various forms of market competition were promoted by a variety of actors as the necessary remedy.

Housing and health – welfare changes in the 1990s in Stockholm

Rental housing policy

Housing policy in Sweden during much of the postwar period has been characterized by Kemeny (1997) as based on the idea of a social rental market,[7] in which rental housing markets are structured to encourage competition between different forms of ownership, principally publicly owned (by local municipalities) and privately owned (by private landlords). In Sweden, which represents a somewhat unusual case among welfare states, the relative size of public sector ownership of rental housing has meant that the public sector effectively establishes the terms for rent-setting, preceding private property owners in negotiations with *Hyresgäst-föreningen*. This has had significant implications for both rent levels and the availability of rental housing, particularly in highly desirable areas such those in central Stockholm and other major cities (Svensson 1998).

In general, rents in mature housing stock, such as in the central cities, have been kept low by the negotiation process and the cost principles (mortgage costs plus maintenance costs) upon which rent levels were negotiated (Kemeny 1993). The basic cost principles were established in the rent control policies initiated during the Second World War, which reacted to previous market failures by requiring rents to be based on actual costs – mortgage plus maintenance and administration – rather than demand for housing. Over time, however, this led to a new problem (and form of inequality) – large disparities in rent levels between 'mature' rental housing stock and recently built rental units. Rents were quite low in highly desirable, older and largely paid-for housing in and near city centres, and comparatively high in more recently-built rental housing that still carried comparatively high debt (often in outlying areas). An effort was made to address these disparities with the phasing out of direct rent controls and the introduction of modified market principles, in the form of the 'use-value' principles (*bruksvärdesystemet*) that were first introduced in 1969 (Svensson 1998). These principles (still negotiated) factor in geographic location, quality of the apartment and other desirability characteristics as a component for negotiating rent levels. The same principles apply to rent-setting negotiations with private owners of rental apartments; Swedish law also explicitly links private sector rent levels to the rent levels of comparable publicly owned rental housing (Svensson 1998).

Numerous political attacks have been directed at the rent setting system and its underlying principles, but broad support for the system among key political constituencies has remained strong enough to prevent major national-level policy changes. As a result, direct attacks on Sweden's rental housing system have made little concrete headway to date. Some significant changes have taken place in recent years, however, suggesting the effectiveness of an incremental approach. The conversion of many municipally owned housing companies (*Allmänyttan*) from public to private ownership is among the most significant.

An increasingly severe housing shortage is helping to drive debate. Stockholm's apartment waiting list in May 2003 included some 79,888 persons, a tenfold increase from 1993 (BF 2003).[8] An informal market in rental contracts dating back at least to the 1980s continues to expand and solidify. The official waiting time in Stockholm for apartments for someone not already in line is a minimum of between three and four years. Given such a severe shortage of rental housing available in the city, rental contracts have great value. It is an open secret that contracts may be purchased or traded for other assets in order to avoid waiting periods that can extend into years. This, of course, generates new inequalities in housing of precisely the type that the system was intended to curb. This development reflects both a normative and cognitive shift – although few seem willing to condone the system, people seeking apartments participate because they are clear that is how the system works. It is nearly impossible to get an apartment in central Stockholm unless one participates in these informal markets. Tight public finances make it difficult for public officials to address either problem by subsidizing the construction of additional housing capacity. In this context, an increasingly private housing market is being argued by property owners' groups and political conservatives as the remedy to a clearly untenable situation.

Between 1976 and the end of 1998, some 46,445 apartments were converted from municipal to private ownership (Svensson 1999). Roughly 40 per cent of these represented entire municipal housing corporations being dissolved and sold off (either whole or in pieces), virtually all since 1987. For example, in 1996, Nackahem, the housing corporation for the Stockholm suburb of Nacka, was broken up into four pieces and its 5,027 rental units sold to four different for-profit companies (Kemeny 1999b), leaving no municipally owned rental housing in Nacka. Some 27,319 apartments were sold off by the municipally owned companies that remain. In some cases, these have been converted to private owner cooperatives (called *bostadsrätt*) (Svensson 1998), but the 2,024 rental units represent only 4 per cent of the total sales as of the end of 1998. In most instances, the sales were to private, for-profit landlords.

The conversions highlighted above took place before the process in Stockholm was moved into high gear with the 1998 election of the Moderate-led municipal government. *Familjebostäder*, one of Stockholm's three municipal housing companies that owns some 30,000 apartments, hired a project leader to assist people living in its apartments in the process of meeting the formal requirements for purchasing their apartment building, including the formation of its governing board (*Familjebostäder* 1999a). *Familjebostäder* indicated in February of 1999, shortly after the new municipal government had taken office, that groups representing some 2,100 renters had already indicated their interest. As of December 1999, the renters of 47 different apartment buildings, accounting for 1,561 individual apartments had formed local boards and been formally approved and invited to take part in negotiations for the purchase of their buildings (*Familjebostäder* 1999b). Virtually all of these were located in the central city. The municipal government indicated its intention to sell the apartment buildings at market prices, but the market value of apartments in very desirable locations raised questions about many renters' ability to handle the financing of such a purchase. Seemingly determined to sell off its public rental housing, discussions turned to the possibility of selling to private for-profit companies as its next step, or of redefining what was meant by 'market prices', although the narrow election loss cut this process short. Overall, between 2000 and 2001, the number of municipally owned rental apartments in the central city dropped by 4,434 (BF 2003).

Subtle but important long-term changes are taking place in the process of this privatization as the shrinking of the size of the public sector weakens its role in both setting rent levels and establishing the underlying values that guide Swedish rental housing markets. Kemeny (1997) points out that the broader conversion from public to private ownership has serious implications for the market-defining role of the public sector in rent-setting negotiations between tenants' organizations and the municipal governments that own much of the housing. The conversion of public to private effectively erodes the size and market power of the public sector. If the process were to proceed to its logical conclusion in a given geographical area, there would be little or no public reference point for rent negotiations, leaving only private owners with whom to bargain and establish rent levels, undermining cost-based principles. This was borne out in Nacka, where the entire municipal housing company was sold to private companies. With no comparable local rental units available to serve as a guide in rent negotiations with the private companies, nearby (and more expensive) Stockholm was used, resulting in substantial rent increases, for example, an additional 750 kronor per month for a three room apartment of 75 square metres (*DN* 14 September 1998).

The privatization has also furthered the shift in guiding principles that permitted the sale of municipally owned housing stock in the first place. One important change, especially for lower income families, is summarized by Lennart Jeding, the chief executive of Stena Fastigheter Stockholm, which purchased roughly half of Nackahem's rental apartments:

> In Fisksätra there are already many low income renters and we do not want the number to increase. We want to improve the area, and we want Fisksätra to get the good reputation it deserves. Those who cannot pay their rent do not fit, we don't sign agreements with them.
>
> (*DN* 24 January 1998)

Such comments demonstrate with unusual candidness one way in which more narrowly-structured interests can increase desire to boost property values, increase rent levels and attract problem-free tenants, leaving the 'problems' to be dealt with elsewhere – ultimately contributing to a level of segregation that has previously been notably absent in Sweden. It also raises questions about what other criteria are being used for determining which prospective tenants 'fit' – and which do not. And while the local government in Nacka argues that it keeps several municipally-rented apartments available for poor residents, the likelihood is that the marginalization, rather than the integration of families experiencing difficulties will be the product of this approach, concentrating them in the least politically sensitive areas. This is quite the reverse of the strategy of Swedish housing policy prior to the 1990s (Olsson 1990). Bostadsrätter are likely to produce a similar problem as the direct interests of residents shift, with individual property owners becoming concerned about the future value of their investment, in most cases a sizeable portion of an individual's or family's assets. In any case, a reasonably healthy economic status and prognosis is required in the first place to meet the lending institution's requirements to make an apartment purchase.

Health care in transition

On December 1, 1999, St. Görans Hospital in Stockholm became Sweden's first private acute-care hospital, owned by Bure Hälsa och Sjukvård AB (recently changed to Capio AB). The sale of St. Görans was not a sudden act; changes that helped pave the way stretch back at least a decade. Groundwork for the privatization of St. Görans began many years earlier, when its management was contracted out to Bure (Saltman 1994) after earlier efforts to sell the hospital outright failed. Thus, by the time a sale was accomplished, the change in ownership was in many ways a formality, since Bure already had its management systems in place, and St. Görans had already been reorganized as a municipally owned stock company. St. Görans follows Sophiahemmet, a non-acute hospital that was taken over by private investors in 1987 (Olsson 1990), although St. Görans is the first overtly for-profit hospital. Other Stockholm area health facilities were also headed towards various forms of privatization. Danderyd and Huddinge Hospitals, for example were converted into municipally owned stock companies in April of 2000. Primary care was also being further privatized, with an estimated 40 per cent of the primary care in the County of Stockholm already in private hands as of 2000.

These developments were preceded by a variety of experiments and ventures that employed market principles – some initiated by individual counties, others by entrepreneurs. For example, a purely private, for-profit initiative re-emerged in 1983 with City Clinic, an out-patient emergency clinic that competed directly with public facilities, and private health care insurance has been available since the early 1980s – marketed in part as a way to avoid the waiting lines that had begun to accumulate (Olsson 1990). This represented a striking departure from the pre-1980s pattern of reforms, which were characterized by a steady expansion of public sector responsibilities for both financing and delivery of health services. Private health insurance, which continues to play an increasingly important role, is further examined below.

During the 1990s, Sweden's health care system confronted the same difficulties faced by other countries, with rising medical costs and typical over-reliance on hospital-based care. In addition, Sweden's system was increasingly criticized as too impersonal and poorly adapted to individual patients' needs. Reorganization and training have helped to address these problems, but one outcome of Sweden's success at keeping health care expenditures in check has been longer waiting times. These vary tremendously by location and by type of service needed, but can vary from no wait at all to months or years for certain elective procedures. Delays for patients seeking services and proposed remedies have been high on the political campaign agenda for the past decade.

Problems with the ability of Sweden's predominantly public health care system infrastructure to keep up with the pace of needed changes had already been apparent for several years when the Swedish Federation of County Councils established the Crossroads project in December of 1988 to investigate future options for Swedish health care. The eventual report, *Crossroads: Future Options for Swedish Health Care*, (*Landstingförbundet* 1991) concluded that while the Swedish health system produced quite good overall results, significant changes were needed to adapt to financial limitations, advances in medicine and changing patient expectations. The report presented three scenarios for reform experiments based on the assignment of responsibility for four specific aspects of health services:

1 ensuring the availability of needed health and medical services;
2 financing health and medical care (and other related services such as long-term care);
3 delivery or production of health services;
4 quality monitoring and assurance.

The broad conclusion was that responsibility for ensuring that needed care is available is a public one, and best carried out by national, county or municipal levels of government – or by some other democratically elected body. Responsibility for financing is treated similarly: care should be publicly financed, and to permit better coordination, financing for health and medical care, sick leave, early retirement, etc. should be consolidated. Several possibilities were entertained on the third question; producing services. These included a variety of mixes of public and private provision of care, typically with a separation of the roles of purchaser and provider of services in an attempt to achieve a greater degree of reorganization and achieve new efficiencies. On the fourth question, quality assurance, the responsibility in all scenarios was seen as remaining with public institutions. In short collective responsibility for the availability, quality and financing of health care was reaffirmed, while the door was opened to allow the flexibility to experiment with private delivery of services as a way of gaining efficiency improvements. Because making efficiency improvements was seen as a growing need, they occupied an increasingly larger priority in terms of time and attention – and in the public debate.

Two years later, under a Moderate-led government, a parliamentary committee was appointed to investigate a more narrowly focused set of alternatives: a county council model reformed to employ market mechanisms between 'purchasers' and 'providers'; a primary care managed model, which would also employ market mechanisms with an eye on British reforms (privatization); and much more radical third proposal, a compulsory health insurance model which would entail abolishing the county councils and replacing them with a system of public or social insurance. This would necessarily entail the privatization of the entire delivery of services. The thread linking the proposals was that the proposals being discussed were 'all, to a greater or lesser extent, market oriented' (Le Grand 1993).

With the same time frame, Saltman and von Otter (1992) recommended an alternative that entailed maintaining public administration, but introducing structured competition within the constraints of publicly organized, planned markets. Resources would follow patients, creating incentives for the kind of quality care that would attract patients who were able to shop around. However, under this plan, no profit would be removed from the system – all health resources would be used in the administration and delivery of health care. Perhaps because it lacked a highly motivated, well resourced constituency, systemic changes have not followed this recommendation.

During the latter half of the 1990s, several experiments employing market-inspired designs were implemented. The key principle of separation between purchaser and provider, with payments being made by the district in which the patient lives, was embraced in different county-level experiments (Stockholm, Sörmland, Bohus, Dalarna), each with its own particular nuances (Bergman 1994). A key development here, in addition to the county authorities gaining experience in contracting for health services, is the re-emergence of private providers of a wide variety of health services. The approach taken by Stockholm was described by Bergman and Dahlbäck (1995) as having the most distinct ideological character of the purchaser–provider experiments, with efforts to foster competition between providers. This has generally meant encouraging private providers to participate by opening new opportunities.

The above developments have largely followed the general outlines of the *Crossroads* report recommendations, with privatization experiments focused on the organization of service delivery. However, the emergence of private health insurance in the 1980s and its growing popularity in the past several years has the potential to be a great deal more problematic.

The Federation of County Councils (*Landstingsförbundet* 2002) noted that the number of privately insured individuals in Sweden had exceeded 100,000 as of 2000, while more recent estimates by news reports place the figure at some 120,000–130,000. This represents a small portion of the Swedish population of nearly nine million, although by all accounts, the figures indicate quite rapid growth in the past five years. It is usually obtained as a non-taxed fringe benefit of employment or organizational membership. Private health insurance is considered to have had little practical effect on health care financing – is essentially dismissed by *LF* report as 'of limited importance and the total turnover . . . less than 0.02 per cent of the cost of health care' (as of 2000; *LF* 2002: 11). Two important reasons for the limited financial impact are apparent. Much of the private insurance sold offers accelerated access to relatively low cost primary care visits. Insurers also practice risk-selection by refusing classes of people most likely to require care.

The important effect of increasingly widespread private health insurance is that it undermines public confidence in the fairness of the system. This effect is all the more powerful when applied to primary care, since that is the type of care with which people typically have the most frequent experience. While those with private insurance are able to jump waiting lines, they are also paying extra for the privilege, even if indirectly. Sweden's equality goals are violated, since resources rather than medical need determines who receives care more rapidly, and the practice does not go unnoticed.

On the production side of the equation, private health care providers have the luxury of specializing in particular types of care where the demand is high and profit margins are greatest. This could have the unintended side effect of making public facilities less viable if they cannot specialize and must provide a full range of services. This effect depends a great deal on how payments are structured, a procedure that remains at best an inexact science. But it is not only private facilities that take privately insured patients on special terms, a number of public hospitals currently supplement revenues by giving scheduling preference to such patients.

Paradigm drift and institutional change in Swedish welfare

The above discussion outlines institutional changes that have been pushed forward in Stockholm (and to a lesser extent, elsewhere in Sweden), primarily under Moderate-led governing coalitions. These institutional changes were not an abrupt departure from earlier policy; they instead represent an extension of the developments of the past decade – even if quite accelerated.

As Kuhn pointed out with regard to science, paradigmatic drift is generated by developments that are seemingly not explainable and not resolvable – anomalies – within the institutionalized paradigm. These anomalies attract attention when they are successfully defined as problematic by important actors; they demand explanation and require remedies. Shortages of available housing and health care services were certainly easy to define as problematic, particularly in light of the long-standing welfare state goal of assuring an adequate minimum standard of living for all. Explanation and remedies proved more difficult. The need for greater efficiency was a natural focus for Social Democratic officials, in part because there was an element of truth to the explanation, and in part because of their long-standing recognition of the need to attend to such issues. But efficiency concerns also fit neatly with a neo-liberal paradigm that defines a central problem of the welfare state as the state itself – considered by definition inefficient, bloated and unresponsive. In this context, equality goals are effectively portrayed not as being temporarily suspended in the interest of sustainability, but rather as having fallen victim to the crushing weight of the overly bureaucratic state.

Equality (and indirectly, decommodification) as a core principle/goal has lost significant ground to efficiency. While equality remains important in Swedish policy discourse, its has slipped by many empirical measures (Palme *et al.* 2002). The importance of equality goals is diminished relative to efficiency, in part because a stubborn set of problems threatens to undermine the equality gains already achieved. Equality receives less public attention both because it is crowded out, and because, since its erosion can be seen as a sign of SAP policy failure, it is less often raised. Unclear about how to make the necessary efficiency gains through other means and blocked by economic conditions from garnering more resources via taxes, the SAP eventually embraced increased competition via market mechanisms as the necessary means.

Competition over cooperation

Competition has gained a central role, and this competition is defined in largely economic terms. This stands in stark contrast to the place of competition in the *Folkhem* (where cooperation rather than competition was the goal), and to the role of competitive economic strategies during the immediate postwar years. Open competition was externalized to a remarkable extent, with corporatist strategies in politics, and with an export-dependent economy. In practice, a shifted emphasis on competition over cooperation has also meant greater pluralism in the political sphere, where a decline has been noted in Sweden's institutionalized consensus-building arrangements (Esping-Andersen 1996; Pestoff 1998). Market-oriented competitive strategies have been increasingly applied over administrative efforts to improve management effectiveness. Such strategies were applied to a limited extent in rental housing, and to an ever-increasing extent in health care. Market-inspired strategies have been embraced almost across the political spectrum (although much less by the Left Party) to supplement or even replace administrative tools for strengthening efficiency and effectiveness.

Collective responsibility undermined?

The dominant pattern that can be seen in the housing sector is a shift from the public sector and collective responsibility to the private sector and individual responsibility. As municipalities sell off their publicly owned housing, municipalities exercise a dwindling influence over both the availability of rental housing and the policies under which apartments are rented out. This conversion from public to private also represents an indirect, though perhaps decisive process leading towards the deregulation of rental housing through shrinking the influence of the public sector in rent setting negotiations with the tenants' organizations. Changes in financing are more ambiguous but, in general, state support directed specifically towards publicly owned housing has been curtailed. Low-interest loans from the national government to municipalities that were intended to subsidize new construction have been phased out. Means-tested housing subsidies are still available, and help subsidize the cost of renting in either public or private settings. Mortgage interest is tax deductible, helping to subsidize private ownership. Overall, the changes taking place broadly reduce the role of the national and local democratic institutions. They do so by shifting ownership and responsibility into a market-governed private sector.

In health care, a similar pattern is emerging, although collective responsibility remains stronger. Delivery of care takes place through an increasingly mixed public/private market, with financing remaining largely public so far. But there does appear to be some lack of clarity about where to set the boundaries. For-profit hospitals are considered problematic, while smaller scale for-profit care is permitted. Public and private health facilities may contract with insurers to give their clients special consideration that conflicts with equality principles and stated policy goals. While this also channels some additional resources into the health care system, it may serve over time to weaken public support for a tax-based financing. Private insurance competes with public insurance, although not on the same terms. Interestingly, Canada, which combines public financing with a largely private health care delivery system, prohibits private insurance from duplicating public coverage.

Paradigm drift to system shift?

Both supporters and critics of Sweden's welfare state have recognized that it was constructed over a period of decades by hundreds if not thousands of individual strategic moves, compromises and policy decisions (Lindbeck 1996; Baldwin 1990; Esping-Andersen 1988). What has been perhaps most remarkable about those decisions in connection with the 'Swedish model' is the relative internal logical consistency among paradigmatic goals and principles, and strong consistency between the paradigm and the institutions established to deliver on its promises. It is that consistency which has been subtly eroded over the past decade, and the erosion is reflected in policy consequences. The efforts of the SAF and its successor *Svenska Näringsliv* directed at influencing public opinion argue these changes are at least in part the product of conscious and calculated efforts.

Changes in welfare rules and structures can be seen as the institutionalization of elements of a particular paradigm in response to new conditions and new demands – or in response to the gaps between what was promised and delivered by earlier institutions built under the guidance of a previous paradigm. With every encounter with welfare institutions, expectations are either confirmed or disconfirmed, beliefs either reinforced or undermined, values either supported or eroded. Thus, changes in institutional structure will tend to influence beliefs and expectations, and what actors are willing to work towards or to defend.

In both housing and health care in Stockholm, a drift towards privatization of service delivery became a headlong rush under a Moderate-led government. Given a shift of a few votes towards the Moderate-led bloc in future elections, the process seems quite likely to resume. Once such privatizations are implemented, whatever the form, the obstacles to re-establishing public ownership are formidable. Along with the erosion of public ownership, the stringent norms governing the new arrangements have also slipped. Contracts for Stockholm's public rental housing are bought and sold, and the resources provided by private health insurance permit people to jump to the front of many waiting lists. These developments conflict with equality goals, but since they may also dampen criticism by offering a pressure valve, they have so far been permitted.

The implication of the arguments made here is that many of the changes in the Swedish welfare state are far from the superficial adjustments that many have suggested. Changes are taking root in the Swedish social and political culture that provides the foundation for Sweden's welfare institutions; they make the institutional changes now underway both conceptually and politically possible. The further institutionalization of the market paradigm in Sweden is by no means inevitable – but it has been made possible in ways that were almost unimaginable only a decade ago.

Notes

1 I am grateful to Steve Turner, Olof Dahlbäck, Stein Kuhnle, Nanna Kildal and Sven Hort for their helpful comments on earlier versions of this paper, and to Jim Kemeny for its original inspiration.
2 Although the term 'Swedish model' was originally coined to describe Sweden's system of political economy, it has also come to describe Sweden's system of social welfare. It is used here in this broader application.
3 Privatization has gone furthest in Stockholm, but has also been noteworthy elsewhere. Significant portions of health services and rental housing have been privatized, for example, in the counties of Skåne and Västra Götaland which, like Stockholm, are or have been governed by majorities influenced by neo-liberal ideas.
4 In practice, this represents two Moderate-led coalitions. Stockholm County is responsible for administering health care services, while Stockholm City is responsible for health-related social services, as well as housing.
5 Stockholm's largest daily newspaper.
6 Translations from the original Swedish are by the author.
7 See Kemeny (1997), for a more detailed elaboration of social rental housing markets and the particular form they have taken in Sweden.
8 Some of those on the list already have apartments, but wish to move within the city.

References

Baldwin, P. (1990) *The Politics of Social Solidarity: Class Bases of the European Welfare State*, Cambridge: Cambridge University Press.

Berger, P. L. and Pullberg, S. (1966) 'Reification and the sociological critique of consciousness', *History & Theory*, 4 (2).

Bergman, S.-E. (1994) 'Purchaser-provider systems in Sweden: an overview of reforms in Swedish healthcare delivery system', *SPRI tryck 250.*

Bergman, S.-E. and Dahlbäck, U. (1995) *Purchasing Health Care: Experiences from Sweden*, Stockholm: Landstingsförbundet.

Burns, T. R. and Carson, M. (2002) 'Actors, paradigms, and institutional dynamics: the theory of social rule systems applied to radical reforms', in R. Hollingsworth (ed.) *Advancing Socio-Economics*, Oxford: Rowman and Littlefield.

Carson, M. (2001) *From the Peoples' Home to the Market: Paradigm Shift to System Shift in the Swedish Welfare State?*, Research Report 1/01, Gävle: Institute for Housing and Urban Research, Uppsala University.

—— (2004) *From Common Market to Social Europe? Paradigm Shifts and Institutional Change in EU Policy on Food, Asbestos and Chemicals, and Gender Equality*. Stockholm: Almqvist and Wiksell International.

Dryzek, J. S. (1996) 'The informal logic of institutional design', in R. E. Goodin (ed.) *The Theory of Institutional Design*, Cambridge: Cambridge University Press.

Esping-Andersen, G. (1988) 'The making of the Social Democratic welfare state', in K. Misgeld, K. Molin, and K. Åmark, *Creating Social Democracy: A Century of the Social Democratic Labor Party in Sweden*, University Park: Pennsylvania State University Press.

—— (1990) *Three Worlds of Welfare Capitalism*, Cambridge: Polity Press.

—— (1996) 'After the Golden Age? Welfare state dilemmas in a global economy', in G. Esping-Andersen (ed.) *Welfare States in Transition: National Adaptations in Global Economies*, London: Sage Publications.

Hall, P. (1993) 'Policy paradigms, social learning and the state: the case of economic policymaking in Britain', *Comparative Politics*, 25: 275–97.

Hjortsberg, C. and Ghatnekar (2001) 'Health care systems in transition: Sweden', Copenhagen: WHO European Observatory on Health Care Systems.

Kemeny, J. (1993) 'The significance of Swedish rental policy: cost renting command economy versus the social market in comparative perspective', *Housing Studies*, 8 (1): 3–15.

—— (1997) *Social Markets in European Rental Housing*, Arbetsrapport No. 3, Institutet för Bostadsforskning, Uppsala Universitet.

—— (1999a) *Narratives, Sagas and Social Policy – State and Society in Housing Research*, Working Paper No. 24, Institutet för Bostadsforskning, Uppsala Universitet.

—— (1999b) 'En social hyresmarknad? Hotet mot den tredje vägens bostadspolitik', *Häften för kritiska studier*, 32 (4): 41–50.

Kuhn, T. (1970) *The Structure of Scientific Revolutions*, (Second Edition), Chicago: University of Chicago Press.

Le Grand, J. (1993) 'Models of Swedish healthcare reform: preliminary assessment', in HSU 2000 *International Perspectives on Healthcare Reform in Sweden: Report from a Hearing on Three Models for Healthcare Reform.* (September 29, 1993), Stockholm: The Committee on Funding and Organisation of Health Services and Medical Care.

Lindbeck, A. (1996) 'The Swedish experiment', *The Economic Journal*, 106 (439):1725–46.

Olsson, S. E. (1990) *Social Policy and the Welfare State in Sweden*, Lund: Archiv

Palme, J., Bergmark, Å., Bäckman, O., Estrada, F., Fritzell, J., Lundberg, O., Sjöberg, O. and Szebehely, M. (2002) *Welfare in Sweden: The Balance Sheet for the 1990s*, Stockholm: Ministry for Social Affairs.

Pestoff, V. (1999) 'Sweden during the 1990s: the demise of concertation and social partnership and its sudden reappearance in 1998', Working paper, Stockholm: Södertörn University College.

Saltman, R. (1994) 'A conceptual overview of recent health care reforms', *European Journal of Public Health*, 4: 287–93.

Saltman, R. and von Otter, C. (1992) *Planned Markets and Public Competition: Strategic Reform in Northern European Health Systems*, Buckingham: Open University Press.

Snow, D. A. and Benford, R. D. (1992) 'Master frames and cycles of protest', in A. Morris and C. McClurg Mueller (eds) *Frontiers in Social Movement Theory*, New Haven: Yale University Press.

Spector, M. and Kitsuse, J. (1987) *Constructing Social Problems*, New York: Aldine de Gruyter.

Svensson, K. A. S. (1998) 'Neither market nor command economy: Swedish negotiative rent setting in practice', *Scandinavian Housing and Planning Research*, 15: 79–94.

—— (1999) 'Assembled data on conversion of municipally owned rental housing to private ownership', unpublished.

Tilton, T. (1990) *The Political Theory of Swedish Social Democracy*, Oxford: Clarendon Press.

Governmental publications

BF (2003) Bostadsförmedlingen, City of Stockholm; www.bostad.stockholm.se.

Familjebostader (1999a) 'Stöd för att bilda bostadsrätter i förorterna': www. familjebostader.com/menyer/foretaget/press/990224.htm.

—— (1999b) 'Ombildningsärenden godkända i Familjebostäders styrelse för erbjudande': www.familjebostader.com/menyer/foretaget/ombildning/forteckning.htm.

Landstingförbundet (1991) *Crossroads: Future Options for Swedish Health Care*, Stockholm: Federation of County Councils.

—— (2002) *Swedish Health Care in the 1990s*, Stockholm: Federation of County Councils.

Newspapers and periodicals

DN (1998) 'Privatisering i Nacka Kommun: Svårare få bostad i Nacka' (Anne Rädestad and Gunnar Sörbring), 24 January.

—— (1999) 'Ständigt detta företag' (editorial, Barbro Hedvall), 31 August.

—— (1999) 'Hyreschock efter ägerbyte', 14 September.

12 Normative foundations of the Icelandic welfare state

On the gradual erosion of citizenship-based welfare rights

Stefán Ólafsson

Introduction

The contemporary Icelandic welfare state is a significant deviant within the Nordic welfare community. At the beginning of the postwar period it was shaped by similar Beveridgean principles as the Scandinavian social security systems, but did not follow the decisive turn towards the 'Scandinavian model' from the 1950s to the 1970s. The Icelandic system remains smaller, less costly, less generous and less redistributive. From the outset the Icelandic system was also more reliant on income-testing of benefits and depended heavily on private and third sector provisions of welfare and caring services, i.e. by non-governmental welfare organizations (NGOs).

The aim of this chapter is to give an account of the principles on which the Icelandic welfare system is based, its deviation from the Scandinavian model and the turn towards more liberalist principles during the 1990s. The consequences of this turn are examined in the light of normative foundations of different types of welfare regimes. The contemporary Icelandic welfare regime is shown to contain significant and growing liberal characteristics, while retaining some fundamental principles of universalism from the formative years of the Beveridge period.

Societal background to the emergence of the welfare state

Modernization of the Icelandic society started during the last quarter of the nineteenth century, with the rise of commercial fishing and enlargement and mechanization of the fishing fleet. At the beginning of the last century Iceland was still one of the poorest countries in Europe, judged by infant mortality rates, life expectancy and economic indicators of living standards. Other indicators of modernization support the general conclusion, that modernization started rather late in Iceland (Ólafsson 1984, 1993a, 1993b; Hálfdanarson and Kristjánsson 1993).

From the 1960s Iceland has enjoyed a much more favourable position, as a persistent member of the league of the 10–15 most affluent nations within the OECD. The pace of development has been particularly rapid in Iceland during the twentieth century.

If we consider the cultural heritage, Iceland has been described as a settlers' society, in the sense that the country was settled by Scandinavians, who came to an uninhabited country, made their own laws (though partly imported from Norway) and established a unique societal organization during the period from the ninth century through the thirteenth (Tomasson 1980). The thesis of a settlers' society suggests that the nation shares many cultural characteristics with other settler societies, such as the United States, Canada, Australia and New Zealand. Such characteristics are typically thought to consist of a particularly strong individualism, a strong ethos of self-help, a strong work ethic, reservation towards a centralized state and rugged manners mixed with a strong sense of equal rights. The small scale of the Icelandic society should also be considered as a shaping force for the social structure, in the sense that it has fostered a sense of community and personal relations characteristic of smaller communities.

In so far as culture is a shaping force for legislation and development of society one should expect to see some traces of the influence of the ideology of self-help, within a context of strong family ties, in Icelandic politics, as well as in the contours of the Icelandic welfare system (Jónsson and Ólafsson 1991; Ólafsson 1996).

Old age pensions: universalism on a tight budget

Modern legislation on social security in Iceland lagged somewhat behind comparable legislation in the leading nations on the European continent and Scandinavia. Nevertheless, the extent of the late development of social legislation is not great, when one considers the generally late modernization of the economy and polity of the country.

New legislation on 'old age grants' was passed in Iceland in 1890. This law cannot in any way be compared with Bismarck's legislation of 1889. It is better characterized as involving a modification of the poor law relating to the older population, despite the fact that it involved a nominal contribution to the funds from farm hands and workers in the age group 20–66. In 1909 a more modern, general law on 'old-age-support funds' was passed. Funds were to be established in every commune in the country, and all individuals between the age of 20 and 60 were required to contribute a fixed amount per year (1.50 *öre* for males and 0.75 *öre* for females, the equivalent of five hours' pay for a manual worker). The state also contributed to the funds. The funds then paid out subsistence grants once a year. These were means-tested and specifically directed at poor and sick or invalid old people. The funds were by law instigated to consider whether the recipients qualified as deserving, i.e. as regards moral condition. This old age pension is thus a curious mixture of a universal contributory insurance form (on the contributory side), which can, however, better be described as a modified form of poor relief on the benefit side. It was indeed universal in the sense that it provided the right to assistance to all poor and infirm pensioners, and all citizens were required to contribute. The grants were, however, very low.

In 1911, about 18 per cent of the population over the age of 60 received an old age subsistence grant, which amounted to less than 1 per cent of the yearly average earnings of workers at the time (Ólafsson 1999). For comparison, in 1910 about 18 per cent of the population in the USA received a pension from the Veterans' pensions funds, amounting on average to about 30 per cent of workers' earnings, and the pension in Denmark, the UK and Germany was also considerably more generous (Skocpol 1992: 131–5).

By 1930 the amount had doubled in relative value, but it was clearly lower than in the other countries from which comparable figures were available (Palme 1990; Ólafsson 1999). The German pioneers were leading in generosity at that time, along with Austria, Italy and Ireland. Australia, Denmark, New Zealand and Canada followed suit. The level of benefits in Iceland was clearly very low by international standards, and remained comparatively low among OECD countries also in 1950 and 1970.

This legislation on old age pensions was in effect with minor modifications, and some increases in the benefits involved, until 1936. At that time a comprehensive legislation on workers' insurance was passed in the Althing (parliament), aimed at constructing an integrated social insurance system. That was the first of the two major landmarks in social security legislation in Iceland and formed the basis of the contemporary system. The other landmark was the general Social Security Act of 1947, to be discussed below.

Figure 12.1 shows the other important feature we want to outline, i.e. the universal nature of the system. Figure 12.1 compares the development of pension coverage (take-up rates) from 1911 to 1990 in Iceland, compared to the average for the OECD nations in Palme's (1990) study. Before 1936 Iceland was a laggard, but the Act from 1936 put it far above the OECD average (with about 70 per cent receiving some pension grant). The rate approached 90 per cent after the major legislation of 1947. During the 1960s it approached universality (Ólafsson 1999).

The comprehensive act on workers' insurance from 1936 had proved rather deficient as regards pensions, health and unemployment insurance, despite noble aims of the reigning government at the time. In fact, the aims of the legislation were more ambitious than the government proved able to fulfil financially. An example of that is the case of the provision of the law for unemployment insurance, which remained a symbolic right until 1955 when it finally became sufficiently financed to be functional.

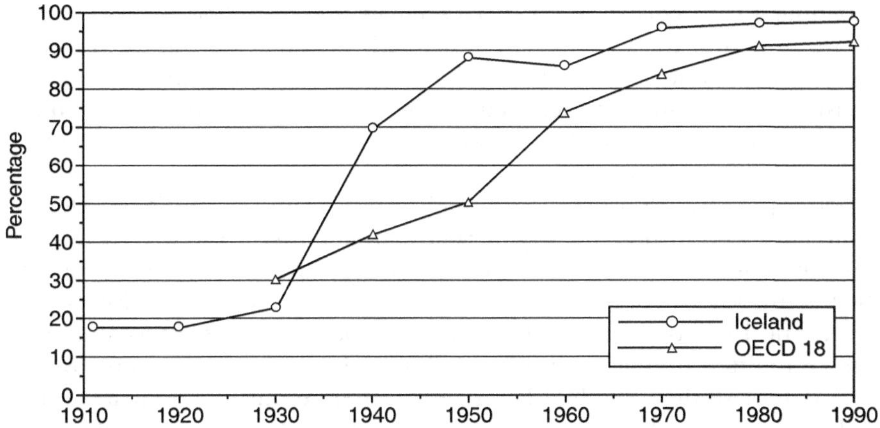

Figure 12.1 Take-up rate of old age and invalidity pensions: Iceland and 18 OECD countries compared (percentage of pensioners receiving pension) (source: based on Palne 1990).

It took the Act of 1947 to firmly lay the foundation of the modern social security and welfare system in Iceland by consolidating the old age (1947) and health insurance (1943–1947), shortly to be followed by the implementation of family benefits (child benefits). The legal framework established with the social security act of 1947 was quite complete and ambitious for its time. What was lacking was primarily the availability of finance and resources for actualizing some of the features to the full, such as the rights to unemployment and family benefits. These were gradually improved in the postwar period.

The political context

The two general laws that were meant to be landmarks in the construction of social security in Iceland, the acts of 1936 and 1947, were both implemented under considerable influence of leftist political parties. The former was proposed by the red–green coalition of Social Democrats, Socialists and the farmers' party (the Progressive Party) which reigned from 1934–1938. The Icelandic Social Democratic Party was instrumental in pressing for implementation of social legislation (Blöndal 1942; Valdimarsson 1984).

In the latter case, in 1947, the Social Security Act was implemented by another coalition, this time led by the right-of-centre Independence Party, with the Socialist Party and the Social Democrats. This was the first parliamentary government to be formed after Iceland gained independence from Denmark in 1944. The forming of the government had proved very difficult. The Social Democrats were not keen on joining the government with the Socialist Party, which had split off from the SDP in 1939.

They therefore raised their demands in the bargaining and insisted on obtaining a new legislation on social security that would be as good as any known system in the world at the time. This demand was put forth in the belief that it would be rejected (Jóhannessen 1981). But the play of circumstances led to the acceptance of this demand by the leading Independence Party and thus Icelanders were to move to the forefront of social security legislation, as a result of a rather unlikely political roulette.

Some preparatory work had already been done by the Social Democratic Party and in the Ministry of Social Affairs during the war years, and this work continued with full force after the governmental negotiations in 1944. This was of course the time of the great success of the Beveridge report and increased interest in affairs of social insurance internationally. The committee preparing the legislation to be put to parliament by the government studied the legislation in the neighbouring countries, especially from Denmark, Sweden, the USA and other European countries. In addition, the committee examined the New Zealand act from 1938. The eventual proposition which was placed before the parliament was based on the Beveridge model, but the law passed was more shaped in the mould of the New Zealand model from 1938, with considerable use of income-testing of benefits to restrain expenditures (Blöndal 1942, 1945). Thus, the old age and invalidity pensions were income-tested from 1947 until 1960, and partial income-testing was again slipped into the system in the early 1970s and fully re-implemented by 1993. Family benefits were at the beginning only provided to families with four or more children. It was not until 1960 that all children were given the right to child benefit.

Developments in the postwar period

Expenditure developments in the postwar period give an indication of Iceland's welfare position in comparison to the other Nordic countries. This is shown in Table 12.1. In Iceland health expenditures are generally high, i.e. on similar levels as in the other Nordic countries, but other

Table 12.1 Expenditures on social security and health in the Nordic countries, 1950–2000 (expenditures as percentage of GDP)

	Iceland	*Denmark*	*Finland*	*Norway*	*Sweden*
1950	6.2	8.0	7.3	6.3	8.5
1960	7.7	9.8	8.3	9.8	10.9
1970	10.1	17.9	13.6	14.7	17.9
1980	16.4	27.8	21.1	21.1	32.6
1990	16.9	28.7	25.1	26.4	33.3
1995	19.1	29.8	31.8	27.3	34.4
2000	19.6	28.7	25.2	25.3	32.3

Sources: NOSOSKO and Nordic Statistical Yearbook (various years).

social security expenditures, especially on benefits, are low both by Nordic and international standards.

In 1950, Iceland had the lowest expenditure rate on social security and health, along with Norway, but the difference between the countries was rather small at that time. At the end of the period the difference was larger. By 1970, Iceland's status as a laggard in the Nordic welfare community was, however, established.

When the expenditures started to grow quite fast in the Scandinavian countries, with increasing generosity of benefits to satisfy the growing ranks of middle class voters (Esping-Andersen and Korpi 1987), Iceland did not follow onto this new track. Instead Iceland tried to remain firm in the Beveridgean/New Zealand model of low benefit levels, with significant use of income-testing in the public system. Unlike in the Antipodes, this strategy in Iceland was at first not particularly directed at obtaining egalitarian goals, as Francis Castles has emphasized regarding Australia and New Zealand (Castles 1993, 1996). In the Icelandic context the strategy primarily served the interest of restraining public expenditures and buttressing the ethos of self-help, in an economy that provided ample opportunities for work.

The main explanations for the low total expenditures on social security in Iceland are low benefits in the public system, extensive use of income-testing which reduces expenditures, lower proportion of old age pensioners in the Icelandic population than in the other Nordic countries, as well as higher employment participation rates of the elderly in Iceland than in any other advanced country. The importance of this last factor is indicated in Table 12.2.

The high participation rate of the elderly in Iceland is at least partly explained by the insufficiency of available social security pensions, and it is made possible by a strong work ethic amongst the population and also by the high demand for labour prevailing in the Icelandic economy.

Table 12.2 Employment participation and retirement in the Nordic countries

	Denmark	*Finland*	*Iceland*	*Norway*	*Sweden*
Employment participation 1996					
Males 55–64	67.9	46.0	92.7	72.3	70.4
Females 55–64	40.1	42.9	56.4	57.4	59.0
Males 65+	4.7	5.1	43.6	14.9	13.9
Females 65+	0.9	2.0	31.8	9.0	9.0
Mean retirement age 1995 (OECD estimate)					
Males	62.7	59.0	69.5	63.8	63.3
Females	59.4	58.9	66.0	62.0	62.1
Life expectancy, males 2000	74.3	74.1	77.9	75.6	77.4
Life expectancy, females 2000	79.0	81.0	81.5	81.1	82.0

Sources: Ólafsson *et al.* (1999); OECD (1998).

As such it may also be taken to be an indicator of the strong self-help ethos in Icelandic society (Ólafsson 1996: 175–224).

While the proportion of elderly people is low in Iceland the proportion of families with children is high (the rate of fertility is high in Iceland and the average number of children in families is higher than in most European countries). In terms of need the expenditures on child benefits and family-related welfare services should therefore be higher in Iceland than in the other Nordic countries, but they are in fact lower, as a proportion of GDP.

Icelandic pensioners can be described as unusually active in work, receiving low pensions from the state and paying on the other hand relatively low taxes (Ólafsson 1999: 256–80, 343–54). That condition is conducive to relatively high disposable earnings for the average citizen with life-time active participation in the labour market, and this fact is reflected in unusually high rates of home-ownership in Iceland (Sveinsson 2000; Ólafsson *et al.* 1999). As occupational pension rights accumulate, the average Icelander, who has a regular working life career, can anticipate a comfortable level of living in retirement (OECD 2002). But, at the same time, this situation is conducive to higher rates of poverty than in the other Nordic countries, especially amongst those who are totally reliant on the public social security system for their level of living or who have a partial or unusual affiliation with the labour market, as well as amongst those that are stuck in relatively low-paying jobs (Ólafsson 1999; Njåls 2003).

General characteristics of the contemporary Icelandic pension system

The Icelandic pension system is now, like the other Nordic systems, fundamentally a three-tiered system, but with significant deviations (Ólafsson 1999; Herbertsson *et al.* 2000). The first tier is a public basic pension financed on a pay-as-you-go basis. It is a flat rate amount divided into two components, a basic pension *(grunnlífeyrir)* and an income supplement *(tekjutrygging)*. The income supplement is heavily income-tested, but the basic amount, which generally amounts to about one-third of the maximum combined amount for the two, has been income-tested since 1992. In addition to these two components there are income-tested provisions for housing allowances. On the whole the first-tier pension from the public social security system (the Beveridgean pension) is a very modest sum, but nearly universal in nature. The public pension is payable from the age of 67. Hence, the public expenditure on pensions is quite low by international standards (Ólafsson 1999: 139–53). The second tier of the system is a mandatory and fully funded occupational pension system, which was shaped by a collectively bargained agreement between the labour market partners in 1969, the LO equivalent part of the unions movement (ASÍ) and the employers' organizations (VSÍ). This provision became mandatory for all employees by law in 1974 and for all gainfully employed by 1980. The pension fund for public employees is, however, only partly funded and as such it is a deviant within the occupational pension funds system, relying partly on a pay-as-you-go provision from government. The occupational pension funds are generally based on occupational classes and administered by representatives of the employers' organizations and the relevant unions. The old age pensions paid out from these funds are similar to the total amount of the old age pensions paid out from the public social security system and growing significantly faster as rights accumulate. When rights will have fully matured, the funds will secure members generally between 50–60 per cent of former pay and the Central Bank of Iceland estimates that the public social security system could add another 10 per cent to that, assuming that present provisions remain (Central Bank 2002: 40). A new legislation from 1997 prescribes that the minimum contribution should be 10 per cent of pay (now 6 per cent from employers and 4 per cent from employees) and the minimum benefit secured is 56 per cent of previous pay after a contribution period of 40 years.

The third tier of the system is the private voluntary individual pension accounts. This part of the pension system is operated by occupational pension funds, banks and other private financial institutions. The government has in recent years provided tax benefits to those who have signed up to pay into such pension accounts and this has given the third tier a great boost in the last five years. All individual pension contributions to these funds are exempt from current taxation, as is the individual's contribution to his mandatory occupational fund. Employers pay an additional 10 per cent on a contribution of up to 4 per cent of present pay. Nowadays close to 40 per cent of wage earners are paying into such individual pension accounts. The spread of these accounts is, as in other western countries, more common amongst the middle and higher income groups.

The most significant deviation of the Icelandic pension system from those of the other Nordic systems is a larger role for the private sector in Icelandic pensions (NGOs), a larger role for funded provisions as against pay-as-you-go provisions, a large role for income-testing in the public social security system and more reliance on defined contributions as against defined benefits. This last feature is, however, a characteristic that the Icelandic systems shares to some extent with the Danish system (Øverbye 1997; Herbertsson *et al.* 2000: 150).

Analysing the Icelandic case: normative foundations and the shift towards liberalism

The main conclusion in my analysis of the Icelandic welfare state in the book *Íslenska leiðin* (The Icelandic Welfare Model), published in 1999, was that the Icelandic regime deviated significantly from the 'Scandinavian model'. This was an important finding since the cultural, economic and political connections of Iceland to Scandinavia, especially Denmark, have been close for a very long time. The Icelanders often looked to the Scandinavian countries for innovative responses to changing societal and political conditions. But having generally been governed by coalitions led by the right-of-centre Independence Party, it should not have come as a complete surprise that the Icelandic case deviated significantly from the social democratic path of the Scandinavian model. The Icelandic governments, while sometimes aiming for similar goals, tended to opt for divergent ways and means of obtaining those goals during the postwar period. In that sense the Icelandic experience was a positive case of the 'politics matter' thesis. But the degree and character of this deviation was generally unclear in the Icelandic policy debates. In Table 12.3 these conclusions are summarized in a comparative perspective, using the four clusters that seemed to fit to the experience of the early postwar period.

Historically two main types of social security emerged in separate waves. The Bismarckian one, implemented from the 1880s onwards, was primarily based on employment-related accumulation of rights, and the Beveridgean one, which aimed at universal coverage and promoted citizenship-based rights to welfare security and services (Kersbergen 1995; Cox 1993). The Beveridge model was primarily implemented during the 1930s and 1940s. Each of these regime types can then be sub-divided into more and less generous types. As is evident from Table 12.3 the German system is exemplary for the more generous employment-based type and the USA for the less generous one. England is exemplary for the less generous countries with citizenship rights, corresponding to T. H. Marshall's social rights with minimum agreeable subsistence levels (1963). The Scandinavian nations are identified as examples of the more generous type of citizenship-based welfare rights.

As shown above, the Icelanders did not follow the Scandinavian neighbours in expanding the welfare system towards more generous citizenship-based rights. The principle of universality with a large role for the state was evident in the Icelandic regime, as it was for the English. The goal of equality was also present in the ideology and in some of the practical features of the system. But the decisive use of income-testing of benefits in Iceland, as in New Zealand, was already a significant hindrance to the realization of the goal of citizenship-based rights. The modern Icelandic social security system was from the beginning less of a citizenship-rights system than that of the Scandinavian countries.

The characteristics of the other regime types are well known from the welfare literature and need no further explications here, except for pointing to the correspondence of the minimalist (USA), Bismarckian (Germany) and Scandinavian (Sweden) regimes to Esping-Andersen's (1990) three worlds of welfare capitalism. But his typology of course joins

Table 12.3 Normative foundations of western welfare systems in the first decades of the postwar period

	A Employment-based rights		*B Citizenship rights*	
	System types			
	Minimalist	*Bismarck*	*Beveridge*	*Scandinavian*
	Primary character			
	Less generous	*More generous*	*Less generous*	*More generous*
Dominant locus of solidarity	Market	Family	State	State
Role of state in welfare provision	Marginal	Subsidiary	Large	Central
Claiming principles	Need	Work/family needs	Citizenship	Citizenship
Degree of universality	Small	Medium-large	Very large	Very large
Main goal of system	Poverty alleviation	Income maintenance	Equality/income maintenance	Equality/income maintenance
Main beneficiaries	The poor	Male breadwinners	All citizens	All citizens
Income-testing of benefits	Large	Small	Large	Small
Type of social security benefits	Flat	Contribution related	Flat	Flat + contrib. related
Primary caring services	Family/market	Family/NGOs	Mixed	Public sector
Typical examples	USA Switzerland Canada	Germany France Italy	England New Zealand Iceland	Sweden Norway Denmark

Source: Based on Ólafsson (1999).

together the first and third columns in Table 12.3. The point to emphasize here is, however, the placing of Iceland outside the Scandinavian regime cluster which is decisive, since one could have expected the forces of the colonial union of Iceland and Denmark until 1945, cultural interactions, geographical proximity and Nordic policy cooperation to have pushed Iceland more into the direction of the Scandinavian model. The fact that Iceland became a society of predominantly right-of-centre politics, whereas the Scandinavian societies were predominantly shaped by social democratic politics in the postwar period, produced different conditions for welfare protectionism in Iceland. The Independence Party, which led most of the coalition governments in the postwar period, was for the most part a reluctant supporter of the welfare state.

In his re-examination of the 'three worlds of welfare' model in 1999,[1] Esping-Andersen remarks that in the immediate postwar period one would almost certainly have put Britain and Scandinavia in the same welfare regime cluster. Both were built on:

> universal, flat-rate benefit programs, national health care, and a vocal political commitment to full employment. Moving ahead into the 1970 and beyond, the two clearly part ways: Britain failed to uphold its full-employment commitment and to supplement modest flat-rate benefits with a guarantee of adequate income replacement.

This failure promoted gradual privatization, which was:

> accelerated by concerted deregulation, more targeting, and privatization during the 1980s: sickness and maternity benefits were transferred to employers, council housing was sold off, the earnings-related pension (SERPS) was 'privatized' through opting out, and both private pensions and health insurance have been nurtured via tax subsidies (Taylor-Gooby 1996). In a contemporary comparison, Britain appears increasingly liberal. Britain is an example of regime-shifting or, perhaps, of stalled social democratization.
>
> (Esping-Andersen 1999: 87)

Similar arguments apply to Australia and even more so to New Zealand, which also would have been classified with Britain and Scandinavia in the immediate postwar period. They can also be considered as examples of regime shifts, moving from citizenship-based rights in the direction of a more liberal type of regime (Castles and Mitchell 1993; Castles 1985, 1996). These cases support arguments for merging the first and third columns in Table 12.3 (the Minimalist and Beveridgean types) into Esping-Andersen's Anglo-Saxon liberal regime type.

The crucial question then is whether Iceland can be considered to qualify as a member of the liberal welfare regime? The characterization in Table 12.3 already gives some ground for doing that, given a certain tolerance for deviations from the 'pure' model, which of course does not exist in reality. In the early postwar period Iceland was a truly mixed welfare regime type, from the perspective of the 'three worlds model', while it fits reasonably well into the cluster with Britain and New Zealand in the 'four clusters model'.

Recent changes and their consequences

To summarize what has happened in Iceland during the last decades and, in particular, with significantly growing force during the 1990s, the following points can be listed:[2]

- Income-testing of social security benefits has been greatly increased. Nowadays all the social security benefits are income-tested.
- Family benefits become more heavily income-tested during the late 1990s, leading to a great reduction in the numbers of recipients.
- Income-testing now to a greater extent 'selects in' the poor rather than 'selecting out' the rich, i.e. its means-testing and poverty alleviation character has been increased.
- Private sector pensions have assumed a larger and rapidly growing role in pension provision.
- The role of user fees in health and education has increased significantly during the 1990s.
- The goal of equalization of incomes has been played down, both in the welfare system and even more so in the taxation system between 1995 and 2001.
- The gap between social security benefits and wages in the labour market has been greatly increased, i.e. public pensions have lagged behind wage developments.
- The role of the market and private sector organizations (NGOs) in welfare provisions has increased.

The great majority of social security benefits in Iceland are now income-tested and, after 1992, when even the basic Beveridge-pension became income-tested, the universality of that very low benefit has declined. In the year 2000 this most universal of benefits in the Icelandic system is paid (partly or fully) to about 94 per cent of pensioners and this proportion declines each year.[3] The income supplement (the previously income-tested part of the basic pension from 1972–1992, amounting to about two-thirds of the basic pension) is paid fully only to about 41 per cent of pensioners and other supplements find their way to even smaller parts of the pensioner population. Universality is not only being eroded, it is also being gradually phased out. This means that the role of social security in providing the general population with basic income maintenance security declines rapidly.

Figure 12.2 indicates the rapidity with which the occupational pension funds take over the role of the public social security system in providing the main income maintenance for the largest part of old age pensioners who have had a working career. It shows the total expenditures of the two systems on pension benefits from 1991 to 2001 as proportions of GDP. In the future, when the occupational pension funds will provide most old age pensioners with about 50–60 per cent of previous pay, the public pension part will only be about one-fifth to one-sixth of that, if present levels are maintained. But if income-testing regulations bite harder into the social security pension as occupational pension benefits are raised, which for a cost conscious government will be very tempting to do, the share of the public pension could be even smaller. Thus, the role of the public social security system could gradually be reduced to providing primarily for the poor and those who cannot lead their life with full participation in the labour market. Such a system of social protection does not of course comply with the principles of Beveridge's system, and much less so does it qualify as a Scandinavian model. It rather approaches the minimalist liberal welfare regime.

But what should we make of this shift of roles from the public social security system to the occupational pension funds managed by the labour market partners? This is a positive development for the majority of the long-term working population as regards the prospective improvement of pension levels, which are proportional to previous pay, thus maintaining the occupational pay structure better into the pension period. In fact the

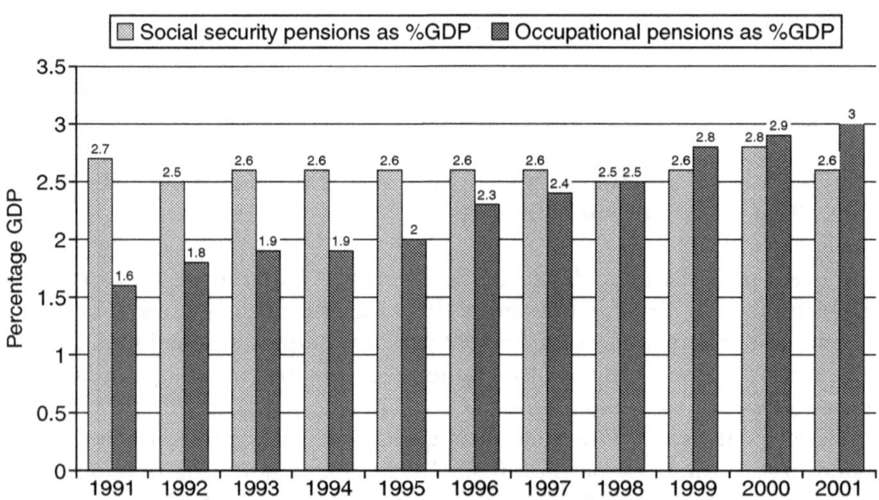

Figure 12.2 Growing share of private sector occupational pensions (managed by NGOs) in the pension regime (source: Social Security Administration of Iceland (Stadtölur almannatrygginga 2002).

union movement can be credited for having added this feature to the Icelandic welfare regime in the face of the low ambitions that characterized the state-run social security system. Another positive aspect is that the funding of the occupational pensions is by many considered better funded than the state run pay-as-you-go system, hence such a form is generally promoted by the World Bank, OECD and various financial analysts.[4] The negative aspect is that it involves a negation of the goal of equalization of living standards and it gradually leaves the social security system as a last resort poverty alleviation provision, increasingly prone to financial squeezing since the average tax payer will have little understanding of needs for tax payments to finance it. With the increasing role also put on extra savings into individual pension accounts and more private provisions through the market the tax payer may be heavily burdened with his own keep, as is typically the case for middle class earners in liberal welfare regimes (Esping-Andersen *et al.* 2002: 13–16). The development spells a clear tendency towards an erosion of social security as a universal organizational principle. The expansion of individual pension accounts strengthens this development quite forcefully. The assets of such accounts grew from 0.9 per cent of GDP in 1991 to about 2.9 per cent of GDP in 1997, and have continued to grow to the present, stimulated by tax incentives (Central Bank of Iceland, website).

Another important development in Iceland in the period since 1995 is the growing gap between pension levels and labour market pay. This can be seen in Figure 12.3, which shows social security pensions for old age and invalidity as a percentage of minimum and average workers' wages.

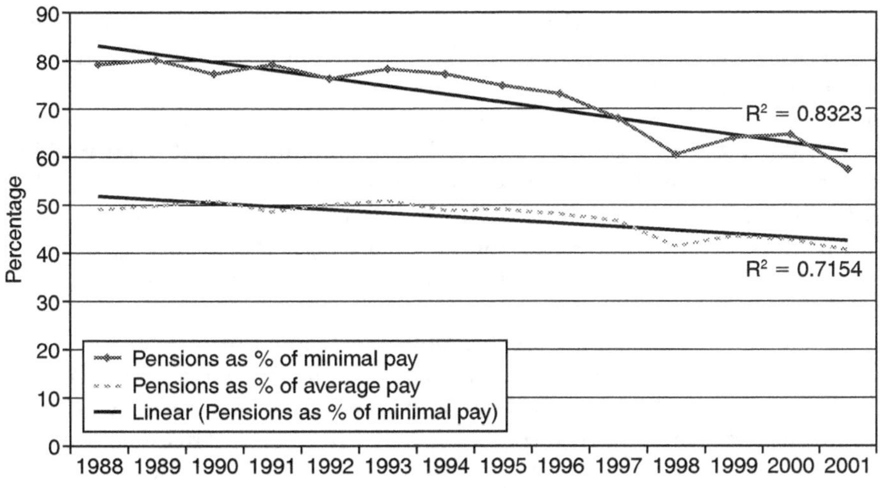

Figure 12.3 Growing gap between social security pension levels and labour market pay. Basic pension as a percentage of minimal and average pay. Iceland 1988–2001 (source: Social Security Administration of Iceland (Stadtölur almannatrygginga 2002).

As of 1995 the government changed the practice of setting the level of social security benefits from year to year. Previously the benefits were tied to average wages, but now they are tied to prices. Increasing purchasing power in the labour market will lead to a greater gap. This would of course be an ideal way of proceeding in a society with high and generous pension levels and a serious problem with work incentives in the population. It might qualify as a progressive 'activation measure' in Germany and Scandinavia or even as a promising 'third way policy packet', as prescribed by Giddens (1998). But in a society with low pension benefit levels, a generally strong work ethic and very high levels of employment participation it is highly misplaced, i.e. the need for such activation measures is relatively absent. What happened with the old age and invalidity pensions is symptomatic for what happened to the daily sickness allowance for the long-term sick, the unemployment benefit and the child benefit. In all cases the benefits lagged behind the minimal wage, which increased significantly during the period. In 2002–2003 the government made agreements with some of the interest groups affected and agreed to give partly back what had previously been lost (this applied to old age pensioners and invalidity pensioners), and in the spring election of 2003, and in the manifesto of the renewed government, promises were made for increasing the child benefit by an amount which, if implemented, would bring it back to the level which prevailed in 1991.

In addition to this the government has, since 1997, taken to taxing more heavily the maximum benefits which those who have no other means of survival than social security benefits receive. These maximum benefits only allow subsistence levels that are below or very close to poverty levels, as measured equally by the methodology of the LIS-group and by assessments of direct minimal costs of living (Ólafsson and Sigurðsson 1996; Harpa 2003). Taxing of such pension levels seems harsh, especially since employment levels are not as high and secure as they were before the 1990s. Those who are landed in unemployment from middle income levels in the labour market, for example, find themselves with the task of living off a flat rate unemployment benefit which is in effect below the poverty line (the average monthly earnings of working people in Iceland in 2003 are about 240,000 *krónur* while the maximum unemployment benefit is about 77,000).

At the same time as the government stretched the claw of taxation further down the low end of the incomes scale, it lowered tax on financial earnings greatly (which primarily benefits the higher income groups) and on businesses from about 50 per cent to 18 per cent.[5] This was done to improve the competitive position of business and is also indicative of the shift from the goal of equality within the tax and welfare systems. The drastic lowering of taxes on businesses came in the wake of a forceful airing of ideas of international low-tax competition and ideas about establishing an offshore financial centre in Iceland as a way of expanding the economy (Gissurarson and Herbertsson 2001). In previous years, the experience of the major restructuring of the welfare state in New Zealand also aroused considerable interest in neo-liberal circles in Iceland.[6] It is quite evident that if such neo-liberal ideas gain further foothold in Icelandic policy-making circles the room for maintaining and expanding the welfare state will be significantly reduced. Some observers may perceive the increased use of income-testing, even of very low benefits, as a measure for increasing equality, i.e. in the sense that the public support goes more directly or solely to the really poor. Experience from other countries shows that, on the contrary, inequality and poverty levels tend to be significantly higher in the liberal welfare regimes that use income-testing to a greater extent (Korpi and Palme 1998).

Lastly, it can be mentioned that the role of the market and NGOs in welfare services has been increased. Specialists working in the state-run hospitals have for a long time also had the possibility of running their own private practice on the side (with a sizeable part of the cost paid by social security). In that sense there has been a considerable degree of public–private mix in that sector. General practitioners have been fighting fiercely in recent years for getting similar privileges outside the public health care centres. In effect, the services of general practitioners within the public system have been greatly affected by these conflicts that seem most likely to end with general practitioners obtaining similar privileges as the specialists. This would further increase user fees in health care. There is a great support within the Independence Party for increasing the role of private practice within the health sector, including the use of fees for queue jumping. In general the role of NGOs in health care provisions has been large and popular in Iceland for a long time. Such activities are often financed with service contracts with government and often involve considerable self-help elements for the target groups in questions. Very few in Iceland would consider a larger role for such organizations as a neo-liberal nor a negative feature. Many would presumably consider their role as one of the more positive aspects of the Icelandic welfare system (Eydal and Sigurðardóttir 2003). But there is considerable opposition amongst the public to increasing the role of private firms in the health sector with higher user fees, even if it is assumed to lower taxes (Ólafsson *et al.* 1998).

In the field of education the governments of the latter part of the 1990s also aimed to increase the role of private schools, not least at the university level. Since 1997, a number of small private universities have been established or upgraded. They receive the same financial contribution per student from government as the state universities, of which the University of Iceland is by far the largest, and in addition the private ones enjoy student fees and can thus be considered to have a financial competitive edge in the market for students.

Despite opposition from the public, the role of user fees in the health sector has been increased significantly during the last decade, not least in the cost of prescribed drugs, but user fees seem more acceptable in the field of education.

Iceland and 'the three worlds of welfare'

Have the normative foundations of the Icelandic welfare state changed? The Icelandic welfare system started on a firm universalist course with the social security legislation of 1947, aiming to provide adequate security of welfare as a part of citizenship rights, on the basis of the Beveridge model. The significant use of income-testing of benefits from 1947 to 1960 meant that the strength of citizenship rights were not as emphatic as in the Scandinavian countries which provided less conditional rights. From the 1950s and 1960s onwards, the Scandinavian countries aimed to strengthen these rights and entitlements further as well as aiming for adequacy of standards. From the early 1970s, Iceland returned again to increasing use of income-testing. During the 1990s this trend culminated in all social security benefits becoming subjected to income-testing, along with child benefits, at the same time that the quality of the security offered by the public system lagged behind the trend in the labour market (i.e. there was a growing gap between the amounts of pension benefits and minimal wages). Occupational pensions evolving from collective bargaining and managed by the labour market partners are gradually taking over the responsibility of providing the main part of pension benefits for those who have a full life-time working career.

From the year 2000 the occupational pensions are treated on the same basis as other earnings, i.e. fully income-tested, and thereby the course has been set on gradually reducing the role of the public social security system as the average occupational pensions increase in value, with growing maturity of rights in that system. The original goal from the 1960s of treating the occupational pensions as additional pension benefits on top of the universal Beveridge pensions has been seriously reduced, if not abandoned. The track seems set for reducing the role of the public social security system to that of alleviating poverty amongst those who are permanently outside the labour market or who have highly irregular careers. This may be considered a trend away from the original principle of universality. If the Icelandic welfare system continues on this track it will gradually take on the principles of employment-based welfare rights (the occupational pensions becoming the main provider of security for the largest part of the population) with a public poor relief system on its side (the remnants of the social security system). Thus I claim that the citizenship basis of welfare rights in Iceland has been eroded gradually since the early 1970s and a significant shift towards more liberalist welfare principles during the last decade has exacerbated that trend.

Let me then indicate how Iceland will fit into the regime characteristics of Esping-Andersen's three worlds model: see Table 12.4 which details characteristics that are commonly associated with each of the three types along with my own characterization of the Icelandic welfare regime. A comparison of some of the items in Tables 12.3 and 12.4 also gives an indication of the changes that have taken place in Iceland during the last decades.

There is no denying that the Icelandic welfare state still has some important principles of universalism in its organizational features. This is most marked in the field of services, especially hospital services. But the role of private practice of doctors employed by the public health care system has been extensive in Iceland, and is likely to be extended further to cover a larger part of general practitioners in addition to the specialists who to a large extent have operated their own private practice along with their roles within the public system. In that sense we can say that the role of private firms or private operations have been significant in Iceland, even within the public health care system. Apart from this role of the private market in health care there is a long tradition for a large role of NGOs in that sector. In 1978 about 65 per cent of service units for old age pensioners and 72 per cent of beds in institutions for sick old people were owned and run by various NGOs (Eydal and Sigurðardóttir 2003). In Scandinavia, the majority of such facilities tend to be owned and run by the state (Lehto *et al.* 1999: 111). In the field of daycare services for children Iceland has progressed quite far towards universal access for children over the age of three to childcare institutions that are run by local communities (NOSOSKO 2000). This is one of the very few areas of welfare services that have significantly expanded during the 1990s. High employment participation rates of women and a relatively large number of children in average families have sustained a great pressure for such services for decades.

Access to university education is also universal in the sense that the state universities have no significant student fees. But the supply of small private universities with student fees has increased lately in the name of increasing competition. Even these universal parts of the welfare system seem to be less universal than is typical in Scandinavia, except perhaps for childcare services, which however require considerable flat rate user fees in Iceland.

But when we turn to the income-maintenance aspect of the Icelandic welfare regime we enter the most liberal, or more accurately, neo-liberal area of the welfare regime in Iceland. As regards the main goal of the social security system, claiming principles, effective universality, main beneficiaries, degree of decommodification and the extent and form of income-testing of benefits, the regime characteristics are quite similar to the liberal model. This is the area in which the Icelandic welfare system is most similar to the Anglo-Saxon welfare regimes. It clearly approaches the

Table 12.4 Contemporary characteristics of the Icelandic welfare regime: Iceland and 'the three worlds of welfare capitalism' compared

System types	*Liberal*	*Conservative*	*Scandinavian*	*Icelandic*
Dominant locus of solidarity	Market	Family	State	State/NGOs
Welfare mix				
Role of state	Marginal	Subsidiary	Central	Large
Role of the market	Central	Marginal	Marginal	Small-medium
Role of NGOs	Large	Subsidiary	Small	Large
Social security system				
Claiming principles	Need	Work/family need	Citizenship	Need/citizenship
Main beneficiaries	The poor	Male breadwinners	All citizens	The poor
Universality of coverage	Small	Medium	Very large	Large
Main goal of system	Poverty alleviation	Income maintenance	Equality/ income maint.	Poverty alleviation
Degree of decommodification	Minimal	High (for breadwinner)	Maximum	Low
Income-testing of benefits	Large	Small	Small	Large
Primary caring services	Family/market	Family/NGOs	State/family	State, NGOs, market, family
Public expenditures on welfare	Small	Large	Large	Small
Distribution effects				
Income equalization effect	Small	Small	Large	Medium
Extent of poverty	Large	Medium	Small	Small-medium
Gender and status effects	Neutral	Differentiated	Pro-equality	Pro-equality
Employment regime				
Employment participation	High	Low	High	Very high
Unemployment levels	Medium	High	Low	Very low
Actual retirement age	High	Low	High	Very high
Labour market regulation	Low regulation	High regulation	Regulated/active	Flexible
Model examples	USA	Germany	Sweden	Iceland

Sources: Adapted from Esping-Andersen (1990, 1999); Scharpf and Schmidt (2000); Ólafsson (1999).

American model, but in a number of ways comes closer to the New Zealand and Australian national systems.

Just as in the Antipodean societies the labour movement has had an equalizing effect on the Icelandic welfare regime. It forcefully pressed for various aspects of 'social wages' during the 1960s and 1970s, often in fact disciplining governments to mend the safety net and increase rights and improve benefits, often even in the face of strong opposition from employers' organizations and the Independence Party (Ólafsson 1999). Even though the labour movement did not succeed in raising wages to the same real level as prevailed in the neighbouring countries, despite GNP per capita being at a comparable level, the unions always placed a great emphasis on maintaining a high employment strategy. This gave wage earners ample opportunities to secure their levels of living in the labour market, and even enjoy higher levels of living by working overtime and moonlighting, both of which have been predominant in the Icelandic labour market for most of the postwar period.

Thus the full employment strategy that was generally successful provided what the welfare state failed to provide. Married women also entered the labour market forcefully quite early and have maintained a strong presence there up to the present, thereby also improving the living standards of the average working families. In fact, this high employment participation of the Icelanders is the main explanation of the generally very high living standard that the average Icelandic family enjoys. Those who could not secure their living standards with active participation in the labour market, such as invalids, the long-term sick and older pensioners, were left with the mean standard of the welfare state. On the whole, the average Icelander enjoys as high a living standard as prevails in the more affluent western societies, but the typical low-income groups and pensioners relying primarily on the public social security system have worse living conditions than similar groups in the Scandinavian welfare states (Ólafsson 1999). This is the negative corollary of the neo-liberal characteristics of the Icelandic welfare system. Inequality and poverty levels seem to be slightly higher in Iceland than in the Scandinavian welfare states. When unemployment levels increased to unprecedented levels in the period from 1992–1995 the proportion of the population which fell under the standard poverty line increased proportionally with the unemployment rate, reflecting the fact that the unemployment benefit was in fact under the poverty level (Gustafsson and Pederson 2000). Similar trends were observed in 2002–2003, but at a lower level. But just as in Australia and New Zealand such a security of living standards that an active and thriving labour market provides is vulnerable in the face of changing competitiveness of the economy and prevailing policies (such as growing emphasis on downsizing, re-engineering, merging and privatization). Increasing globalization makes security in the labour market more vulnerable (Scharpf and Schmidt 2000; Castles 1996; Esping-Andersen 1999; Esping-Andersen *et al.* 2002; Beck 2000).

Although I hypothesize that the Icelandic welfare regime has significantly shifted its character towards the American/Anglo-Saxon liberal welfare regime, especially in the area of social security benefits, I would also concur with Castles and Mitchell' (1993) description of Australia and New Zealand as liberal-labour welfare regimes and claim that the Icelandic case shares those features to some extent. This, however, is a matter of minor deviation and finesse within the liberal regime cluster. These Antipodean societies also share similar aspects of universalism with Iceland, with the restraining features of the income-testing principles.

To conclude, it may be said that the normative principles of the Icelandic welfare system have shifted somewhat in the direction of eroding the principle of universal welfare rights, grounded as citizenship rights. That change, which at present is not fully matured, involves a shift towards employment-based rights, in the spirit of Chancellor Otto von Bismarck (as outlined in Table 12.3). Such a change has different implications for different classes of society. Those who can have a regular and successful life-time working career may profit, while those who endure more irregular careers, those who get stuck in low-income jobs or those who remain wholly outside the labour market may be in a more vulnerable position. The capacity for universal measures to affect the distribution of levels of living between the classes of society may be reduced. The status of the goal of equality, so prominent in the more universal Scandinavian welfare model, would seem to be lowered with such a change.

Notes

1 In the book *Social Foundations of Postindustrial Economies*, pp. 73–94.
2 Empirical data to support these contentions is available at http://www.borg.hi.is/islvelf.ppt., i.e. data on welfare expenditures, benefit levels in relation to wages, child benefits expenditures, and lastly taxation rates by income levels and development of earnings during the late 1990s, which show a significant increase of inequality in the distribution of levels of living in Iceland at that time.
3 Figures from the Social Security Administration show a slow and regular decline after 1992, as would be expected from the logic of the system (Staðtölur almannatrygginga 1999–2002).
4 This is, however, subject to debate. See for example the discussions about the pros and cons of public and private ways in pension regimes in the World Bank book of 1994, *Averting the Old Age Crisis: Policies to Protect the Old and Promote Growth*, and Lawrence Thompson (1998), who argues more for the importance of a continued strong role for the state in social security provisions, in the book *Older and Wiser: The Economics of Public Pensions.*
5 This came in two steps, from about 50 per cent to 32 per cent and then to 18 per cent.
6 Ruth Richardson, the influential proponent of the major policy shift in New Zealand, was for example invited to Iceland to lecture on her experiences.

References

Beck, U. (2000) *The Brave New World of Work*, Cambridge: Polity Press.

Blöndal, J. (1942) *Félagsmál á Íslandi*, Reykjavik: Ministry of Social Affairs.

Castles, F. G. (1985) *The Working Class and Welfare*, Sydney: Allen and Unwin.

—— (ed.) (1993) *Families of Nations: Patterns of Public Policy in Western Democracies*, Aldershot: Dartmouth Publishing Company.

—— (1996) 'Australia and New Zealand: needs-based social guarantees and working class life cycles', in G. Esping-Andersen (ed.) *Welfare States in Transition*, London: Sage.

Castles, F. G. and Mitchell, D. (1993) 'Worlds of welfare and families of nations', in F. G. Castles (ed.) *Families of Nations*, Aldershot: Dartmouth.

Central Bank of Iceland (2002) *The Economy of Iceland*, Reykjavík: Central Bank Homepage.

Cox, R. H. (1993) *The Development of the Dutch Welfare State*, Pittsburgh: University of Pittsburgh Press.

Esping-Andersen, G. (1990) *The Three Worlds of Welfare Capitalism*, Cambridge: Polity Press.

—— (ed.) (1996) *Welfare States in Transition*, London: Sage.

—— (1999) *Social Foundations of Postindustrial Economies*, Oxford: Oxford University Press.

Esping-Andersen, G. and Korpi, W. (1987) 'From poor relief to institutional welfare states', in R. Erikson, E. J. Hansen, S. Ringen and H. Uusitalo (eds) *The Scandinavian Model*, New York: M. E. Sharpe.

Esping-Andersen, G., Gallie, D., Hemerijck, A. and Myles, J. (2002) *Why We Need a New Welfare State*, Oxford: Oxford University Press.

Eydal, G. B. and Sigurðardóttir, S. H. (2003) 'Äldreomsorgen i Island utveckling och framtidstendenser', *Nordisk Socialt Arbeid*, 23 (3): 162–71.

Giddens, A. (1998) *The Third Way: The Renewal of Social Democracy*, Cambridge: Polity Press.

Gissurarson, H. H. and Herbertsson, T. Th. (eds) (2001) 'Tax competition: an opportunity for Iceland?', Reykjavik: Institute of Economic Studies, University of Iceland.

Gustafsson, B. and Pedersen, P. (eds) (2000) *Poverty and Low-Incomes in the Nordic Countries*, Aldershot: Ashgate.

Hálfdanarson, G. and Kristjánsson, S. (eds) (1993) *Íslensk þjóðfélagsþróun 1880–1990: Ritgerðir*, Reykjavík: University of Iceland, Social Research Institute.

Herbertsson, T. Þór, Orzag, J. M. and Orzag, P. R. (2000) *Retirement in the Nordic Countries*, Copenhagen: TemaNord: 548.

Jóhannesen, M. (1981) *Ævisaga Ólafs Thors*, Reykjavík: Almennabókafélagið.

Jónsson, F. H. and Ólafsson, S. (1991) 'Lífsskoðun í nútímalegum þjóðfélögum', Reykjavík: Social Research Institute.

Kersbergen, K. van (1995) *Social Capitalism: A Study of Christian Democracy and the Welfare State*, London: RKP.

Korpi, W. and Palme, J. (1998) 'The paradox of redistribution and strategies of equality', Stockholm: SOFI.

Lehto, J., Moss, N. and Rostgaard, T. (1999) 'Universal public social care and health services', in M. Kautto, M. Heikkilä, B. Hvinden, S. Marklund and N. Ploug (eds) *Nordic Social Policy: Changing Welfare States*, London: Routledge.

Marshall, T. H. (1963) *Sociology at the Crossroads and Other Essays*, London: Heinemann.

Njåls, H. (2003) *Fátækt á Íslandi: Hin dulda félagsgerð borgarsamfélagsins*, (Poverty in Iceland: The Hidden Aspect of the Urban Society), Reykjavík: University of Iceland, Urban Studies Centre.

NOSOSKO (various years) *Social tryghed i de nordiske lande*, Copenhagen: Nordic Council Statistical Secretariat.

OECD (1998) 'Resources during retirement. Maintaining prosperity in an ageing society: the OECD study on policy implications of ageing', Working Paper AWP 4.3, Paris: OECD.

—— (2002) *Society at a Glance*, Paris: OECD.

Offe, C. (1985) *Disorganized Capitalism*, Cambridge: Polity Press.

Ólafsson, S. (1984) *Modernization and Social Stratification in Iceland*, D.Phil. Thesis, University of Oxford, Nuffield College.

—— (1993a) 'Variations within the Scandinavian Model: Iceland and Scandinavia compared', in E. J. Hansen, S. Ringen, H. Uusitalo and R. Erikson (eds) *Welfare Trends in Scandinavia*.

—— (1993b) 'Innreið nútímþjóðfélags á Íslandi', in M. Snaedal and T. Sigurðardóttir, *Frændafundur*, Reykjavík: University of Iceland Press.

—— (1996) *Hugarfar og hagvöxtur*, Reykjavík: University of Iceland Press.

—— (1999) *Íslenska leiðin: Almannatryggingar og velferð í fjölþjóðlegum samanburði*, University Press and Social Security Administration of Iceland.

Ólafsson, S. and Sigurðsson, K. (1996) 'Poverty in Iceland', in A. Puide (ed.) *Den nordiska fattigdomens utveckling och struktur*, Copenhagen: ThemaNord; also in Gustafsson and Pedersen (2000) *Poverty and Low-Incomes in the Nordic Countries*.

Ólafsson, S., Kaldalóns, I. and Sigurðsson, K. (1998) 'Viðhorf til velferðarríkisins á Íslandi', Reykjavík: Social Research Institute.

Ólafsson, S., Sigurðsson, K. and Ammendrup, M. (1999) 'Lífskjör, lífshættir og lífsskoðun eldri borgara á Íslandi 1988–1998', Reykjavík: Social Research Institute, University of Iceland.

Øverbye, E. (1997) 'Mainstream pattern, deviant cases: the New Zealand and Danish pension systems in an international context', *Journal of European Social Policy*, 7 (2): 101–17.

Palme, J. (1990) *Pension Rights in Welfare Capitalism*, Stockholm: SOFI.

Scharpf, F. W. and Schmidt, V. A. (2000) *Welfare and Work in the Open Economy*, Vols. I and II, Oxford: Oxford University Press.

Skocpol, T. (1992) *Protecting Mothers and Soldiers*, Boston: Harvard University Press.

Sveinsson, J. R. (2000) *Society, Urbanity and Housing in Iceland*, Gävle: Meyers.

Tomasson, R. F. (1980) *Iceland: The First New Society*, Minneapolis: University of Minnesota Press.

Valdimarsson, V. U. (1984) *Alþýðuflokkurinn og stjórn hinna vinnandi stétta 1934–38*, Reykjavík: Sagnfræðistofnun HÍ.

13 Welfare as if deliberative democracy mattered

Jørn Loftager

Introduction

The securing of democracy was an important general motive behind the development of the postwar welfare state. Dearly bought experience from the preceding decades had revealed that neither the planned economy of state socialism nor free-market capitalism made up an adequate basis of democratic government. By means of a politically regulated market economy and a basic measure of welfare for all (Korsgaard 1999), the welfare state was supposed to lead society along a new and democratic Third Way. In a long-ago classic essay, T. H. Marshall outlined how an equal status of citizenship was progressing on the basis of universal civil, political and – especially – social rights in spite of the continuing prevalence of economic inequalities inherent in market capitalism (Marshall 1966 [1950]).

This idea of compatibility between capitalism and democracy was realized during the next two decades to such an extent that around 1960 it became a widespread belief that the old ideological battle between socialism and liberalism was fading away and replaced by a widespread consensus on 'welfare democracy' (Rasmussen 1968).

Only a few years later, however, the trust in the welfare state as a mediator between capitalism and democracy was severely questioned. According to the New Left of the late 1960s and the 1970s, the welfare state was to be seen as a class state predestined to protect the rule of capital or, at least, as a contradictory 'peacekeeper' that would eventually end in crisis (Offe 1985). Nor did the neo-liberalism of the 1980s have any confidence in the idea of welfare democracy. The belief in Keynesian regulatory economic policies was strongly questioned and, moreover, the expanding public sector was said to produce paternalism, encroaching the integrity and autonomy of the individual and so eroding the basis of democracy.

After the intensive discussions in the 1970s and 1980s, during the 1990s the problematic of democracy and capitalism disappeared to a large extent as a perspective and theme for discussions on the welfare state (Eriksen and Loftager 1996). An immediate reason for that was no doubt the collapse of the former socialist regimes in the late 1980s and the ensuing almost complete consent to the institutions of liberal democracy. With one stroke, democracy became something trivial, something 'without enemies' (Beck 1998), and correspondingly the question of the socio-economic conditions of democracy lost its relevance. From this 'taking-for-granted' premise, attention has concentrated instead on democratizing the public sector on an institutional level by means of decentralization, user and customer influence on policy implementation and the managing of institutions.

However, such democratizing remedies seem to concern effectiveness rather than democracy proper, and as far as I can see, there are still good reasons to maintain an interest in the relationships between the welfare state, capitalism and democracy. Generally because the structural tensions between capitalism and democracy are still with us, and more specifically because of certain current trends concerning both 'what kind of democracy' and 'whose welfare' we are talking about. What I am thinking of is, on the one hand, a profound and growing interest in democracy as deliberative democracy, according to which the democratic role of the citizen is not merely that of expressing preferences, choosing and voting but also, and most importantly, that of taking part in public reasoning and deliberation; and the latter role is much more vulnerable to disturbances caused by socio-economic inequalities and asymmetric power relations than is the former. On the other hand, I am referring to the theory and practice of new welfare policies under headlines like 'from welfare to workfare' or 'from passive to active policies', which have been introduced as central parts of a (new) Third Way (Giddens 1998; Rose 1999). Although something like deliberative democracy seems to be endorsed by Third Way proponents, the delicate question is, I shall contend, if this is a promising cocktail.

Against this background, the overall concern of this chapter is to discuss what kind of welfare system can nurture deliberative democracy, and my basic contention is that the former Third Way comes much better off in that respect compared to the present-day version of the Third Way.

In the first section of the chapter I shall outline the idea of deliberative democracy by profiling it against the 'economic' theory of democracy and with a special focus on the question of its socio-economic base. In the second section, Habermas' historical analysis of the decay of the public sphere is confronted with Marshall's theory of social class and citizenship, and referring to the Danish case it is argued that Marshall's vision of an equal status of citizenship to a large extent has been realized by the Nordic universal welfare state.

The third section briefly portrays the new Third Way, stressing how it introduces new ideas of community and of the proper relationship between the individual and the state. As an empirical case, I shall refer to the strategy of activation implemented under the Danish welfare reforms of the 1990s, and it will be shown how it embraces elements which challenge the ideals of equal citizenship.

The last section will briefly summarize some key results from analyses on the effects and basic assumptions of activation and I shall speculate a little on possible alternative third way strategies.

Deliberative democracy

The strong consensus after 1989 on the institutional content of democracy – the basic institutions and rights of liberal democracy – has not been followed by a similar agreement about the deeper meaning of democracy. On the contrary, the 'end of history' has given rise to widespread discussions on its 'regulative ideal' (Miller 1993). One of the most significant theories is that of deliberative democracy (Bohmann and Regh 1997; Eriksen 1995; Elster 1998). Even though this theory is represented by several different positions, they all focus on public reasoning and debate as the cornerstone of democracy. Likewise, although it has in no way won hegemonic status, the work of Jürgen Habermas serves as a common point of reference, and it is interesting to observe the expansion of the debate which followed after the translation into English of Habermas' classic analysis on the public sphere from 1962 (Habermas 1989).

In this section I shall in a few words present some important features of deliberative democracy, stressing the way in which this theory differs from – broadly speaking – economic conceptions of democracy.

The phrase 'economic theory of democracy' was used by Anthony Downs as the title of his – also classic – book from 1957 (Downs 1957). Its basic idea is that political man is identical to economic man. Voters are considered as consumers on the political market, choosing among commodities supplied by the political parties as producers. And as a parallel to the capitalist company's motive of profit maximization, 'parties formulate politics in order to win elections rather than win elections in order to formulate politics' (ibid., p. 28). In his likewise classic account, Schumpeter similarly states: 'we must . . . start from the competitive struggle for power and office and realize that the social function is fulfilled, as it were, incidentally – in the same sense as production is incidental to the making of profits' (Schumpeter 1976 [1943]: 282).

Lacking a 'real' market mechanism in the political sphere, the basic problem of democracy on this premise is how to aggregate pre-given preferences in order to respect the principle of political equality – one man, one vote. And much of the debate within the tradition of public choice has been concerned with the question of constructing solutions to this problem of aggregation (Kurrild-Klitgaard 1999).

However, the democratic ideal of what I prefer to call mirroring is not limited to positions that (explicitly) share the economic-man premise.

It is a much more widespread ideal, also in the public at large, that democracy is fundamentally popular government, meaning that political decisions ought to be in accordance with the will or the preferences of the people or – in practice – its majority. For instance, the grand old man of democratic theory, Robert A. Dahl's definition points to 'the continuing responsiveness of the government to the preferences of its citizens considered as political equals' (Dahl 1971: 1).

In spite of its prevalence, the economic theory of democracy has several important limitations. On its own premise, the problem of aggregation is difficult and in principle impossible to solve, in the sense that there is no single voting procedure which can aggregate the preferences of the voters in an unambiguous and optimal way (Kurrild-Klitgaard 1999). So there happens to be a necessary element of arbitrariness detrimental to the basic democratic values of political equality. Another limitation concerns the assumption of pre-given preferences. The problem is that the dynamics of preference-shaping and opinion-formation, which seems to count a lot in real world democratic politics, are excluded by definition from the democratic process. The ideal of mirroring makes up a third problem, in the sense that this ideal is not only generally appreciated, but also highly contested. On the one hand, representatives should be responsive to the electorate and act according to its demands. On the other hand, populism, opportunism and 'Gallup politicians' form negative expressions, referring implicitly to quite another ideal of representation. A fourth challenge to the economic theory of democracy is that it makes no room for rational political reasoning and argumentation. Whereas the actual existence of ideals of dialogue and rational political debate cannot be denied, it can be maintained, of course, that such ideals make up illusions and that in the last instance politics is essentially a game of power and interests and/or subjectively chosen preferences that will only allow of self-oriented strategic behaviour and pure instrumental rationality.

Precisely on this point the contrast vis-à-vis deliberative democracy is evident and pronounced. According to this theory, the regulative ideal and basic promise of democracy is not aggregation of preferences. Rather, the ideal is that political decisions should be based upon public reasoning, discussion and deliberation. Political man is not identical to the man acting in the textbooks of economics; arguments rather than preferences make up the atoms of democracy. Of course, preferences, interests, attitudes etc. are there, but they are to be seen as results as well as starting points of political processes in which the force of the better argument ought to prevail.

Deliberative democracy is also different from the economic conception of democracy, in that it involves the presence of a political community or citizenship: reasoning – as opposed to mere choosing – presupposes someone to reason with. Furthermore, that kind of democratic interplay forms a positive-sum game somehow similar, for instance, to a scientific community of researchers. Problem-solving is the primary aspect of both types of conduct (Dewey 1927).

Regarding the question of political participation, I myself find it important to stress that whereas economic theories of democracy to a large extent have been focusing on voting – in some cases just as an instrument of choosing among competing elites (Schumpeter) – the very ideal of mirroring does not preclude extensive participation. 'Voice' is also a way of expressing preferences, for instance by means of user boards in public institutions or grass-root actions, which seems to be fully in accordance with the premise of an economic conception of democracy. On the other hand, deliberative democracy is not participatory democracy in the sense that participation is considered as something good in itself. The crucial thing is that everyone should have the opportunity of taking part in the processes of political deliberation and reasoning, but in so far as one does not have any contribution to make, it is certainly not a deed to demand an equal share of influence in particular policy processes.

Likewise, the notion of deliberative democracy that I am trying to expound, does not consider political representation as a necessary second best compared to direct democracy. The public sphere is not a forum of governance, and it can fulfil its undertakings of deliberation, enlightenment and debate – and so function as a 'sounding-board' (Habermas 1992) for social needs, problems and aspirations – only if there exists a distinct and separate formal governmental structure including elected representatives. Similarly, the kind of 'common good' that corresponds to the claim of political rationality must be understood as a 'for the time being' common good in the sense that the better argument will always and necessarily be the provisional better argument.

Socio-economic conditions of deliberative democracy

Habermas' history of the structural transformation of the public sphere is a history of decay (Habermas 1989). Surely the actual public sphere was never fully in accordance with its own ideal, but the analysis certifies that for one thing, in the late eighteenth century the British Parliament had to give up its exclusivity and recognize the public as a partner of discussion. For another thing, although only a minority of the (male) population was included, at the time it was possible to believe in a future in which everyone would have the chance of fulfilling the admission requirements in the shape of property and general education or enlightenment ('*Bildung*'). However, in the course of the nineteenth century it was revealed how the ideal of generalized possession of property would never be realized. The initially expected identity between the roles of *citoyen* and bourgeois turned out to be an illusion. Instead the political sphere was gradually opened to groups that did not meet the demands concerning economic independency and general education. As a consequence, politics proved not to be a matter of rational discussion and problem solving in order to realize a common good. Rather, it was essentially about conflicting groups fighting to promote their distinctive interests – in agreement with what should become the standard idea of politics in political science. History seemed to demonstrate the incompatibility between capitalism and (deliberative) democracy.

And to make a long and complicated story very short, according to the early Habermas, the overall socio-political development in the twentieth century does not change this conclusion. Especially, he does not believe that the evolving social rights connected with the expanding postwar welfare state would be able to serve as a kind of new basis for the securing of economic independency and autonomy for each and every citizen. Whereas the welfare state might to a certain extent succeed in neutralizing class positions, it would at the same time define a new 'class' of dependent clients incompatible with an equal citizenship. What the idea of welfare democracy portrayed as something close to the final of society Habermas envisioned as a nightmare of technocracy.

In that respect, the conclusion in Marshall's seminal essay on social class and citizenship is totally different. The basic message here is that the class inequalities of capitalism can be met by establishing an equal status of citizenship – 'the inequality of the class system may be acceptable provided the equality of citizenship is recognized' (1996: 6). According to Marshall, citizenship is constituted by three sets of universal rights: civil, political and social rights evolving in the eighteenth, the nineteenth and the twentieth century, respectively. A crucial point is that the different rights make up a system of rights, so that the accomplishment of each of them presupposes the completion of the others. Especially, Marshall stresses how the equal fulfilment of civil and political rights is conditioned by the establishing of universal social rights. Whereas public support under the poor law resulted in withdrawal of civil and political rights the fundamental novelty of the twentieth century is that such support is given as rights:

> social rights imply an absolute right to a certain standard of civilisation which is conditional only of the discharge of the general duties of citizenship. Their content does not depend on the economic value of the individual claimant ... thus creating a universal right to an income which is not proportionate to the market value of the claimant.
>
> (1996: 26, 28)

The same universalism, which is constitutive for the state governed by law should also characterize the welfare state. And it is precisely because social rights are given as universal rights of citizenship that the problems of stigmatization and clientelization are avoided.

> What matters is that there is a general enrichment of the concrete substance of civilised life ... Equalisation is not so much between classes as between individuals within a population which is now treated for this purpose as though it were one class. Equality of status is more important than equality of income.
>
> (1996: 33)

Now, comparing Marshall's hopes and visions to Habermas' pessimistic outlook, I would argue that the former are in much better accordance with the actual main trends during the last four decades than is the latter, especially if one thinks of the Nordic welfare state. As a matter of form, it should be added that in his later works Habermas has changed his appraisals considerably (Habermas 1989, 1996); however, with regard to the question of the basic conditions of a functioning political public sphere, I find it still fruitful to refer to the original analysis.

In what follows I shall substantiate this assessment by referring briefly to the Danish development, which seems to have accomplished Marshall's anticipations to a high degree. First, the Danish welfare state is an example of the universalistic model, where relatively generous social goods and services are tax-financed and given as rights of citizenship. Referring both to the political forces that brought about the Nordic welfare states historically and to their so-called de-commodifying qualities, it has been commonplace to label these states 'social democratic' (Esping-Andersen 1990). However, at least regarding the Danish welfare state, I think that 'social-liberal' is a much more appropriate designation. On the one hand, the liberal or bourgeois political parties have played a major role in important formative decisions (Nørgaard 1999). On the other hand, and more importantly, the principle of universalism belongs basically to a liberal universe. And whereas it is important to stress the de-commodifying aspects of social rights of citizenship, it is just as well crucial to notice and recognize the market conformity characterizing universalistic rights and schemes.

Historically, the development of the Danish welfare state nicely illustrates Marshall's theory of a progressing citizenship (Bjørn 1998; Loftager 2002), but here we have to concentrate on the period since the early 1970s. In that period the Danish welfare system has contributed to a practical 'universalization' in the specific sense that virtually all grown-up Danes have become individual income-receivers, which amounts to no less than a basic historic novelty. The expansion of the public service sector played an important role for a profound increase in women's labour-market participation rate; the same did undoubtedly the extension of the system of income transfers, and in all cases it meant that almost all people without an earned income of their own were guaranteed an income from the state. In that respect, it is crucial to notice that various job-offer and educational schemes made it possible to regain entitlement to unemployment benefits without any time limit. A so-called principle of income-replacement in the social security system was pointing in the same direction, and so was an early-retirement scheme, which quickly became a universal right, partly by virtue of its being financed by general taxes and partly by virtue of the fact that it covered most of the work force. In addition, for some years a so-called transitional benefit allowed long-term unemployed people above 50 years of age to go on (very) early retirement. At the other end of the age scale, the child allowance was universalized, in the sense that it was granted without income test, and the same became true of the educational benefit system. Altogether, this development indicated a scenario towards the ultimate universalistic welfare system, namely that of a basic or citizen income given unconditionally as a right to every citizen (Goul Andersen 1996; Loftager 1996).

In a broad historical perspective, it seems both instructive and obvious to appraise the resulting securing of universal economic independency as a kind of substitute for the general possession of property which used to make up a necessary – although not sufficient – requirement for a deliberative democracy based upon a status of equal citizenship. Certainly, Marshall did not imagine a development like the Danish, neither regarding the size of the workforce, nor concerning the large proportion – around 20 per cent – of the population on public transfer income. However, these conditions don't seem to be inconsistent with his ideal. This is self-evident with regard to the emergence of an independent basis of support for women, and actually it can be brought up as a rather serious problem in Marshall's analysis that he ignores the question of women's (previous) economic dependency on the husband. It might seem more difficult to bring a situation in which around 20 per cent of the population of working age live on transfer payments into accordance with a notion of equal citizenship. In principle, however, it is unproblematic. As mentioned above, the decisive thing is that a person's status is not determined by his or her market capacity but by universal rights of citizenship. Quite another thing is, of course, if the condition of receiving 'passive' support results in marginalization and exclusion. Precisely that has been a main point of view in the Danish political debate on welfare in general and a central argument behind the activation reforms in particular, but, as will become apparent, it is an argument without firm empirical foundation.

The new third way of activation

It is disputed how radical a change the activation strategy represents. Some argue that it is in good accordance with traditional policies (Green-Pedersen *et al.* 2001), others find that it involves a heavy tightening, but not qualitative changes (Abrahamson and Oorschot 2002), and still others claim that the changes amount to a shift of paradigm (Cox 1998). My own conclusion is that it is in fact justified to talk about a change of paradigm.

Although at present much looks the same as before, potentially far-reaching changes have been implemented, and a new discourse has clearly manifested itself (Jespersen and Rasmussen 1998).

First and foremost and very simple: whereas so-called 'passive' support used to make up the obvious general solution to the generic social-order problems of capitalist society, such public support is now conceived of as the basic problem. The inspiration behind this 'Copernican turn' clearly comes from the idea of workfare rather than welfare, which in turn forms a basic part of the politics of the current Third Way (Jordan 1998; Rose 1999). In that connection, it is important to stress that workfare is not concomitant to a neo-liberal minimal-state strategy. Rather, it is primarily coupled to communitarian concerns for community and inclusion accompanied by a strong conviction that it is both the right and the duty of the state to take responsibility for its protection (Mead 1986, 1997; Etzioni 1993). Second, however, the discourse of activation also includes economic-liberalistic notions of 'give and take' (Jespersen and Rasmussen 1999; Nørskov Toke 2002), and precisely the combination of neo-liberal supply-economic beliefs and a communitarian philosophy of community appears to be characteristic of the present Third Way. For a more elaborate and general analysis, readers are referred to Nicolas Rose, who shows how notions of human and social capital make up mitigating elements in that they introduce 'etho-politics into economics through the capitalization of morality in the service of national economic advantage' (Rose 1999: 282). Here I shall content myself with discussing the way in which this mixture appears in the Danish politics of activation.

It finds an immediate expression in a typical doubleness regarding the anxiety for societal solidarity. That is to say, the anxiety does not only relate to the (asserted) negative consequences of welfare benefits to the recipients. It also concerns the legitimacy of the benefits in the eyes of the taxpayers – how can one expect them to accept high tax levels in order to support people who don't do anything in return?

The basic assumption of the activation strategy is that passive support is de-qualifying as well as de-motivating. It takes away the incitement to seek and accept jobs and so it produces marginalization from the labour market, which in turn results in further social marginalization and exclusion.

However, the answer should not be 'laissez faire, laissez passer'. Rather, the response should be what Giddens in his *The Third Way* labels 'generative policies', aiming at 'positive welfare' (Giddens 1998). Whereas the old welfare state passivated and clientelized its citizens, the new Third Way welfare state is going to ensure that each individual becomes able to support himself and so contribute to the community. In that respect, the central instrument is the duty to do something immediately in return for any public support received.

But, one might object, is this something new? Has it not always been the case that the right to support is conditioned by an obligation to work? The answer, of course, is yes. The difference – and the difference that really makes a difference – is, however, that previously the duty of availability was a duty to accept an offer of a job on ordinary conditions on equal terms with everybody else. In other words, the difference is between duties and requirements that are universally in force and duties that are not known in advance and are not the result of a freely negotiated contract. General duties and obligations are totally in accordance with the liberal ideal of an equal citizenship. Because of their universality, duties to pay taxes, to education and to military service etc. express equality of status. In contrast to that, the activation duties as they are defined – in the last instance – by the authorities signalize and institutionalize differences and inequality of status.

Compared to other descriptions of the activation policies, the above way of characterizing it may look rather biased. In his analysis, for instance, Torfing stresses how the Danish government has succeeded 'to detach workfare from its neo-liberal "origin" and to reformulate its content in accordance with the socio-political legacy in Denmark' (Torfing 1999: 17). It is emphasized, that the Danish success in fighting unemployment does not reflect an increasing number of 'working poor', and Torfing also gives a basically positive account of the activation measures and demands vis-à-vis each individual unemployed. In that respect, the so-called individual action plans are of crucial importance. They are plans that are prepared for each unemployed person in order to improve the effectiveness of the efforts. In accordance with the officially formulated intentions, Torfing stresses that the plans make it possible to target activities and demands in ways that are meaningful, and he states that 'activation through participation in "futile work-for-the-sake-of-working projects" is limited, as the law does not aim at repressing and punishing the unemployed' (ibid.: 18).

Immediately, this is correct. At the same time, however, it must be added that no one has tried to disguise that activation is not only about carrots. It is also about sticks, and the authorities does not try to deny that the expected effect of activation to a considerable degree is due to the factor of motivation which is connected both to the demand of activation and to the prospect of losing one's income for good (Arbejdsministeriet 2000).

In some cases the element of targeting may result in greater effectiveness compared to universal 'passive' measures, and evaluation studies indicate that a majority of the involved persons express positive attitudes towards the activation projects (Hansen 2001). Nevertheless, it appears to be more than doubtful to characterize the politics of activation in general, and the action plans in particular, as being in good accordance with the Danish socio-political legacy. These action plans correspond to a potential far-reaching encroachment on the autonomy of the individual. The very idea that it should be the task and duty of the state – i.e. the employment officer – to make a legally binding agreement with each individual concerning her or his choice of life projects seems to represent a paternalism which is very hard to bring into harmony with the Danish legacy of welfare liberalism (Nørskov Toke 2002). Certainly, in some cases paternalism might be in accordance with the liberal premise, namely if the people in question have lost their autonomy, for instance because of old age, illness or drug dependency but it goes without saying that this is a very exceptional situation regarding unemployed people. So there has evolved an apparent discrepancy in Danish social policy between on the one hand a subject area like compulsory treatment of drug addicts, where the authorities have been very cautious not to encroach the integrity and autonomy of the individual, and on the other hand the area of activation, where this hardly has been an issue at all (Nørskov Toke 2002).

People on activation are not only obliged to work on other and poorer conditions than people in ordinary jobs, they also don't enjoy what Marshall termed 'collective civil rights' stemming from collective agreements. Another, principally far-reaching change of the 1994 labour-market reform is that participation in activation measures no longer means renewed entitlement to unemployment benefits. As a result, the previous guarantee of upholding the status of individual income-receiver no longer exists. The period of support is limited to four years; after that, unemployed persons might get social security payments, but these are tested against the family income so that even a rather modest income of the spouse eliminates the entitlement.

In this way (involuntary) private support has re-emerged as a socially recognized and legitimate form of support. In the light of communitarian ideals of strong family ties, this may be appraised as a step of progress, but it seems difficult to bring into harmony with liberal ideas of equal citizenship.

In the Danish debate it has been a main argument against passive transfers that they generate dependency on the state and undermine the ideal of taking care of oneself. However, apart from the fact that people on activation still get their livelihood from the state, what matters according to a citizenship perspective is not dependency as such but different sorts of dependency. Again, in perspective of the ideal of equal citizenship, the critical types of dependency are those that do not appear from general rules but stem from unpredictable bureaucratic discretion. In those cases, there is a principal risk of encroachment of the citizens' autonomy and integrity and so – ultimately – of weakened civil and political rights.

As mentioned above, according to the deliberative conception of democracy the opportunity of public participation in political reasoning and opinion formation is of crucial importance, but such participation presupposes the presence of the kind of private autonomy that the course of activation potentially threatens. If your economic subsistence is dependent on the good will of the authorities, then this makes up a rather weak basis for (critical) political activity – parallel to the intimidation of electors by employers before the ballot was made secret (Elklit 1989).

In addition to that kind of potential direct consequences, the activation might also weaken the status of citizenship more indirectly by producing stigmatization: activated persons are 'weak' persons, who need special treatment and help in order to develop appropriate attitudes and personal qualities (Carstens 1998). And activation as upbringing is, of course, a primary example of communitarian paternalism.

In general, the difference between the old and the new Third Way can be said to consist of two categorically different notions of community. Whereas Marshall's citizenship is to be understood as a liberal socio-political community of citizens with equal rights and duties, the community associated with the politics of activation is identical to the community of work. It appears – mechanically – as a reflex of everyone's respecting the norm of doing paid work. So, activation is not merely a means to get more people into ordinary jobs, it is also an end in itself, because it ensures 'that people are included in meaningful (work) communities. I.e. participation in this connection is an aim in itself, because it is considered to be good to the individual – also if it does not lead to self-support' (Socialministeriet 2000: 50–1, *author's translation*).

As shown in several analyses, such communitarian argumentation is widespread in the Danish discourse of activation (Jespersen and Rasmussen 1998; Nørskov Toke 2002). Referring to Durkheim's famous conception of solidarity, this indicates the presence of a mechanical understanding of solidarity, according to which inclusion is based on the sharing of common values and norms (Loftager 2000). If one defines community as community of work, activation becomes a categorical imperative, i.e. a claim and a duty that does not need to be argued further by means of reference to specific consequences.

This interpretation is in good accordance with the fact that the belief in the principle of activation has not been disturbed by several studies that to a large extent have questioned its results in terms of effects on employment and its basic assumptions in general. So there has been serious doubt cast on the core supposition, namely that passive support produces marginalization and exclusion. Certainly, it has been well documented that there is co-variance between (long-term) unemployment and a lot of social problems and calamities such as problems of abuse, family dissolution, illness and early death (Nygaard Christoffersen 1996). But what is the cause and what is the effect? It goes without saying that serious illness, for instance, might be the cause of long-term unemployment rather than the other way round. On the other hand, studies of people on public transfers clearly indicate that passive support only to a very small degree produces marginalization. The striking and perhaps surprising fact is the extent to which long-term unemployed people and people on early retirement manage to continue their usual daily lives concerning habitation, contact to family and friends and participation in various social activities (Goul Andersen 1996, 2002; Lund Clement and Goul Andersen 1999). Likewise, the fear of a shrinking solidarity among the taxpayers towards the receivers of public transfer payments also seems to be unfounded (Goul Andersen 1996).

With regard to the profound reduction of the number of Danish unemployed persons during the 1990s, it is commonplace to explain it as an effect of the activation policies. However, this assumption is not in accordance with available facts and figures either. A recent overview of the existing evaluation studies in Holland and Denmark concludes that the employment effect of activation has been rather limited, and in some cases even negative (Abrahamson and Oorshot 2002). Furthermore, a panel study that followed a number of unemployed persons over four years casts heavy doubt on the validity of the basic premise of unemployment as primarily structural unemployment. The study in question shows that renewed labour–market integration can only to a very small extent be explained by the expected factors: the length of the period of unemployment, the level of education and job motivation (Albrekt Larsen 2002). Instead it seems likely to explain the rise in employment as primarily a result of improving market conditions.

As suggested by these few remarks, it is hard to discern the social or economic necessities that forced the decision-makers to strike into the new Third Way. In other words, it seems difficult to point out any merits which can offset the above-mentioned shortcomings regarding the equal status of citizenship.

Concluding remarks: beyond the (new) Third Way?

The realization of the ideal of deliberative democracy presupposes that everyone can take part in public reasoning and deliberation as autonomous and independent citizens. Originally, the fulfilment of this requirement was associated with the emergence of a market society that allowed every person to become possessor of property. Thus, the course of development marked by capitalist class divisions made up a hard stroke towards the idea of an equal citizenship, and the delicate relationship between capitalism and democracy became a returning main theme in political sociology. In the postwar period, the attention has to a large extent concentrated on the welfare state and its potentials as a guarantor for democracy. The basic idea was that the establishment of social rights might constitute a basis for an equal citizenship. A principal problem with this solution is, however, that the welfare state itself, depending on its structure and way of functioning, might create new dependencies detrimental to the preconditions of democracy and especially deliberative democracy.

Based upon general observations and theoretical arguments as well as Danish evidence, the main conclusion of this chapter is that with regard to that, the former Marshall-like Third Way comes better off than the currently dominating Third Way. It should be stressed that this chapter has not dealt with the actual deliberative working of democracy under the condition of the new Third Way. Probably, it would be very difficult to register any immediate effects of the shift of welfare paradigm. The focus has been on (one of) the pillars on which deliberative democracy rests and it goes without saying that the consequences will appear only in the longer run.

It is not my ambition to make a forecast of democracy's future development, but that much seems certain that although democracy has become a democracy without enemies – if that holds true after 11 September 2001 – its prospects will still be dependent on its socio-economic conditions.

To the extent that my conclusions are valid, the interesting question is, of course, what kind of a future welfare system might nurture deliberative democracy? In line with the main argument of the chapter, the general answer is that instead of following the current Third Way of activation and selectivity, it seems appropriate to suggest an expanded universalism as an obvious alternative. It is beyond this chapter to appraise the realism and practicality of a basic or citizens' income, but the general positive Danish experiences concerning the 'passive' – but not passivating! – transfers might indicate that such an income scheme is much more sensible and imaginative than the currently dominating discourse on welfare politics would lead us to believe (cf. Kildal 2001; Loftager 2000). It might be an interesting new chapter in the history of expanding citizenship.

References

Abrahamson, P. and Oorschot, W. V. (2002) 'The Dutch and Danish miracles revisited: comparing the role of activation policies within two different welfare regimes', paper prepared for presentation at the 2nd COST Action 15 Conference, Oslo, April 2002.

Albrekt Larsen, C. (2002) 'Challenging the hegemonic discourse of structural unemployment', *CCWS Working Paper No. 2002-24*, Aalborg University.

Arbejdsministeriet (2000) *Effekter af aktiveringsindsatsen*, Copenhagen: Arbejdsministeriet.

Beck, U. (1998) *Democracy without Enemies*, Cambridge: Polity Press.

Bjørn, C. (1998) *Dengang Danmark blev moderne. Historien om den virkelige danske utopi*, Copenhagen: Gyldendal.

Bohman, J. (1998) 'Survey article: the coming age of deliberative democracy', *The Journal of Political Philosophy*, 6 (4): 400–25.

Bohman, J. and Regh, W. (eds) (1997) *Deliberative Democracy*, Cambridge: The MIT Press.

Carstens, A. (1998) *Aktivering – klientsamtaler og socialpolitik*, København: Hans Reitzels Forlag.

Cox, R. H. (1998) 'From safety net to trampoline: labour market activation in the Netherlands and Denmark', *Governance*, 11 (4): 397–414.

Dahl, R. A. (1971) *Polyarchy: Participation and Opposition*, New Haven and London: Yale University Press.

Dewey, J. (1927) *The Public and its Problems*, Chicago: Gateway Books.

Downs, A. (1957) *An Economic Theory of Democracy*, New York: Harper & Row.

Elklit, J. (1989) *Fra åben til hemmelig afstemning*, Århus: Politica.

Elster, J. (ed.) (1998) *Deliberative Democracy*, Cambridge: Cambridge University Press.

Eriksen, E. O. (ed.) (1995) *Deliberativ Politikk: Demokrati i teori og praksis*, Oslo: Tano.

Eriksen, E. O. and Loftager, J. (ed.) (1996) *The Rationality of the Welfare State*, Oslo: Scandinavian University Press.

Esping-Andersen, G. (1990) *The Three Worlds of Welfare Capitalism*, Cambridge: Polity Press.

Etzioni, A. (1993) *The Spirit of Community*, London: Fontana Press.

Giddens, A. (1998) *The Third Way: The Renewal of Social Democracy*, Cambridge: Polity Press.

Goul Andersen, J. (1996) 'Marginalisation, citizenship and the economy: the capacities of the universalist welfare state in Denmark', in E. O. Eriksen and J. Loftager (eds) *The Rationality of the Welfare State*, Oslo: Scandinavian University Press.

—— (2002) 'Coping with long-term unemployment: economic security, labour market integration and well-being', CCWS Working paper 2002-23, Aalborg University.

Green-Pedersen, C., Kersbergen, K. V. and Hemerijck, A. (2001) '"Neo-liberalism, the 'Third Way' or what?" Recent Social Democratic welfare policies in Denmark and the Netherlands', *Journal of European Public Policy*, 8 (2): 307–25.

Habermas, J. (1989) *The Structural Transformation of the Public Sphere*, Cambridge: MIT Press.

—— (1996) *Between Facts and Norms*, Cambridge: MIT Press.

Hansen, H. (2001) *Arbejde, aktivering og arbejdsløshed*, Frederiksberg: Samfundslitteratur.

Jespersen, S. P. and Rasmussen, S. L. (1998) 'Fra velfærdsstat til velfærdssamfund – en analyse af 90'ernes velfærdsdebat', specialeopgave, Institut for Statskundskab, Aarhus Universitet.

Jordan, B. (1998) *The New Politics of Welfare*, London: Sage.

Kildal, N. (ed.) (2001) *Den nya sociala frågan*, Göteborg: Daidalos.

Korsgaard, O. (1999) 'Demosstrategien', Arbejdspapir nr. 5, Forskningsprojektet Voksenuddannelse, folkeoplysning og demokrati; København: Danmarks Lærerhøjskole.

Kurrild-Klitgaard, P. (1999) 'Demokrati, magt og kollektive valgs rationalitet', in U. Jakobsen and M. Kelstrup (eds) *Demokrati og demokratisering: Begreber og teorier*, København: Forlaget Politiske Studier.

Loftager, J. (1996) 'Citizens income – a new welfare state strategy?', in E. O. Eriksen and J. Loftager (eds) *The Rationality of the Welfare State*, Oslo: Scandinavian University Press.

—— (2000) 'Medborgarinkomst och deliberativ demokrati', in N. Kildal (ed.) *Den nya sociala frågan*, Göteborg: Daidalos.

—— (2002) 'Aktivering som (ny) velfærdspolitisk tredjevej', *Politica*, (3): 296–312.

Lund Clement, S. and Goul Andersen, J. (1999) 'Ny marginaliseringsundersøgelse af førtidspensionister mv.', in *NYT*, No. 2, 1999: 1–2, Institut for Økonomi, Politik og Forvaltning, Aalborg Universitet.

Marshall, T. H. (1966) *Class, Citizenship and the State*, New York: Doubleday & Company.

Mead, L. M. (1986) *Beyond Entitlement*, New York: The Free Press.

—— (1997) 'Welfare employment', in L. M. Mead (ed.) *The New Paternalism*, New York: The Free Press.

Miller, D. (1993) 'Deliberative democracy and social choice', in D. Held (ed.) *Prospects for Democracy*, Cambridge: Polity Press.

Nørgaard, A. S. (1999) 'Viden og videnskab om velfærdsstaten: er der én dansk velfærdsstat?', *GRUS*, (56–7), 20 (1999): 6–39.

Nørskov Toke, K. (2002) 'Paternalisme i dansk socialpolitik – autonomi eller moralisme?', specialeopgave, Institut for Statskundskab, Aarhus Universitet.

Nygaard Christoffersen, M. (1996) *Opvækst med arbejdsløshed*, København: Socialforskningsinstituttet, 96: 14.

Rasmussen, E. (1968) *Ideologi*, København: Gyldendal.

Rose, N. (1999) 'Inventiveness in politics', *Economy and Society*, 28 (3): 467–93.

Schumpeter, J. A. (1976 [1943]) *Capitalism, Socialism and Democracy*, London and New York: Routledge.

Socialministeriet (2000) *Socialpolitik som investering, Socialpolitisk Redegørelse 2000*, København: Socialministeriet.

Torfing, J. (1999) 'Workfare with welfare: recent reforms of the Danish welfare state', *Journal of European Social Policy*, 9 (1): 5–28.

Index

www.ingramcontent.com/pod-product-compliance
Lightning Source LLC
LaVergne TN
LVHW011120300926
849160LV00008B/455
9780415429764